Tourism and Hospitality in 21st Century

TOURISM AND HOSPITALITY in 21st Century

Lalita Sharma

CENTRUM PRESS
NEW DELHI-110002 (INDIA)

CENTRUM PRESS
H.O.: 4360/4, Ansari Road, Daryaganj,
New Delhi-110002 (India)
Tel: 23278000, 23261597, 23255577, 23286875
B.O.: No. 1015, Ist Main Road, BSK IIIrd Stage,
IIIrd Phase, IIIrd Block, Bengaluru-560085 (INDIA)
Tel: 080-41723429
Email: centrumpress@gmail.com
Visit us at: www.centrumpress.com

Tourism and Hospitality in 21st Century

First Edition, 2011

ISBN 978-93-81293-76-8

PRINTED IN INDIA

Printed at Tarun Offset, Delhi

Contents

Preface

All over the world more people than ever travel and stay from home. Tourism and hospitality are the world's main industries, which are in huge part responsible for a great deal of economic growth, balance of payments, employment and regional balance in their countries. They are also significant socially, culturally and environmentally-for those who become tourists and for their hosts. The future of tourism and hospitality is of importance to many businesses and other organizations, as well as governments. The book sets out to introduce educators and practitioners as well as others with an significance in the future, to the new century and the form of things to come.

'Tourism and Hospitality in the 21st Century' is appropriate for: senior personnel in private and public area of tourism and hospitality operations; international and national official tourism bodies and added organizations; universities and other higher education institutions; universities and other higher education institutions; consultancy; finance, construction and supply industries; and as a reference point for students.

Author

1

Introduction

Tourism is travel for recreational, leisure or business purposes. The World Tourism Organization defines tourists as people who "travel to and stay in places outside their usual environment for more than twenty-four hours and not more than one consecutive year for leisure, business and other purposes not related to the exercise of an activity remunerated from within the place visited." Tourism has become a popular global leisure activity. In 2008, there were over 922 million international tourist arrivals, with a growth of 1.9% as compared to 2007.

International tourism receipts grew to US$944 billion (euro 642 billion) in 2008, corresponding to an increase in real terms of 1.8%. As a result of the late-2000s recession, international travel demand suffered a strong slowdown beginning in June 2008, with growth in international tourism arrivals worldwide falling to 2% during the boreal summer months. This negative trend intensified during 2009, exacerbated in some countries due to the outbreak of the H1N1 influenza virus, resulting in a worldwide decline of 4% in 2009 to 880 million international tourists arrivals, and an estimated 6% decline in international tourism receipts.

Tourism is vital for many countries, such as Egypt, Greece, Lebanon, Spain, Malaysia and Thailand, and many island nations, such as The Bahamas, Fiji, Maldives, Philippines and the Seychelles, due to the large intake of money for businesses with their goods and services and the opportunity for employment in the service industries associated with tourism. These service industries include transportation services, such as airlines, cruise ships and taxicabs, hospitality services, such as accommodations, including hotels and resorts, and entertainment venues, such as amusement parks, casinos, shopping malls, music venues and theatres.

ETYMOLOGY OF TOURISM

Theobald (1994) suggested that "etymologically, the word tour is derived from the Latin, 'tornare' and the Greek, 'tornos', meaning 'a lathe or circle; the movement around a central point or axis'. This meaning changed in modern English to represent 'one's turn'. The suffix –ism is defined as 'an action or process; typical behaviour or quality', while the suffix, –its denotes 'one that performs a given action'. When the word tour and the suffixes are combined, they suggest the action of movement around a circle. One can argue that a circle represents a starting point, which ultimately returns back to its beginning.

Therefore, like a circle, a tour represents a journey in that it is a round-trip, *i.e.*, the act of leaving and then returning to the original starting point, and therefore, one who takes such a journey can be called a tourist." In 1941, Hunziker and Krapf defined tourism as people who travel "the sum of the phenomena and relationships arising from the travel and stay of non-residents, insofar as they do not lead to permanent residence and are not connected with any earning activity."

In 1976, the Tourism Society of England's definition was: "Tourism is the temporary, short-term movement of people to destination outside the places where they normally live and work and their activities during the stay at each destination. It includes movements for all purposes." In 1981, the International Association of Scientific Experts in Tourism defined tourism in terms of particular activities selected by choice and undertaken outside the home.

In 1994, the United Nations classified three forms of tourism in its Recommendations on Tourism Statistics:

1. Domestic tourism, involving residents of the given country traveling only within this country.
2. Inbound tourism, involving non-residents traveling in the given country.

3. Outbound tourism, involving residents traveling in another country.

HISTORY OF TOURISM

Wealthy people have always traveled to distant parts of the world, to see great buildings, works of art, learn new languages, experience new cultures and to taste different cuisines. Long ago, at the time of the Roman Republic, places such as Baiae were popular coastal resorts for the rich. The word tourism was used by 1811 and tourist by 1840. In 1936, the League of Nations defined foreign tourist as "someone traveling abroad for at least twenty-four hours". Its successor, the United Nations, amended this definition in 1945, by including a maximum stay of six months.

LEISURE TRAVEL

Leisure travel was associated with the Industrial Revolution in the United Kingdom – the first European country to promote leisure time to the increasing industrial population. Initially, this applied to the owners of the machinery of production, the economic oligarchy, the factory owners and the traders. These comprised the new middle class. Cox and Kings was the first official travel company to be formed in 1758. The British origin of this new industry is reflected in many place names.

In Nice, France, one of the first and best-established holiday resorts on the French Riviera, the long esplanade along the seafront is known to this day as the Promenade des Anglais; in many other historic resorts in continental Europe, old, well-established palace hotels have names like the Hotel Bristol, the Hotel Carlton or the Hotel Majestic – reflecting the dominance of English customers. Many leisure-oriented tourists travel to the tropics, both in the summer and winter. Places of such nature often visited are: Bali in Indonesia, Brazil, Cuba, the Dominican Republic, Malaysia, Mexico the various Polynesian tropical islands, Queensland in Australia, Thailand, Saint-Tropez and Cannes in France, Florida, Hawaii and Puerto Rico in the United States, Barbados, Sint Maarten, Saint Kitts and Nevis, The Bahamas, Anguilla, Antigua, Aruba, Turks and Caicos Islands and Bermuda.

WINTER TOURISM

Although it is acknowledged that the Swiss were not the inventors of skiing it is well documented that St. Moritz, Graubünden, became the cradle of the developing winter tourism: Since that year of 1865 in St. Moritz, many daring hotel managers choose to risk opening their hotels in winter but it was only in the seventies of the 20th century when winter tourism took over the lead from summer tourism in many of the Swiss ski resorts. Even in Winter, portions of up to one third of all guests (depending on the location) consist of non-skiers. Major ski resorts are located mostly in the various European countries (*e.g.* Andorra, Austria, Bulgaria, Czech Republic, France, Germany, Iceland, Italy, Norway, Poland, Serbia, Sweden, Slovenia, Spain, Switzerland), Canada, the United States (*e.g.* Colorado, California, Utah, New York, New Jersey, Michigan, Montana, Vermont, New England) New Zealand, Japan, South Korea, Chile, Argentina, Kenya and Tanzania.

MASS TOURISM

Mass tourism could only have developed with the improvements in technology, allowing the transport of large numbers of people in a short space of time to places of leisure interest, so that greater numbers of people could begin to enjoy the benefits of leisure time. In the United States, the first seaside resorts in the European style were at Atlantic City, New Jersey and Long Island, New York.

In Continental Europe, early resorts included: Ostend, popularised by the people of Brussels; Boulogne-sur-Mer (Pas-de-Calais) and Deauville (Calvados) for the Parisians; and Heiligendamm, founded in 1793, as the first seaside resort on the Baltic Sea.

ADJECTIVAL TOURISM

Adjectival tourism refers to the numerous niche or

specialty travel forms of tourism that have emerged over the years, each with its own adjective. Many of these have come into common use by the tourism industry and academics. Others are emerging concepts that may or may not gain popular usage.

Examples of the more common niche tourism markets include:

- Agritourism
- Culinary tourism
- Cultural tourism
- Ecotourism
- Extreme tourism
- Geotourism
- Heritage tourism
- LGBT tourism
- Medical tourism
- Nautical tourism
- Pop-culture tourism
- Religious tourism
- Slum tourism
- Space tourism
- War tourism
- Wildlife tourism

DEVELOPMENTS OF TOURISM IN 21ST CENTURY

There has been an upmarket trend in the tourism over the last few decades, especially in Europe, where international travel for short breaks is common. Tourists have high levels of disposable income, considerable leisure time, are well educated, and have sophisticated tastes. There is now a demand for a better quality products, which has resulted in a fragmenting of the mass market for beach vacations; people want more specialised versions, quieter resorts, family-oriented holidays or niche market-targeted destination hotels.

The developments in technology and transport infrastructure, such as jumbo jets, low-cost airlines and more accessible airports have made many types of tourism more affordable. WHO estimates that up to 500,000 people are on planes at any time. There have also been changes in lifestyle, such as retiree-age people who sustain year round tourism. This is facilitated by internet sales of tourism products. Some sites have now started to offer dynamic packaging, in which an inclusive price is quoted for a tailor-made package requested by the customer upon impulse. There have been a few setbacks in tourism, such as the September 11 attacks and terrorist threats to tourist destinations, such as in Bali and several European cities.

Also, on December 26, 2004, a tsunami, caused by the 2004 Indian Ocean earthquake, hit the Asian countries on the Indian Ocean, including the Maldives. Thousands of lives were lost and many tourists died. This, together with the vast clean-up operation in place, has stopped or severely hampered tourism to the area. The terms tourism and travel are sometimes used interchangeably. In this context, travel has a similar definition to tourism, but implies a more purposeful journey. The terms tourism and tourist are sometimes used pejoratively, to imply a shallow interest in the cultures or locations visited by tourists.

SUSTAINABLE TOURISM

"Sustainable tourism is envisaged as leading to management of all resources in such a way that economic, social and aesthetic needs can be fulfilled while maintaining cultural integrity, essential ecological processes, biological diversity and life support systems." (World Tourism Organization) Sustainable development implies "meeting the needs of the present without compromising the ability of future generations to meet their own needs" (World Commission on Environment and Development, 1987) Sustainable tourism can be seen as having regard to ecological and socio-cultural carrying capacities and includes involving the community of the destination in tourism development planning.

It also involves integrating tourism to match current economic and growth policies so as to mitigate some of the negative economic and social impacts of 'mass tourism'. Murphy (1985) advocates the use of an 'ecological approach', to consider both 'plants' and 'people' when implementing the sustainable tourism development process. This is in contrast to the 'boosterism' and 'economic' approaches to tourism planning, neither of which consider the detrimental ecological or sociological impacts of tourism development to a destination.

However, Butler (2006) questions the exposition of the term 'sustainable' in the context of tourism, citing its ambiguity and stating that "the emerging sustainable development philosophy of the 1990s can be viewed as an extension of the broader realization that a preoccupation with economic growth without regard to it social and environmental consequences is self-defeating in the long term." Thus 'sustainable tourism development' is seldom considered as an autonomous function of economic regeneration as separate from general economic growth.

ECOTOURISM

Ecotourism, also known as ecological tourism, is responsible travel to fragile, pristine, and usually protected areas that strives to be low impact and (often) small scale. It helps educate the traveller; provides funds for conservation; directly benefits the economic development and political empowerment of local communities; and fosters respect for different cultures and for human rights.

PRO-POOR TOURISM

The pro poor tourism has to help the very poorest in developing countries has been receiving increasing attention by those involved in development and the issue has been addressed either through small scale projects in local communities and by Ministries of Tourism attempting to attract huge numbers of tourists. Research by the Overseas Development Institute suggests that neither is the best way to encourage tourists' money to reach the poorest as only 25% or less (far less in some cases) ever reaches the poor; successful examples of money reaching the poor include mountain climbing in Tanzania or cultural tourism in Luang Prabang, Laos.

RECESSION TOURISM

Recession tourism is a travel trend, which evolved by way

of the world economic crisis. Identified by American entrepreneur Matt Landau (2007), recession tourism is defined by low-cost, high-value experiences taking place of once-popular generic retreats. Various recession tourism hotspots have seen business boom during the recession thanks to comparatively low costs of living and a slow world job market suggesting travellers are elongating trips where their money travels further.

MEDICAL TOURISM

When there is a significant price difference between countries for a given medical procedure, particularly in Southeast Asia, India, Eastern Europe and where there are different regulatory regimes, in relation to particular medical procedures (*e.g.* dentistry), traveling to take advantage of the price or regulatory differences is often referred to as "medical tourism".

EDUCATIONAL TOURISM

Educational tourism developed, because of the growing popularity of teaching and learning of knowledge and the enhancing of technical competency outside of the classroom environment. In educational tourism, the main focus of the tour or leisure activity includes visiting another country to learn about the culture, such as in Student Exchange Programmes and Study Tours, or to work and apply skills learned inside the classroom in a different environment, such as in the International Practicum Training Programme.

CREATIVE TOURISM

Creative tourism has existed as a form of cultural tourism, since the early beginnings of tourism itself. Its European roots date back to the time of the Grand Tour, which saw the sons of aristocratic families traveling for the purpose of mostly interactive, educational experiences. More recently, creative tourism has been given its own name by Crispin Raymond and Greg Richards, who as members of the Association for Tourism and Leisure Education (ATLAS), have directed a number of projects for the European Commission, including cultural and crafts tourism, known as sustainable tourism. They have defined "creative tourism" as tourism related to the active participation of travellers in the culture of the host community, through interactive workshops and informal learning experiences.

Meanwhile, the concept of creative tourism has been picked up by high-profile organizations such as UNESCO, who through the Creative Cities Network, have endorsed creative tourism as an engaged, authentic experience that promotes an active understanding of the specific cultural features of a place. More recently, creative tourism has gained popularity as a form of cultural tourism, drawing on active participation by travellers in the culture of the host communities they visit. Several countries offer examples of this type of tourism development, including the United Kingdom, the Bahamas, Jamaica, Spain, Italy and New Zealand.

DARK TOURISM

One emerging area of special interest has been identified by Lennon and Foley (2000) as "dark" tourism. This type of tourism involves visits to "dark" sites, such as battlegrounds, scenes of horrific crimes or acts of genocide, for example: concentration camps. Dark tourism remains a small niche market, driven by varied motivations, such as mourning, remembrance, education, macabre curiosity or even entertainment. Its early origins are rooted in fairgrounds and medieval fairs.

DOOM TOURISM

Also known as "Tourism of Doom," or "Last Chance Tourism" this emerging trend involves traveling to places that are environmentally or otherwise threatened (the ice caps of Mount Kilimanjaro, the melting glaciers of Patagonia, The coral of the Great Barrier Reef) before it is too late. Identified by travel trade magazine TravelAge West editor-in-chief Kenneth Shapiro in 2007 and later explored in The New York Times, this type of tourism is believed to be on the rise. Some see the trend as related to sustainable tourism or ecotourism due to the fact that a number of these tourist destinations are considered threatened by environmental factors such as global warming, over population or climate change. Others worry that travel to many of these threatened locations increases an individual's carbon footprint and only hastens problems threatened locations are already facing.

GROWTH IN TOURISM INDUSTRY

The World Tourism Organization (UNWTO) forecasts that international tourism will continue growing at the average annual rate of 4%. With the advent of e-commerce, tourism products have become one of the most traded items on the internet. Tourism products and services have been made available through intermediaries, although tourism providers (hotels, airlines, etc.) can sell their services directly.

This has put pressure on intermediaries from both on-line and traditional shops. It has been suggested there is a strong correlation between tourism expenditure per capita and the degree to which countries play in the global context. Not only as a result of the important economic contribution of the tourism industry, but also as an indicator of the degree of confidence with which global citizens leverage the resources of the globe for the benefit of their local economies.

This is why any projections of growth in tourism may serve as an indication of the relative influence that each country will exercise in the future. Space tourism is expected to "take off" in the first quarter of the 21st century, although compared with traditional destinations the number of tourists in orbit will remain low until technologies such as a space elevator make space travel cheap. Technological improvement is likely to make possible air-ship hotels, based either on solar-powered airplanes or large dirigibles. Underwater hotels, such as Hydropolis, expected to open in Dubai in 2009, will be built. On the ocean, tourists will be welcomed by ever larger cruise ships and perhaps floating cities.

SPORTS TOURISM

Since the late 1970s, sports tourism has become

increasingly popular. Events such as rugby, Olympics, Commonwealth games, Asian Games and football World Cups have enabled specialist travel companies to gain official ticket allocation and then sell them in packages that include flights, hotels and excursions.

LATEST TRENDS

As a result of the late-2000s recession, international arrivals suffered a strong slowdown beginning in June 2008. Growth from 2007 to 2008 was only 3.7% during the first eight months of 2008. The Asian and Pacific markets were affected and Europe stagnated during the boreal summer months, while the Americas performed better, reducing their expansion rate but keeping a 6% growth from January to August 2008. Only the Middle East continued its rapid growth during the same period, reaching a 17% growth as compared to the same period in 2007.

This slowdown on international tourism demand was also reflected in the air transport industry, with a negative growth in September 2008 and a 3.3% growth in passenger traffic through September. The hotel industry also reports a slowdown, as room occupancy continues to decline.

As the global economic situation deteriorated dramatically during September and October as a result of the global financial crisis, growth of international tourism is expected to slow even further for the remaining of 2008, and this slowdown in demand growth is forecasted to continue into 2009 as recession has already hit most of the top spender countries, with long-haul travel expected to be the most affected by the economic crisis. This negative trend intensified as international tourist arrivals fell by 8% during the first four months of 2009, and the decline was exacerbated in some regions due to the outbreak of the influenza AH1N1 virus.

TOURISM IN THE FACE OF 21ST CENTURY'S CHALLENGES

It is difficult to pin-point in a short publication all the problems which will determine the direction of tourism's development in the twenty-first century. This difficulty results from dynamic transformations which are in our modern civilization. Twenty years ago in his book entitled „The Third Wave", A. Toffler wrote that humanity will stand in the face of new challenges, and it appears that these processes are in the future. According to the author the title „The Third Wave", like the previous two indicate, „...will squeeze out previous cultures and civilizations bringing it's morals into effect, which was inconceivable for people who had been born earlier".

The speed of our everyday life was considerably slower, as the first wave, the agricultural revolution, needed one thousand years to run its course. The Industrial revolution, or the second wave, needed only three hundred years from the beginning to the end. However, these prior transformations are incomparable to the speed and progress of our modern civilization. This third wave has been dubbed the technological revolution and is now in process. Some of the more visible processes in our modern life include; the quick development of the technology, the revolution in genetics, the conquest of outer space, the rapid development of cities, and the changes in our jobs and lifestyles. With this information we can state that A. Toffler was correct in saying „The third wave will burst into history within a few decades time.

Thus we will feel the effects of the third wave in our lifetime". Toffler's vision of radical changes in economics accompanied by worldviews of new "liberal opportunities" will create the disintegration of the industrial society. Traditional industries will be replaced with new industries based on modern technology, causing transformation between the relationships of our home and work place, working time and free time, and prosperity versus poverty.

The meaning of the natural environment will become more important as the world will be seeking new values resulting in changes of cultures and ideologies. Lifestyles and family functions will change, taking on new meaning with concepts such as science, careers, and unemployment. However, the question remains, what impact will these new changes have on tourism? Will tourism use these opportunities, or will it be an enclave in which we can rest from civilization. Tourism is a dynamic discipline and is affected by these processes previously discussed. The analysis of trends in the modern tourist market show there are many changes suggesting that tourism in the future will differ from present day affairs. The complexity of tourism will bring about many difficulties throughout its development. J. Krippendorf stated, „ it is possible that tourism, an antidote for the industrial world, has become an industry and predacious devourer of the environment".

The more difficult challenge of the twenty-first century will be the protection of the environment. Fortunately the tourism industry has begun using modern technology in the fields of computer science, communications, and the building of transportation to preserve the environment. The development of tourism is also known to be an asset to social economics, however, there tends to be strong speculations to the overall benefits in this aspect.

THE CONDITIONS AND PROGNOSIS IN THE DEVELOPMENT OF TOURISM AT THE BEGINNING OF THE 21ST CENTURY

Consider the further of tourism and the challenges it will face at the beginning of the twenty-first century. The prognosis is very optimistic as suggested in publicised rapport. The rapport talks about quick development and states that during the next twenty years tourism will be one of the fasts growing departments in the world's economy. However, tourism is far from the end of its development, as for now it consists of a small percentage of the world's citizens.

The main hazards in development are problems with the political situation in the world, especially conflicts within the Balkans, the instability of the Arab world, and the disorganisation between authorities and conflict in the former territory of the Soviet Empire. Slightly less hazardous factors deal with economics such as recession and the increase of gas prices. Nevertheless the outlook on tourist development remains optimistic. The quantitative development of tourism is accompanied by multi-aspects including qualitative and structural transformations. The recent geopolitical changes made in different regions of the world has had a great influence on the scale and structure of tourism.

The downfall of communism and democratisation of societies in former socialist countries are events which have an impact on modern tourism, and other parts of the world have witnessed similar processes within their societies. The development of international tourism will take on new dynamic and important changes in spatial structures. Generally speaking an increase in share of the tourist structure shows no connection with an increase in share of the profit structure.

There is no guarantee of an even distribution in the benefits of tourism. A good example is Africa, which last years shares in total scale of tourist arrivals increased while the total scale of shares in receipts from tourism rapidly decreased. Some interesting changes in the quality of the tourist market are connected with the supply and demand. These aspects of needs, motivations, and demands lead to new directions in tourist firms. A quick tempo of bringing modern technologies into tourism may herald a real revolution in the organisation of the tourist system.

These examples show that tourism, like all repeats of civilization, odder-go changes and the question remains; what tasks will tourism face in the beginning of the new century? There are many factors which will shape the future of the tourist market and it should be noted that some are out of the control of the market. In an attempt to answer some of these questions there must be an analysis of the trends involved with tourism. The diagram presents two basic groups of factors which will decide about tourism in the twenty-first century. The first group are exterior factors called "megatrends".

The second group are interior factors connected with the tourist market. Because of the limited frames in this publication the developing megatrends are on table one, while the factors from the second group are in the complex tables. For more convenient analysis they are split into two groups, one concerned with the demand and one the supply.

MEGATREND INFLUENCES ON THE TOURIST MARKET

The end of the twentieth century was a time of great transformation in all fields of life. There were many fast paced changes throughout social conditions, the economy, and technology, which brought about many transitions within tourism. The constant tendencies to observe and gain knowledge about the markets basic condition are needed to succeed with each activity and the trends within tourism can change quickly. The ability to forecast and stimulate these developmental processes is the key to making the correct decisions for the future.

The fluxuation and competition within the tourist market not only requires constant observation and the ability to anticipate change, but also being able to react to the new trend before it becomes the norm. This shows the importance of knowledge in the action of these megatrends, which can be classified into six basic groups; demographics, politics, social and cultural, economics, technology, and ecology. In each of these groups there are positive factors, which will either stimulate or deter the development of tourism, each with variability in strength and effect. These constituents will decide about the dynamics and expansion of tourism with the difficulty being verification. These megatrends, especially demographics, social, cultural, ecology, and technology hold such a strong influence on the maturation of tourism that such events as a political crisis or economic recession (in some regions) would be unable to hinder such progress.

THE MAIN TRENDS IN TOURIST DEMANDS

There are many interesting publications about change within the field of tourist demands and many studies, which analyse the direction of these changes in development, have been publicised recently. The majorities are unanimous regarding the expansion and direction on the transformations of demands, so much so that there is even an accepted concept known as "Hard and Soft Tourism". It is based on the observational changes within the sphere of former and actual clients in travel agencies and set the standard characteristics of two opposite kinds of tourism: the traditional tourist and the modern tourist.

There is a vision of which tourism will dominate the future, characterised by a more active tourist and less interest in passive tourism. The prediction is that traditional tourism, refereed to as 3 × S (sun sea and sand) will be squeezed out by tourism based on a new formula involving 3 × E (entertainment, excitement, and education). During recent years there has become intensified interest in travelling to historical cities, the so-called "green tourist" with additional concern for a tendency in business tourism.

Nevertheless it could be halted through the development of telecomm- unications and shorter but more frequent trips consisting of sightseeing and holiday could become more popular. The useful system of "bridges" between a national holiday leading to the extension of weekends has brought about a prognosis for a renaissance in national tourism. V.T.C. Middleton claimed that for tourists, who quite often may be 'experienced,' a trend in national tourism may become more attractive now then ever, including the sixties. The smaller interest in international tourism is in the neighbouring countries, or places where many Europeans have had vacation.

In 1990 European travel represented about seven per cent of all international travel, although this number was up to about ten per cent in 1996, and Europeans are not the only ones concerned with these numbers. A poll conducted recently by the Travel Trade Gazette concerning international tourism showed these tendencies in change also pointed to the tourist industry representatives.

One director of a travel agency was quoted saying 'a person who was in Spain ten years ago at present is probably in Penang". The quick increase in numbers of individual trips along with package tours is the prediction of the future. Today Individuality has a strong influence on cars, clothes and other daily needs as well, and the gaining interest of individual travel is one of the most important tendencies in today's tourist demands.

THE MAIN TRENDS IN TOURIST SUPPLY

The advancements and inclinations characterised previously have caused fundamental changes in present and future actions of travel agencies. During the last thirty years the developed markets have been dominated primarily by the supply, however, in the future we can expect to see increased importance in the demand factors as well. Agencies, which are not well informed about the market, could feel the effects and begin losing clients. Today a tourist offer has a different meaning then it did several years ago, when the identical packaged product was selling to a maximum number of clients. This is when the main task of an agency was to secure transportation and hotels for the tourists in an identified town near similar beaches and the local supply had to answer the whimsical requirements of the tourist. Today's tourists expect something different and the prognosis for the twenty-first century is different then it has been in past centuries.

The totality of tourists activities will be one of the most characteristic features in the early dawn of the twenty-first century, and covering borders in economical activity and the concentration of capital are visible in all spheres of the international economy. These inclinations at the tourist market level are quite visible where huge companies are creating the new direction in trend bringing the end of the small travel agencies drawing to a close. The tourist market has been captured by the huge American and Western European companies with Asian, Japanese, and Chinese companies expected to join them in the near future.

Obviously there are some smaller travel agencies which will be needed to look after some special services, but for the most part this will be the change of the movement in the international tourist structure. The expected changes in Russia and China could bring the largest investments into these two countries. It seems that the tourists supply will have a more violent nature than the demand and the odds are that the supply, at the same time, will be the main point of stimulation and transformation.

2

Hospitality and Tourism Industry

AN OVERVIEW

For people who think this is the industry for them, strongly suggest that they really think about their personality and be sure they can thrive (and survive) in the atmosphere. It truly is different from anything else. It is critical that they work for a hotel while they are still in school, preferably in a few different hotels, and departments, so they can get a feel for it and know where they would be the happiest and most successful. The growth in the services sector of the worldwide economy has been phenomenal in the last 25 years. In the United States, services currently account for more than 75 per cent of the gross domestic product (GDP), which is a popular measure of an economy's productivity.

Similarly, on an international scale, services continue to account for an ever-increasing percentage of economic activity. Most new jobs are created in the service sector, and the growth in the hospitality and tourism industry is a major contributor. Until the mid-1980s, the emphasis within the marketing community was on products. Now services have surpassed products and have taken on a more important role in marketing.

Services, such as those offered by providers in the hospitality and tourism industry, have developed marketing strategies and practices that are unique. It has been established that the strategies, tactics, and practices that have been used successfully for product marketers do not always work successfully for those who market services. With the distinct differences between products and services in mind, the field of services marketing has evolved.

SERVICES DEFINED

Unlike products, which are tangible, services are usually intangible. A service is not a physical good; rather, it is the performance of an act or a deed. This performance often requires consumers to be present during the production or delivery of the service. Service industries, including hospitality and tourism, are actually selling consumers an experience. Services have been defined to "include all economic activities whose output is not a physical product or construction, is generally consumed at the time it is produced, and provides added value in forms (such as convenience, amusement, timeliness, comfort or health) that are essentially intangible concerns of its first purchaser."

Service employees such as front desk agents, housekeepers, hostesses, wait staff, car rental agents, flight attendants, and travel agents are responsible for creating positive experiences for customers. These frontline employees are critical to the success of service firms and play boundary-spanning roles because of their direct contact with customers.

These roles are important because customers' perceptions of service firms are formed as a result of their dealings with the boundary-spanning employees. Several reasons underlie the remarkable growth in services. Two leading services marketing experts, Christopher Lovelock and Lauren Wright, cite numerous reasons for this growth:

Changing patterns of government regulation: The reduction in government regulation has spurred the growth of services. In recent years, there has been a very noticeable shift towards the government taking a much less active role in the regulation of business activities. The most noteworthy of these shifts have been in the airline, trucking, telecommunication, and electrical generation and distribution industries. All of these industries have seen significant changes, as the barriers to entry have been removed and regulations governing such marketing elements as price have also been relaxed or entirely removed.

Relaxation of professional association restrictions on marketing: A new element of competition has been introduced into professions such as law and medicine as more of the practitioners in these areas advertise their services. Bans or restrictions on promotion have been largely removed. Within the hospitality and tourism industry, standards have also changed. We have seen an increase in advertising focusing on direct comparisons, or attacks, on competitors' products and services. This type of advertising strategy creates, or sustains, the perception of superiority in the mind of the consumer in favour of the brand being advertised.

Privatization of some public and nonprofit services: The term privatization was first used in Great Britain when the government adopted the policy of returning national industries from government to private ownership. This transformation has resulted in a greater emphasis on cost containment and a clearer focus on customers' needs. Later, in Central and Eastern Europe, following the fall of communism, we witnessed a continuing transformation from planned or government-run economies to market-driven economies fueled by private companies. Many of these countries' governments have released the control of airlines and travel agencies to private firms.

Technological innovation: Technology continues to alter the way firms do business and interact with consumers. In all types of businesses, consumers take a more active role in the service delivery process. For example, airlines, in an effort to reduce labour costs and increase speed of service to customers, have aggressively promoted self-check-in, both at the ticket counter and through their Web sites prior to arrival at the airport. Customers print boarding passes, receipts, and other documents without intervention by an airline employee. Express checkout for hotel guests has been in place for many years, but hotel chains continue to experiment with ways to enhance the service, thereby reducing labour costs and/or increasing the customers' perceived value.

In other settings, touch-screen computers collect feedback from guests, in much the same manner that comment cards have been used previously. The ease with which a company can maintain and access a database has permitted the development of sophisticated reservation systems and has led to more sophisticated frequent traveller programmes. The use of more sophisticated reservations and property management systems has allowed hospitality and tourism firms to improve the level of service provided to guests. Guest history data serve as another example of how a hospitality organization can use technology to gain a competitive advantage. If a hotel guest requests a specific type of pillow, staff can record this preference within the individual's guest history file. When this guest checks into another hotel operated by the chain, the items that were previously requested can be waiting, without the guest even having to request them.

Growth in service chains and franchise networks: Much of the growth in service firms, including the hospitality industry, has been the direct result of franchising efforts by some of the major companies. Franchising represents a contractual arrangement whereby one firm (the franchisor) licenses a number of other firms (the franchisees) to use the franchisor's name and business practices. Notable lodging organizations such as Choice Hotels International and Marriott International, as well as food service firms such as McDonald's, Burger King, Taco Bell, and Wendy's, have all used franchising as a major vehicle for growth. The continued growth of the hospitality industry by means of franchising has put additional stress on independent owners and operators. In fact, each year the percentage of hospitality and tourism operations that are independently operated decreases.

Internationalization and globalization: Increasing shareholder value often remains directly associated with increasing company sales and profits, and globalization is one means of achieving this. As more and more of the prime locations are developed domestically, companies look internationally for expansion opportunities. This has been particularly true for fast-food franchisors: a significant proportion of their expansion during the last few years has occurred outside of their traditional domestic markets.

Pressures to improve productivity: In many industries within the service economy, competition stays very intense. This factor, when combined with the pressure from investors for higher returns on capital, has resulted in pressure to increase productivity and reduce costs. In many cases, managers seek to reduce labour costs by running leaner operations or using technology to replace humans for some tasks An example of this was when Delta Airlines encouraged passengers to check in via the Internet, thereby reducing the number of passengers who wanted to check in at the airport. They offered an incentive of 1,000 extra frequent-flyer miles to any passenger who used this service. While increasing productivity and profits remains a highly desirable goal, it must not be done at the expense of long term customer satisfaction. Without long-term satisfaction, future profitability may exist in jeopardy.

The service quality movement: With the advent of consumerism, the public's perception is that service quality has declined. In response, successful firms are using the customer's perception of quality to set performance standards, rather than relying solely on operationally defined standards for service quality. They often conduct extensive research to determine the key elements that impact the customer's perception of service quality. When Ritz-Carlton won the Malcolm Baldrige National Quality Award, this was tangible evidence that paying careful attention to customers' service expectations can have a dramatic impact on the firm.

Expansion of leasing and rental businesses: The expansion of businesses that lease equipment and personnel to firms has been a contributing factor in the growth of the service sector. More and more firms are looking to outsource some elements of their operation, and they often start with elements that are not part of the firm's core product or business. For example, most hotels that host meetings and conventions have outsourced the servicing of the audiovisual needs of groups to a company that specializes in that type of business. The company in turn leases the audiovisual equipment to groups that are holding meetings in the hotel. The company is able to provide more up-to-date and specialized equipment to groups than the hotel might if it provided the service itself. The hotel does not have to maintain an inventory of equipment, and therefore capital costs are reduced.

Manufacturers as service providers: Some of the firms that traditionally manufactured and distributed tangible products have found it profitable to provide services as well. For example, most automobile manufacturers have consumer credit agencies to facilitate the leasing and purchasing of automobiles.

In the hospitality industry, PepsiCo decided to enter the restaurant industry and distribute its products through acquisitions such as Taco Bell and KFC, but the company later reconsidered this strategy and sold these brands to Yum! Brands, Inc. In the computer industry, firms such as IBM and Hewlett-Packard provide services in addition to hardware and software. In most cases, the profit margins on services are higher than on products, contributing significantly to the bottom line of the firm.

Pressures on public and nonprofit organizations to find new income sources: All organizations are under pressure to increase sales, which often becomes difficult within the traditional products that a firm sells. There are many reasons for this, but increasing competition and mature industries are often contributing factors. In an effort to find new sources of income, firms often seek new services that will generate new net sales, without cannibalizing sales of existing products. For example, a limousine company might expand its city tour business in addition to the other services offered.

Hiring and promotion of innovative managers: In the past, managers in the service industries often spent their entire careers within a single industry, or perhaps even with the same firm. This situation no longer reintroduction to services marketing mains the same, especially at the corporate level of management. Firms often hire individuals from other industries to provide a fresh perspective and fresh ideas. The results can become dramatic. One such individual is Steven Bollenback, president and CEO of Hilton Hotels. Prior to his very positive impact on Hilton Hotels, he had engineered innovative financing at both Marriott International and Trump Hotels and Resorts.

THE NATURE OF SERVICES

Along with the growth in services, an appreciation for the ways in which services are different from products has developed. The traditional ways of marketing tangible products are not equally effective in services marketing. In many industries, marketing involves tangible manufactured products, such as automobiles, washing machines, and clothing, whereas service industries focus on intangible products such as travel and foodservice. However, before we can explore how services get successfully marketed, we need to examine the ways services differ from products. Lovelock and Wright have identified nine key differences.

No ownership by customers: A customer does not take ownership when purchasing a service. There is no transfer of assets.

Service products as intangible performers: The value of owning a high performance car or the latest computer lies in the physical characteristics of the product and to some extent the brand image it conveys. The value of purchasing services lies in the nature of the performance. For example, if you decide to celebrate a birthday or anniversary by dining at an expensive restaurant, the value lies in the way in which the service actors perform. When servers come to the table and present all the entrees simultaneously, the choreographed presentation appears in the same manner as a choreographed play or performance.

Greater involvement of customers in the production process: Because consumers tend to be present when receiving service within a hospitality operation, they remain involved in the service production. In many instances, they are directly involved through the element of self-service. Examples of this can be seen in fast-food restaurants as well as in hotels that provide automated check-in and checkout by means of either a machine or a video connection through the television. Airlines have greatly expanded self-service within their operations as a means of reducing labour costs. In any case, the customer's level of satisfaction depends on the nature of the interaction with the service provider, the nature of the physical facilities in which the service gets provided, and the nature of the interaction with other guests present in the facility at the time the service is provided.

People as part of the product. People or firms that purchase services come in contact with other consumers as well as the service employees. For example, a hotel guest waits in line at the front desk or the concierge desk with other guests. In addition, the guests share facilities such as the pool, the restaurant, and the fitness centre. Therefore, service firms must also manage consumer interactions to the best of their abilities to ensure customer satisfaction. For example, a hotel's sales office would not want to book group business with a non drinking religious group at the same time as a reunion of military veterans. The two groups are significantly different in behaviour, and the expectation is that they would not mix well within the facilities at the same time. Similarly, restaurants separate smokers and nonsmokers, and they should try to separate other patrons that show some potential for conflict.

Greater variability in operational inputs and outputs: In a manufacturing setting, the operational production can be controlled very carefully. For example, staff carefully manage inventory and precisely calculate production times. Services, however, are delivered in real time, with many variables not being fully under the control of managers.

For example, if a guest has been promised an early check-in but all of the guests from the preceding night are late in checking out, it becomes more difficult for the hotel to honour the arriving guest's request. A service setting remains a more difficult site in which to control quality and offer a consistent service experience. Service firms try to minimize the amount of variability between service encounters, but much of the final product stays situational. There are many uncontrollable aspects of the delivery process, such as weather, the number of consumers present, the attitudes of the consumers, and the attitudes of the employees. Therefore, it becomes impossible to consistently control the quality for services in the same manner as the quality of manufactured products. *Harder for consumers to evaluate:* Consumers can receive considerable information regarding the purchase of products; however, they often do not obtain it for services. Prior to buying a product, a consumer can research the product attributes and performance and use this information when making a purchase decision, especially an important one.

No inventories for services: Due to the intangible nature of services, they cannot be inventoried for future use. Therefore, a lost sale can never be recaptured. When a seat remains empty on a flight, a hotel room stays vacant, or a table stays unoccupied in a restaurant, the potential revenue for these services at that point in time becomes lost forever. In other words, services are perishable, much like produce in a supermarket or items in a bakery. It remains critical for hospitality and tourism firms to manage supply and demand in an attempt to minimize unused capacity. For example, restaurants offer early-bird specials and airlines offer deeply discounted fares in an attempt to shift demand from peak periods to non peak periods, thereby increasing revenue and profits.

Importance of time: Hospitality services are generally produced and consumed simultaneously, unlike tangible products, which are manufactured, inventoried, and then sold at a later date. Customers must be present to receive the service. There are real limits to the amount of time that customers are willing to wait to receive service. Service firms study the phenomenon of service queues, or the maximum amount of time a customer will wait for a service before it has a significant (negative) impact on his or her perception of service quality. Airline companies offer curbside check-in for the most time-conscious passengers, and restaurants have devised practices such as providing guests with pagers and expanding the bar area in order to reduce the negative effect that results from waiting for service.

Different distribution channels: The distribution channel for services is usually more direct than the traditional channel (*i.e.*, manufacturer-wholesaler retailer- consumer) used by many product firms. The simultaneous production and consumption normally associated with service delivery limits the use of intermediaries. The service firm usually comprises both the manufacturer and the retailer, with no need for a wholesaler to inventory its products. Consumers are present to consume the meals prepared in a restaurant, to take advantage of the amenities in a hotel, and to travel between cities by plane.

SEARCH, EXPERIENCE, AND CREDENCE QUALITIES

Consumer behaviour is covered in greater depth, but a brief introduction to the subject as it relates to services becomes useful at this point. When consumers make purchase decisions, they move through a series of steps that explain the thought process leading up to and following the purchase of a product or service. Prior to making a purchase decision, consumers look for information about the product or service. Search qualities are attributes that the consumer can investigate prior to making a purchase.

When purchasing hospitality and tourism services, consumers rely heavily on word of mouth and on promotional elements such as advertising and publicity. Since services are intangible, search qualities can be difficult to evaluate. However, advances in technology and the increase in consumer advocacy groups have resulted in more information being available to consumers prior to purchase. The second set of qualities consumers use to evaluate services are experience qualities.

These refer to the attributes that can be evaluated only after the purchase and consumption of a service. The intangible nature of services forces consumers to rely heavily on experience qualities in the final evaluation of services. Therefore, a high risk remains associated with the purchase of services. For example, consumers who want to purchase an automobile will test-drive the car and review and consult the consumer performance data that are available on that model. Conversely, consumers who rent cars cannot evaluate their purchases until after they have committed their payment. Few consumers will take the time or make the effort to test-drive potential rental cars prior to making a decision at the time of rental. Similarly, consumers are taking a risk when they choose a restaurant because they cannot sample meals before they are purchased. Finally, credence qualities are those attributes that are difficult to evaluate even after the service is consumed. Even though you arrive safely at your destination after a flight, you cannot evaluate the pilot's work in any real depth. In many cases, you know a service was not performed correctly only when an obvious mistake exists. For example, bacteria often appear on food served in restaurants, but the public becomes aware of it only when major ramifications such as food poisoning or deaths get publicized.

Purchase decisions related to services are more difficult to make because of the lack of search qualities and the difficulty in evaluating credence qualities. Consumers tend to rely on their own past experiences and those of others when making purchase decisions. Therefore, service firms must obtain as much feedback from consumers as possible. If consumers do not return, the firm may not know why, and the consumers will probably tell others about their experience. Service firms should know if consumers are not satisfied so that appropriate actions can be taken to improve the quality of service and increase repeat business.

SERVICE QUALITY

Firms use two basic strategies to compete: become a low-cost provider of a particular service and focus on price competition, or focus on quality and try to differentiate your service from those offered by your competitors. Firms that can project high-quality images can charge higher prices. Service quality is a perception resulting from attitudes formed by customers' long-term, overall evaluations of performance.4 Maintaining high quality service in the hospitality and tourism industry remains difficult because of the variability in service delivery mentioned earlier in this chapter.

Service quality is affected by all of the individuals who have contact with customers. If one employee provides below-standard service or fails to satisfy the customer, a negative experience could result. Therefore, it is important to understand the entire process of service delivery that leads to consumer perceptions of quality.

THE SERVICE QUALITY PROYCESS

The service quality process is the product of the expectations and perceptions of a firm's management, its employees, and the customers it serves. Whenever there are differences in expectations or perceptions between the people involved in the delivery and the consumption of services, a potential for a gap in service quality exists. Firms should diagnose any service quality gaps because there is a direct relationship between service quality and customer satisfaction. Simply stated, when customers are satisfied, they are much more likely to purchase from the service provider again. Over time, if they remain satisfied, they become loyal customers.

The service gap is the final gap that exists when there is a difference between customers' expectations of a service and their perceptions of the actual service once it is consumed. When this difference occurs, it is the result of one or more gaps that occur earlier in the service quality process. The first potential gap is referred to as the knowledge gap, which occurs when management's perception of what consumers expect is different from the consumers' actual expectations. This gap may lead to other gaps in the service quality service quality process, and it is usually the result of a failure in the firm's research programme or organizational structure. Firms need to obtain feedback from customers and employees that can be used to design services that will appeal to customers.

If the current service offering is not satisfying customers, then the firm should know from its customer surveys or because its employees are willing, and able, to provide valuable information that they obtain from customers, either voluntarily or involuntarily. The second potential gap is referred to as the standards gap, which refers to the discrepancy that can occur between management's perception of what customers expect and how the service delivery process is designed to meet those expectations. Management establishes the specifications to provide the desired service at the desired level of quality. Therefore, even if management remains accurate in its perception of customer expectations, a gap could still exist in service because the delivery process does not accomplish the goals of the firm. For example, management may have correctly determined the amount of time that customers are willing to wait to check in to a hotel, but they may not schedule enough front desk clerks to meet the customers' expectations.

This could result from a lack of commitment on the part of management or the result of management trying to reduce the firm's operating costs. One of the techniques used by management is to develop a service blueprint— a flow chart that details the delivery process, including the points of contact with customers. This will help to uncover any shortcomings in the delivery process that may lead to a gap in service quality. Management should document each step in the process to identify areas for improvement.

The third potential gap is referred to as the delivery gap, which occurs when there is a difference between the service delivery specifications and the actual service delivery. Management may have correctly assessed customer expectations and developed specifications that will meet these expectations, but employees may not deliver the service properly. For example, a restaurant may specify that wait staff should approach customers within two minutes of seating. However, the wait staff may stand around discussing their plans for later in the evening and ignoring the specifications. Firms must find ways to create an atmosphere for employees that ensures their willingness to perform the job tasks as desired by management.

Employee selection and training are critical in this process, as are the rewards and recognition provided for good performance. The fourth potential gap is referred to as the communications gap, which occurs when there is a difference between the service delivered and the service quality promised through the firm's external communications with customers. Many firms have a tendency to promise more than they can deliver in an attempt to persuade customers. For instance, advertisements for hospitality and tourism firms lead customers to believe that in the event of a problem or mishap the firms will do whatever they can to satisfy customers. Making promises to consumers that cannot be delivered is a big mistake that service providers often make. It results in service performance levels that are below consumer expectations, leading to dissatisfaction. Each individual consumer makes purchase decisions and has established, based on past experiences, a set of expectations for the performance of a product or service.

Anyone who travels on a regular basis can provide stories related to experiences with airlines, hotels, and restaurants. Ironically, firms that advertise 100 per cent satisfaction guarantees are banking on the fact that most customers will not complain or force the issue. In other cases, firms simply neglect to inform customers about procedures or policies that would affect their expectations. For example, a good waitress will make sure that customers know that a dish is spicy or that a certain entree will take longer to properly prepare, so that customers can make informed decisions and are less likely to become dissatisfied, because the actual performance will more closely match consumer expectations.

If any of the first four gaps occur, then the service gap will occur because the actual service will not meet the customer's expectations. Comment cards and basic surveys will often uncover a service gap, but they may lack the detail needed to evaluate the other potential gaps. Therefore, firms should have a mechanism in place to obtain feedback from customers and employees that can be used to examine the entire service quality process. If services do not meet customers' expectations of quality, then the customers become dissatisfied and will likely not return. Also, they will convey these negative experiences to their friends and colleagues.

MANAGING SERVICE QUALITY

To provide high-quality service, all members of the staff, from the highest to the lowest level on the organizational chart, must view the guest as the highest priority. Delivering high-quality service is based on an attitude of serving customers. For example, the mission statement of The Greenbrier, a well-known resort, states, "We are ladies and gentlemen serving ladies and gentlemen." Developing an attitude that places the customer as the highest priority for the business remains critical. Without satisfied customers and repeat patron- age, the business will not succeed in the long term.

To develop a service quality orientation, customers should be perceived in the following way:

- Each customer is the most important person in any business.
- Customers are not dependent on us, but we are dependent on them.
- Customers do not interrupt our work. They are the purpose for it.
- Customers do us a favour when they call. We are not doing them favours by providing them services.
- Customers are part of our business, not outsiders.
- Customers are human beings like us, with the same feelings and emotions.
- Customers bring us their wants, and it is our job to fulfill them.
- Customers deserve the most courteous and attentive service we can provide.
- Customers are the lifeblood of every business.

Firms that use a customer orientation become more successful at providing products and services that meet customers' needs and expectations. In contrast, firms that assume they know what is best for the customer are more likely to fail. This is further illustrated by those firms that successfully engage in relationship and internal marketing.

RELATIONSHIP MARKETING

All progressive companies devote marketing resources to attract and retain new customers. Relationship marketing is based on the proposition that it is less expensive to keep the customers you already have than to acquire new customers.

It is shortsighted to think that merely attracting new customers will keep the business headed in a successful direction. Rather, an equal amount of attention and resources should be devoted to keeping the customer base that already exists. In times of slow market growth and increasing competition, it will be less expensive to maintain an existing customer base than to seek new customers.

Relationship marketing involves attracting, developing, and retaining customer relationships. This long-term view towards the customer must be seen as being equal in importance to attracting new customers. Many firms make the mistake of focusing on new customers at the expense of existing customers, and the level of service quality diminishes. For example, hotel sales managers are expected to develop new accounts with corporate and association groups.

Sometimes they spend so much time trying to get these new accounts that they neglect some of their existing accounts. This lack of attention may cost the hotel the group's future business because they took the customer for granted. Service firms should build relationships and maintain them.

A relationship marketing approach is highly desirable upon meeting the following conditions:

- A customer has an ongoing or periodic desire for the service.
- The service customer controls the selection of the service organization.
- Alternative service providers make it easy for customers to switch.

All three of these conditions are present in the hospitality and tourism industry. Many firms offer special prices and additional services to highly desirable customers in an attempt to build long-term relationships. These practices are most commonly used with business accounts and frequent users. For example, hotels provide contract rates for corporations that supply a high volume of annual business. Airlines receive one of the lowest rates possible in hotels near airports because they have flight crews who need guest rooms on a daily basis. Also, airlines build relationships with frequent flyers by providing them with additional services such as preboarding, free upgrades, and airport clubs where they can rest or conduct business away from crowded lounges at departure gates.

INTERNAL MARKETING

In addition to focusing efforts on consumers, firms can achieve higher levels of service quality by marketing to their employees. Internal marketing encompasses all activities used by a firm in an effort to improve the marketing effectiveness of its employees. Efforts should be made to communicate with all employees, especially those in boundary spanning roles who come in contact with customers. The ability to deliver consistent, high-quality service depends on the organization's ability to recruit, train, retain, and motivate dedicated service personnel. First, service firms need to select and hire employees who are willing and able to provide high-quality service. There are many people in the job market, and firms need to create attractive positions that appeal to highly motivated individuals.

A range of potential service exists that an employee can provide from the minimum necessary to retain the position and not be penalized to the maximum possible service. This variability in the level of possible service is referred to as discretionary effort. For example, if an airline passenger leaves a carry-on item on a flight, the airline's personnel have some discretion as to the level of service they will provide. They can take their time and forward the item to the traveller's next destination, or they can try to deliver it to the traveller before he or she boards the next plane or leaves the airport. Second, service firms should provide employees with adequate training so they possess the skills that are required in performing their job tasks.

In addition, the firm should communicate with employees so they are aware of changes within the organization as well as upcoming events. If service personnel are well trained and they understand what management expects, the environment is right for success. Firms can use both internal communications, such as newsletters and e-mail, and external communications, such as advertising and public relations, to convey their expectations to employees.

An advertisement can be used to create and manage consumer perceptions and expectations, but at the same time, the ad can be used to educate employees as well. One of the major airlines aired a commercial on television that showed an athletic employee running through the airport to catch a traveller who left his briefcase at the check-in counter.

This commercial served two purposes:

1. It let customers know that the airline provided high-quality service, and
2. It gave employees an idea of the firm's service expectations.

Finally, firms need to provide employees with rewards and recognition when they perform at a high level of discretionary effort. This motivates service providers to continue performing at high levels and to remain loyal to the firm. Retaining good employees is important in providing high-quality service, and it reduces the costs associated with turnover. It takes a great deal of time and effort to hire and train good employees.

Firms can use extrinsic rewards such as salary increases and bonuses or intrinsic rewards such as recognition and job satisfaction to motivate employees. Many firms recognize "employees of the month" by honouring them with plaques displayed where customers can see them or allowing them to use special parking spaces close to the building.

CUSTOMER SATISFACTION

Most firms understand the importance of customer satisfaction and will provide basic training to their employees. The more sophisticated firms actually have instruments that they use to measure customer satisfaction and establish benchmarks for future comparisons. Benchmarking is a process whereby a firm establishes a level of performance by comparing current performance against past performance, or by comparing current performance against the performance of other companies or an entire industry.

Data are used to create benchmarks, which then become the standard against which current and customer satisfaction future performance is evaluated. Unfortunately, many firms still only pay lip service to customer satisfaction and the complaints received from customers.

The following information was collected through the efforts of the Technical Assistance Research Programme in the 1980s, but it remains accurate today:

- The average business does not hear from 96 per cent of its unhappy customers.
- For every complaint received, 26 other customers have the same problem.
- The average person with a problem tells 9 or 10 people, and 13 per cent will tell more than 20.
- Customers who have their complaints resolved to their satisfaction tell an average of 5 people about the experience.
- Complainers are more likely to do business with you again than non complainers who have a problem: 54–70 per cent if resolved, and 95 per cent if resolved quickly. These statistics support the contention that a dissatisfied customer tells people about a bad experience more often than a satisfied customer tells people about a good experience. However, firms should take note that it is beneficial to have customers voice their complaints so that they can be resolved and increase the likelihood that the customers will return.

IMPROVING CUSTOMER SERVICE AND CUSTOMER SATISFACTION

Improving customer service should be a top priority of all managers working in the hospitality and tourism industry. Customer satisfaction occurs when a firm's service, as perceived by customers, meets or exceeds expectations. Firms that can consistently meet or exceed customer expectations will develop good reputations and often good quality images. When we travel, we encounter service providers in hotels and restaurants who provide exceptional service. This type and consistency of service does not happen by accident; it begins with a commitment by management to make it that way.

Conversely, when the opposite occurs, the finger should be pointed at management as well:

- *Define your standards of quality service with measurable indicators:* Before you can evaluate the level of service provided by employees within your organization, you must establish the standards by which they will be judged. These standards, or benchmarks, should be observable and measurable. For example, it might be reasonable to expect front desk agents to answer the telephone within four rings or room service to deliver meals within 30 minutes of when the order was received. Once these standards are developed, they must be communicated to all personnel. It remains crucial that standards be clearly defined before any plans are developed to improve the level of service. Martin suggests two major dimensions to define quality service: the procedural dimension and the convivial dimension. The procedural dimension includes incremental flow of service, timeliness, accommodating consumer needs, anticipating consumer needs before they occur or are requested by the consumer, communicating in a clear and concise manner, customer satisfaction obtaining consumer feedback, and coordinating through proper supervision. The convivial dimension includes displaying a positive attitude and body language, using the guest's name as a means of delivering personal attention, attending to the guest on a personal basis, providing guidance to guests who are indecisive, and solving problems that arise.
- *Assess your current situation*: As in any continuous improvement programme, before you move forward, you must determine your current position. This can be done by objectively assessing the level of service currently provided within the organization; this

involves conducting an audit of the services provided by service personnel within the organization. As a result of the audit, the strengths and weaknesses of the firm can be determined; this will provide a means of building on the aspects of service that are positive and improving the areas that are deficient. Audits can be conducted using mystery shoppers, or corporations may use staff members to audit the performance of units within the company.

- *Develop effective service improvement strategies:* This must be accomplished through well-planned and thorough training of service providers. Attention must be paid to identifying objectives for the training and providing specific instructions and clear descriptions of the expected outcome (s) of the training.
- *Initiate your solutions carefully:* As with any plan, implementation is the most critical stage. You should proceed with caution, taking steps incrementally rather than all at once. You should build on small successes, rather than trying to accomplish too much too soon.
- *Provide feedback, recognition, and rewards:* Positive feedback must be provided if the change in behaviour continues. A reward structure must be provided that will maintain the level of interest and enthusiasm among the service providers throughout their careers. This represents a major challenge for management, but one that is well worth the effort. Finally, management must continually evaluate the performance of its employees and make the appropriate changes. Over time, customers' expectations of service firms change, and competitive firms may increase the level of service that is considered the standard in an industry. Therefore, firms must constantly reassess their strategies and redefine their service standards. Service performance and customer satisfaction should be measured and

evaluated using benchmarks established during previous periods. Also, direct comparisons with the performance of firms considered industry leaders are an excellent way to establish goals for future improvement.

Service Failures, Customer Complaints, and Recovery Strategies

Service failures occur at critical incidents, or "moments of truth," in the service encounter, when customers interact with a firm's employees. It is important to provide service personnel with the authority and the recovery tools necessary to correct service failures as they occur. This section will discuss the types of service failures, common consumer complaints, and recovery strategies that can be used to repair the service failures.

SERVICE FAILURES

The timeliness and form of response by service providers to service failures will have a direct impact on customer satisfaction and quality perceptions.

Service failures are assigned to one of three major categories:

1. Responses to service delivery system failures,
2. Responses to customer needs and requests, and
3. Unprompted and unsolicited employee actions.

The first category, system failures, refers to failures in the core service offering of the firm. These failures are the result of normally available services being unavailable, unreasonably slow service, or some other core service failure that will differ by industry.

For example, a hotel's pool may have a leak and be closed, a customer may have to wait a long time for the shuttle to an airport car rental agency, or an airline might mishandle a passenger's luggage. The second category, customer needs failures, are based on employee responses to customer needs or special requests. These failures come in the form of special needs, customer preferences, customer errors, and disruptive others (*i.e.*, disputes between customers). For example, a hotel guest may want to have a pet in the room, a customer may want to be switched to an aisle seat on an airplane, a customer at an event may lose his ticket, or a customer in a restaurant may be smoking in a nonsmoking section. The third category, unsolicited employee actions, refers to the actions, both good and bad, of employees that are not expected by customers. These actions can be related to the level of attention an employee gives to customers, to unusual actions that can be performed by employees, to an action's reinforcement of a customer's cultural norms, or to an employee's actions under adverse conditions.

For example, a hostess in a restaurant could anticipate the needs of a family with a small child, a hotel front desk clerk could give a free upgrade to a guest who waited in line too long, a flight attendant could ignore passengers with children, or a cruise ship employee could help to evacuate passengers during a crisis customer satisfaction

CUSTOMER COMPLAINT BEHAVIOUR

As mentioned earlier in this chapter, certain undesired outcomes are associated with dissatisfied customers. Two of the most common are to engage in negative word of mouth and to change service providers. A third, less common reaction is to engage in some form of retaliation. This retaliation can range from a negative word-of-mouth campaign to causing physical damage or launching a major protest.

The way a firm approaches and handles complaints will determine its long-term performance. Some firms show a dislike for customers who complain, while other firms create an atmosphere that encourages customers to voice their concerns.

For example, Bertucci's Brick Oven Pizzerias, headquartered in Massachusetts, offers customers a tollfree number that they can call to register a complaint. One of the primary reasons for doing this is to provide dissatisfied customers with an outlet to have their concerns heard and to take immediate steps to resolve the complaint. By doing so, the firm hopes to reduce negative word of mouth and to retain customers. Most customers complain in an attempt to reverse an undesirable state. Other more complicated reasons for complaining are to release pressure, to regain some form of control over a situation, or to get the sympathy of others. Whatever the reason, the outcome is that customers are not completely satisfied, and it is in the firm's best interest to know when this occurs. There are many other dissatisfied customers who do not complain because they don't know what to do or they don't think it will do any good.

RECOVERY STRATEGIES

When customers complain, firms are presented with the opportunity to recover from service failures. Recovery strategies, and actions occur when a firm's reaction to a service failure results in customer satisfaction and goodwill. In fact, customers who are involved in successful service recoveries often demonstrate higher levels of satisfaction than customers who do not report service failures or complain. The following list describes popular service recovery strategies:

Cost/benefit analysis: Service firms should compare the costs of losing customers and obtaining new customers with the benefits of keeping existing customers. Most firms place a high value on retaining customers. However, some guests take advantage of satisfaction guarantees and complain on every occasion. Many hotel chains, such as Doubletree, maintain a database on complaints and will flag chronic complainers.

Actively encourage complaints: It is better to know when customers are not satisfied so that action can be taken to rectify the situation. It is important to note that while unhappy customers may not complain to service firms, they will often complain to their family and friends. Hospitality and tourism firms use comment cards and toll-free numbers to encourage customers to provide feedback. Also, service personnel are trained to ask customers whether everything was satisfactory.

Anticipate the need for recovery: Service firms should "blueprint" the service delivery process and determine the moments of truth, or critical incidents, where customers interact with employees. The process can be designed to avoid failures, but recovery plans should be established for use in the event that a failure occurs.

- *Respond quickly:* The timelier the response in the event of a service failure, the more likely that recovery efforts will be successful. Once a customer leaves a service establishment, the likelihood of a successful recovery falls dramatically. Based on this principle, firms such as Marriott International provide service hotlines at each hotel to help resolve problems quickly. Managers and associates know that the speed with which they respond is often as critical as what the final resolution becomes.
- *Train employees:* Employees should be informed of the critical incidents and provided with potential strategies for recovery. For example, some hotel training programmes use videotaped scenarios of service failures to show employees potential problems and the appropriate solutions.
- *Empower the front line:* In many cases, a successful recovery will hinge on a frontline employee's ability to take timely action and make a decision. Firms should empower employees to handle service failures at the time they occur, within certain limits.

For example, Ritz-Carlton allows its employees to spend up to $1,000 to take care of dissatisfied customers. One of the classic examples of a service failure involved Northwest Airlines during a major winter storm at the Detroit airport. Unfortunately, due to the heavy snow, many outbound flights were canceled, and no gates were available for unloading passengers from the inbound flights. This traffic jam left many passengers stranded as the airplanes sat on the taxiways for as long as eight hours. Northwest's inability to provide the passengers with information or a solution resulted in hundreds of unhappy passengers and a class action lawsuit. Having delayed flights and a shortage of gates is not a new phenomenon at airports in climates such as Detroit's, and Northwest Airlines should have had a viable service recovery programme in place that could have lessened the severity of the problem.

TECHNIQUES TO ASSESS CUSTOMER SATISFACTION

One of the critical components of a firm's commitment to customer satisfaction is feedback that provides an assessment of the firm's performance. Then benchmarks can be established and future progress can be evaluated. Also, these measures can be used to reward service personnel in a way that stays consistent with a firm's customer satisfaction goals. The following section describes the most common techniques used by firms to assess customer satisfaction.

SPOKEN COMMENTS AND COMPLAINTS

Listening to consumer comments and complaints remains the most straightforward way to evaluate customer satisfaction. Service firms should set up formal systems that encourage customer and employee feedback regarding service experiences. Management should not overlook the value of the information obtained by boundary-spanning personnel through their normal contact with customers. One of the most recent approaches is providing toll-free numbers so that customers can call to voice complaints.

SURVEYS AND COMMENT CARDS

Many hospitality and tourism firms leave comment cards in guest rooms, on tables in restaurants, and at other points of contact so that they can obtain feedback. One of the problems associated with this method is the lack of representation. The response rate is small, and it tends to be biased towards those who are most upset and chronic complainers. Larger operations will conduct surveys through the corporate offices by either telephone or mail. Surveys will normally be more representative than comment cards and provide more detailed information. These types of surveys also provide for a more representative sample of customers.

NUMBER OF REPEAT CUSTOMERS

Service firms can gauge customer satisfaction by keeping track of repeat business. Higher levels of satisfaction would be associated with higher percentages of repeat customers. This models an unobtrusive method of assessing customer satisfaction, but it does not provide much detail.

TRENDS IN SALES AND MARKET SHARE

Another way to evaluate customer satisfaction without direct contact with customers is to examine the firm's internal sales records. Comparisons can be made on a month-to-month basis and with the same period of the previous year. Higher levels of satisfaction would be associated with increases in sales. However, firms should be careful with this method because there are many possible explanations for increases in sales. For example, the firm may have launched a new advertising campaign, a competitor may be renovating or going out of business, or the firm may have decreased its prices. In addition to examining sales records, firms should also look at market share.

This measure considers sales in relation to the competition, which is a more accurate assessment of improved market performance. However, there could also be other explanations for changes in market share besides customer satisfaction.

SHOPPING REPORTS

Another approach used by hospitality and tourism firms involves having someone consume a service just like any other customer. The "secret shopper" can be an employee of the firm, an outside person chosen by the firm, or an employee of an outside firm that specializes in this service assessment activity. These shoppers are normally equipped with detailed evaluation forms based on company guidelines that can be used to record the desired information.

It is often recommended that someone outside the firm be used in an attempt to maintain some level of objectivity. It is important to have a particular operation evaluated by more than one shopper on several occasions throughout the desired period. Doing so will result in a more representative sample of service experiences.

SERVICE TRENDS AFFECTING THE HOSPITALITY AND TOURISM INDUSTRY

Identifying trends within any business is one of the keys to success. Being in a position to identify what is occurring and what is likely to occur in the future remains very important. As discussed earlier, when studying trends in a broad sense, one should examine five major areas: the competitive environment, the economic environment, the political and legal environment, the social environment, and the technological environment.

Several issues and trends are critical to understanding hospitality and tourism marketing. They help put into proper perspective what occurs within the competitive marketplace. Three trends that are having an impact on the hospitality industry and will continue to do so are shrinking customer loyalty, increasing customer sophistication, and increasing emphasis on the needs of individual customers.

SHRINKING CUSTOMER LOYALTY

Advertising and promotion for the hospitality and tourism industry's product-service mix have traditionally focused on the product, the services service trends affecting the hospitality and tourism industry provided, and the physical plant or atmosphere in which the customer enjoys the product-service mix. Today, many hospitality and tourism firms focus their promotions on price; that is, heavy price competition exists along with a good deal of discounting. Unfortunately, price discounting exists as a short-term strategy that seldom builds brand loyalty. Consumers often shop around for the best deal and are loyal only to organizations that give them a consistently superior one.

Recognizing this, companies have sought ways to increase brand loyalty, especially among heavy users of the product service mix. The best examples of this approach are the frequent flyer programmes promoted by the airlines and the frequent traveller programmes promoted by the lodging companies. These loyalty programmes are commonplace in the lodging industry; all of the major chains use loyalty programmes to encourage and reward frequent guests. The strategy behind loyalty programmes is to hook the customer with points which can be redeemed for products or services. The more frequently the customer stays at a hotel operated by the company, the more points are earned.

The basic concepts common to all of these programmes are:

- Identify individuals who frequently purchase your product-service mix.
- Recognize the contribution those individuals make to the success of your company.
- Reward those individuals with awards and incentives that will increase their loyalty to your company and its brands.

Tie-ins with other companies providing travel-related services are also frequently used. For example, airlines, hotels, and car rental companies frequently offer bonus points within their programmes if the traveller uses the services offered by one of the companies participating in the tie-in. Both the airlines and the hotel companies are constantly making minor alterations to their programmes.

Increasing Consumer Sophistication

The budget segment of the lodging industry has undergone significant growth in the last several years. This growth has been fueled by the consumer demand for affordable accommodations that provide good value. In fact, consumers focus more on value and less on quality or price alone. Consumers have become more sophisticated and understand the concept of value at any price level.

Hotels have responded that offer good quality service at an affordable price. Each of these brands features nicely appointed guest rooms, limited or no public meeting space, limited or no food service provided on the hotel site, and a complimentary continental breakfast for guests. These limited-service brands incur lower development and operating expenses and thereby can provide guests with a lower price and good value, something that all consumers are seeking. Hotels in the upscale segment are also trying to increase the consumer's perception of value. They continually provide a broad assortment of amenities, such as health clubs on the property, business centres, rooms that provide more work space for business travellers, and personalized concierge service. These properties are striving to become "one-stop" destinations, providing a complete product-service mix that includes many food and beverage outlets, in-house office services, a wide variety of meeting room configurations, and other services, such as recreation, that will appeal to potential guests.

Within the fast-food service segment, companies often "bundle" their products in an attempt to increase sales and provide a better value for their customers. For example, they combine a sandwich, a large order of french fries, and a large soft drink at a price lower than what the items would cost if purchased separately. Similarly, tour operators and travel agents attempt to provide customers with more value by "bundling" the various components of travel (*e.g.*, airline ticket, hotel room, car rental, and tickets for tourist at service trends affecting the hospitality and tourism industry tractions) at a price lower than the sum of the individual components. This approach is known as product bundling.

Increased Emphasis on the Needs of Individual Customers

The markets within both hospitality and tourism segments have been segmented for a long time. In the past 5 to 15 years, this trend has become even more pronounced. Mass marketing has become a thing of the past as more firms extend their product lines to meet the specific needs of smaller segments of travellers and diners. This phenomenon has become most apparent in the lodging industry.

During the last decade, most of the major lodging chains developed several new brands or types of lodging properties to appeal to market segments that they were not currently serving. In addition, many hotel chains have merged with or acquired other hotel chains that focus on different market segments. Improvements in technology have given firms the ability to maintain large databases that detail consumer purchasing behaviour and preferences.

This information can be used to direct marketing efforts towards individual customers or market segments. Instead of relying on the mass media for promotions, a marketer can target past customers through direct mail and e-mail with special promotions and incentives that have a higher probability of being successful. There is more customization of products and promotions and less wasted coverage with media campaigns.

It began by defining services and explaining the characteristics that separate tangible products and services. Services are intangible and cannot be inventoried. This requires changes in the distribution process, and it makes it difficult to maintain consistent quality. It also requires more involvement on the part of customers, who actually become part of the product. The intangible nature of services results in more of an emphasis on experience qualities that are evaluated after a product becomes consumed, and less on search qualities that can be evaluated prior to purchase.

The concept of service quality remains important because consumers form perceptions of a firm based on its ability to provide a consistent level of service. This chapter introduced the service quality process and the potential gaps that could occur throughout the process. These gaps in service will decrease the level of service quality and lead to a decrease in customer satisfaction. Firms learn to manage service operations and improve quality through employee selection and training.

Once a firm focuses on the needs of consumers, it can build customer loyalty through relationship marketing. The overall performance of the firm can be improved through internal marketing efforts that attempt to communicate with employees and provide them with an environment for success. Customer satisfaction exists as the ultimate goal for a firm because it leads to brand loyalty and repeat purchases. Firms must meet or exceed customer expectations on a consistent basis in order to satisfy them. This chapter discussed ways to improve customer service and increase customer satisfaction. There are critical incidents, or moments of truth, when customers interact with employees and service failures can occur. Firms should encourage customers to voice their complaints so that the firms can anticipate and avoid possible failures. Also, firms can prepare service recovery strategies and train their employees to use them.

A firm's progress concerning customer satisfaction can be assessed using the techniques provided in this chapter, and benchmarks can be set for future comparisons. Finally, the chapter discussed some of the current trends in the hospitality and tourism industry that affect service operations. First, there is shrinking customer loyalty. Customers have many alternatives for fulfilling their needs, and it is easy to compare these alternatives using all of the information that is available. The stronger the competition, the more incentives customers are given to switch service providers. Second, consumers are becoming more sophisticated. Consumers have access to a proliferation of information about products and services. This information allows them to focus on overall value, rather than price or quality alone. Also, consumer advocacy organizations provide helpful tips for getting bargains and avoiding firms with poor reputations. Finally, there is an increased emphasis on the individual needs of customers. Improved technology has made database marketing possible, allowing more precise targeting of markets and less wasted coverage with promotions. Firms are able to service more market segments by introducing new brands or forming relationships with other firms (*e.g.*, strategic alliances, mergers, and acquisitions).

3

Tourism Modelling

INTRODUCTION

The TPF model consists of an innovative integration of tourism and travel analysis within a computable general equilibrium (CGE) modelling framework, to assist the formation of government policies relating to tourism and travel. The current research with Tourism Satellite Accounts (TSAs) can be complemented and extended by the use for analysing tourism and travel. These models are formal economic models that extend, rather than replace, tourism satellite accounts (TSAs). Indeed, the increasing implementation of TSAs is a stimulus to the use of TPF models because they provide data that is ideal for implementing a TPF model.

These models allow the full potential of the detailed data contained within TSAs to be realised and facilitate:

- The assessment of tourism's overall economic impact,
- The analysis of tourism policy,
- Tourism forecasting, predicting long-term trends in tourist numbers and expenditures.

TOURISM SATELLITE ACCOUNTS AND TPF MODELS

Tourism satellite accounts are being formulated by countries across the world, in order to provide accurate measures of the size of tourism sectors, the nature of demand for tourism, the nature of supply in tourism sectors, and the direct contribution of tourism to GDP and employment. This makes an invaluable contribution to our knowledge of the tourism sector. When measuring the economic impact of tourism, input-output (IO) models have often been used in the past. While these models successfully capture some of the economic impact of tourism, they do not capture all of the economic impact, leading to estimates of the economic impact of tourism that are not only unreliable but heavily biased.

Computable general equilibrium (CGE) models have their historical origins in input-output methodology, but were developed to overcome the many shortcomings of IO models. In particular, CGE models allow prices to vary and resources to be reallocated between production sectors. Tourism Policy and Forecasting (TPF) models build upon this framework by including tourism data from TSAs to provide a consistent means of modelling tourism in the entire economy.

Computable general equilibrium modelling is one of the most flexible and innovative economic techniques developed in recent decades. It has been used extensively by such international organisations as the World Bank, the World Trade Organisation and the OECD as well as in academia. It has been used in the fields of international trade, economic development, agricultural economics and environmental economics. Tourism impact models have traditionally relied on input-output (IO) modelling.

More recently, there have been initial applications of CGE models in the tourism field. The use of CGE models uses the latest methodology and gives more accurate predictions than techniques such as IO modelling. CGE models are formulated in a way that is radically different from input-output modelling, macroeconomic modelling, partial equilibrium modelling or, indeed, any other form of numerical simulation. Whereas the other modelling techniques rely on an initial stimulus which is then traced through the economic system in a systematic and deterministic manner, CGE models are formulated by specifying how economic agents react to changes in the economy. A CGE model is then solved simultaneously for all markets, production sectors and economic agents. This gives CGE models a significant advantage in flexibility over other forms of modelling, because other forms of modelling can only trace the effects of specific initial stimuli, and do so in a one-way deterministic system. In a CGE model, the initial stimulus can originate anywhere in the economy, and can be literally anything that can occur in an economic framework, ranging from changes in taxes and subsidies, to technological change, population growth, shifts in demand and regulatory changes. CGE models are not deterministic in the same way that other simulation approaches are.

The initial stimulus affects markets, production sectors and economic agents who react to the stimulus and provide further changes to the economy. These changes do not work in a one-way direction, so effects can feed back to where the stimulus started. Broadly speaking, the construction of a CGE model is a process of setting up a series of markets (for goods, services and factors of production), production sectors and demand groups (households). Each market, sector and household has its own set of economic rules that determine how it reacts to external changes.

Typically, markets for goods and services are market clearing, so that if demand exceeds supply, the price of the good or service will increase until the market clears. If the price of the good that a production sector produces increases, the output of the sector will increase. Consequently its use of factors of production will increase and the supply of the good will increase. Eventually these demand and supply changes will (due to the demand-supply correcting behaviour of prices in markets) increase the price of factors of production and decrease the price of the output good, until it is no longer profitable to increase output any further.

By setting up the economic conditions whereby each market, sector and household reacts to changes in the economy, a CGE model can then model a variety of possible scenarios. In other forms of numerical simulation, models are set up whereby the simulation follows a direct causal relationship from one effect to the next. CGE models by their very nature allow interactions between markets, and between sectors, that may be very complex. IO models rely on an input-output table for data, and trace the intermediate demands for goods and services that are needed to satisfy final demands by consumers, the government, investment and exports.

Hence, they calculate the indirect effects of final demand. The earnings of income (by private consumers and the government) can also be included to calculate the induced effects, which are similar to Keynesian multipliers. CGE models include other effects through factor markets and foreign currency. In doing so, the CGE models include not only the indirect effects but also the induced effects. Tourism Policy and Forecasting models extend the CGE framework to incorporate tourism and travel, with data on tourism demand and the supply of tourism industries, and frameworks for modelling tourism and travel.

Four basic characteristics differentiate Nottingham TPF models from IO models of tourism and travel:

- A TPF model includes flexible prices and wages. This enables factors of production, such as labour and capital, and foreign exchange markets to be modelled.
- Income-expenditure consistency must be maintained for all private households, the government, firms and any other economic agents that are modelled.
- Consumers' responses to changes in prices and income levels are taken into account by behavioural assumptions.
- Substitution between intermediate inputs and factors of production, as prices and wages change, is taken into account by production assumptions.

A TPF model contains four types of equation:

- Equilibrium conditions for each market ensure that supply is equal to demand for each good, service, factor of production and for foreign exchange.
- Income-expenditure identities ensure that the economic model is a closed system. All earnings must be accounted for through expenditure or savings. These conditions apply to all private house holds, the government, firms and any other economic agents that are modelled.

- Behavioural relationships state how economic agents react to changing prices and income levels. These then determine consumers' demand levels for each good and service.
- Production functions determine how much is produced for any given level of factor employment. With assumptions regarding market structure, these determine what levels of labour employment, capital usage and intermediate input usage are required to satisfy a given level of output for a set of prices.

One of the strengths of the TPF models is their flexibility. The TPF models usually contain certain core components of the model structure, and can be expanded by extending the scope of the model to suit the circumstances of the tourist origin/destination country or region.

Model structure components include:

- Market competition. Various forms of market competition can be included, from perfect competition to monopoly.
- Labour markets can be modelled in various forms, with the possibility of allowing for unemployment.
- Foreign trade can be treated in several different ways, to enable the modelling of small and large countries.
- Dynamics can be incorporated to show how the economy moves through time, with economic agents' expectations about future events incorporated into their decision-making processes.

In addition, extensions to the model scope can be made, such as:

- Income distribution can be modelled by incorporating many household groups. The distributional effects of tourism or tourism policies could then be examined.
- Inter-regional effects could be modelled by modelling distinct regions within a country.
- International effects can show how tourism's effects are spread between countries.
- The environment can be incorporated to show the

effects of tourism and tourism policy on environmental issues.

IMPACT MODELLING

TSAs represent a major step forward in the measurement of the economic size of tourism, but do not assess the total impact of tourism. Estimating the impact of tourism has the advantage of showing the desirability of tourism, in addition to measurement of size. It can also show what impact tourism has on different sectors, regions or on income distribution, depending on the specification of the model.

One problem with any attempt to measure the size of a sector such as tourism is that it is usually measured from the demand-side and it is difficult to compare results with sectors such as mining, agriculture or manufacturing that are usually measured from the supply- side. The direct impact of tourism is, on the surface, the most comparable with supply-side sectors, but falls into definitional problems. If an aircraft is owned by an airline, for example, a proportion (corresponding to the proportion of airline services consumed by tourists) of the aircraft will be included in the direct measurement of tourism. If, however, the airline rents the aircraft from another company, the value of the rental service will be attributed as an intermediate input into tourism, and the corresponding returns to investment will not be included in tourism value added. In an attempt to rectify this situation, various countries have included indirect effects through input-output (IO) models as an alternative in their TSAs.

While this solves problems relating to definitions of intermediates, it goes beyond the measurement of the size of tourism in an accounting sense and loses direct comparability with supply-side sectors. IO models include some intermediate purchases (such as food and fuel, for example) that should clearly be thought of as intermediate purchases and not as being within the tourism sector itself. In short, the IO models go some way beyond measuring the size of the sector to measuring its economic impact. IO models do not, however, measure the full impact of tourism.

These models make various assumptions that evidently exclude some of the economic effects that a sector has. Therefore the measurement of indirect impacts through IO models gives only a partial picture of the full impact of tourism. In fact, the TPF results are more comprehensive and IO results more misleading because they incorporate only some of the impact of tourism.

TOURISM POLICY ANALYSIS

The TPF models can be readily utilised to provide other forms of economic analysis. Policy analysis is an important way in which the potential of TPF models can be further demonstrated.

The TPF models offer the ability to perform "what-if" simulations:

- Examine the economic effects of existing policies on tourism or of proposed alternatives. For example, they can show the net effective taxation of tourism that exists or provide a quantitative assessment of policy alternatives.
- Provide a theoretical viewpoint or an applied quantitative estimate.
- Examine purely taxation issues, or other policy instruments such as investment incentives and planning regulations.
- Examine the effects of tourism policy, or the effects that other policies have on tourism.

These examples demonstrate that the scope for tourism policy analysis with the TPF models is large.

Cases of particular relevance include:

- Examination of the current levels of tourism taxation, *i.e.* whether tourism is taxed at too low or too high rates relative to the rest of the economy.
- Quantitative estimates of tourism policy alternatives, such as planned tax changes or tourism development plans.
- Quantitative estimates of the effects of other policies on tourism, such as trade liberalisation or general taxation changes.

FORECASTING

TPF models can be used to forecast future trends in the tourism industry. Such forecasting models show how changes in the world economy will feed through to tourism.

Three main causes of change are highlighted here:

1. Factor accumulation, including capital accumulation through investment, labour growth through population growth, and changes to the skills of labour through education and training.
2. Technological change, through technical progress.
3. Policy changes, which may be foreseeable.

These factors influence both income growth on the demand side and production costs on the supply side. As each factor may be changing at different rates in different sectors and in different countries, forecasting their total effect requires a TPF model. Relative prices balance the demand and supply side factors to achieve equilibrium in each market. Continuing increases in overall skill and education levels will, for example, lead to high growth rates in sectors that use highly skilled and highly educated labour.

How this affects tourism depends very much on the skill and education levels in tourism characteristic sectors, and on the intermediate relationships between tourism characteristic sectors and the rest of the economy. Differential growth rates between tourist source countries will affect international tourism growth rates in different destination markets. Tourism growth will, in general, be highly responsive to increases in income levels in source countries, and will depend on the relative prices for tourism and other goods and services.

The TPF models provide the opportunity to assess the potential long-term growth of tourism in response to changes in the economy (such as population growth and changing education levels) that are highly predictable, as well as the short-term impact of macroeconomic changes such as currency market crises and natural disasters.

TSAS AND A TPF MODEL OF THE USA

Tourism satellite accounts provide detailed data on

tourism activities that are not otherwise available in national accounts because national accounts provide data classified according to production activities and commodities, and tourism spans many of these standard classifications. The U.S. TSA used here specifies 18 industries and 23 commodities.

The tables that it provides are:

- *Production Account of Tourism Industries and All Other Industries*: This is a "make" matrix showing the output of each commodity in each industry and a breakdown of costs by industry into three categories: intermediate inputs, compensation of employees, and other value added.
- Supply and Consumption of Tourism and All Other Commodities.

  This shows:

  - A breakdown of total supply of each commodity into various categories—such as domestic production, imports government sales; and
  - A breakdown of demand into categories—intermediate, personal consumption, investment, exports and government expenditures.
- *Tourism Demand by Type of Visitor*: This provides expenditures on each category by visitors, broken down into the following categories: business, government, resident and non-resident.
- *Tourism GDP of Tourism Industries and Other Industries*: . Using a tourism industry ratio derived as tourism output divided by industry output, this details of how much GDP is generated by tourism in each industry.
- *Tourism Employment and Compensation of Employees*: Using the tourism industry ratio, this derives tourism employment and compensation of employees by industry. The ability to define different categories of tourism expenditure and trace the effects of this expenditure through the economy is an important and substantial step in tourism research. The data

provided by such tables are invaluable for economists when modelling tourism.

The data requirements of tourism policy and forecasting models are that input-output tables and tourism demand data are available for a consistent classification of industries and commodities.

Therefore, where published input-output tables adequately classify tourism and travel sectors, only the demand data is required from TSAs. Where published input-output tables do not adequately define tourism industries, data from the TSAs on the structure of supply may also be necessary. The U.S.

TPF model combines the tourism demand data for 1997 with the published 1997 benchmark input-output table containing data for 494 sectors and 37 categories of final demand, in addition to other sources of data. We present illustrative results here of an aggregated version of the Tourism Policy and Forecasting Model for the USA.

It has 18 sectors and commodities that correspond as closely as possible, given the necessary matching of TSA data, IO data and data from other sources, to the published TSA.

THE EFFECT OF A 10% INCREASE IN FOREIGN TOURIST EXPENDITURES

In order to measure the impact of foreign tourism, we simulate a 10% increase in foreign tourist expenditures. This 10% increase is $9.6bn. Economic welfare, as measured by equivalent variation rises by $5.8bn, just under 0.1% of GDP. These comparative illustrate that just over half of the expenditure is captured as an increase in welfare, as markets adjust to reallocate resources, imports increase, and other exports are crowded out.

The impact of this expenditure is captured by GDP, in terms of:

- Direct expenditure impact,
- Input-output estimates, and
- General equilibrium estimates with the TPF model. While the direct impact of the $9.6bn extra

expenditures is $4.5bn and the input-output estimate is $9.4bn, the TPF estimate is $6.0bn.

This indicates that:

- A large proportion of the expenditures leads directly to purchases of intermediate inputs, hence the low figure for the direct expenditure impact.
- Almost all of the expenditure leads to increased GDP in the input-output estimate. The IO estimate has no crowding-out, and there is very little import leakage.
- The TPF estimate includes significant levels of crowding-out and resource reallocation.
- Some tourism and travel sectors have significantly higher increases in GDP in the TPF model than the IO model suggests. Here, the initial stimulus of foreign tourism expenditures is reinforced by domestic expenditures as firms benefiting from the initial expenditures increase there own expenditures on business tourism, and private households which have increases in income spend more on domestic tourism.
- Others tourism and travel sectors, such as water and rail transport, have a lower GDP increase than the IO model suggests. These are sectors that sell products that are relatively small proportions of the foreign tourist's expenditures. Resources are reallocated to other sectors that are able to pay higher wages. These reallocation effects outweigh the induced effects that these sectors experience from higher incomes.
- Non-tourism industries (here, 'all other commodities') have a decline in sector GDP that the IO model completely misses, because it does not include price crowding-out effects and resource allocation. Here, there is no direct stimulus from the foreign tourism expenditures. Indirect (intermediate demands, as captured

through the IO model) and induced effects are positive, but are outweighed by resource allocation effects.

INDIRECT TAXATION

The overall effect of indirect taxation exposes the levels of effective protection that the structure of taxation gives to industries, and shows how distortions that indirect taxes introduce lead to economic loses. As such, it is an important indicator as to how economically efficient taxes are in each sector. The results therefore remove arguments about the motives for taxation because the total level of taxation is maintained. The changes to the GDP contribution of labour and capital are given in the first column.

Changes to the GDP contribution of taxation are given in the second column. Changes to the total GDP contribution by sector, and in total, are given in the third column, and in the fourth column as a percentage of the 1997 GDP contribution. Overall, removing all indirect taxes and replacing them with non-distorting direct taxes leads to an improvement to GDP of $528.4bn, which is 2.1% of GDP in 1997. This therefore is the measure of the total distortionary impact of the indirect taxation system.

This improvement to GDP comes about through an increase in the GDP contribution of labour and capital ($1,033.8bn) outweighing the loss in indirect taxation revenue ($-505.4bn). With some exceptions, tourism and travel sectors have a lower GDP increase than the national average of 2.1%. Non-tourism sectors ('all other commodities' is a much larger sector than 'gasoline and oil' or the wholesale sector) have a larger GDP effect than the national average. This implies, since tourism sectors do not expand by the national average when indirect taxation is removed, that the tourism sectors have levels of effective taxation that are higher than the national average. The results of these 17 separate simulations are summarised as the welfare effect of removing the individual taxes. Taxes in a range of sectors such as auto and truck rental, recreation and entertainment and retail margins, impose distortions on the economy that lead to a higher welfare loss than the tax revenue that they raise. Some sectors, such as water transport, air transport and hotels and lodging places, have much lower distortionary impact when compared to the tax revenue.

There are many reasons why sectors have different distortionary impacts, including:

- The distortionary impact of tax rates are often more than proportional to the tax revenue raised, so that higher tax rates lead to a higher distortion/revenue ratio.
- The distortionary impacts are related to other sectors through intermediate demands, and substitution in final demand. Sectors that have high distortions can effectively pass some of these distortions to related sectors.
- The distortionary impacts are related to how readily supply and demand change in response to price changes, in other words to the elasticities of supply and demand. Sectors with inelastic supply and demand (*i.e.* low levels of supply and demand response to prices) tend to have lower distortionary impacts from taxation. In a general equilibrium framework, the responsiveness of supply and demand depends on many factors, such as who purchases the product (a product mainly purchased by firms will often have a lower demand elasticity than one purchased by households) and the structure of production (an industry that relies heavily on one type of input will tend to have a lower supply elasticity than other industries).

If scenarios can simulate the effects of anything from productivity growth, changes to competition (anti-trust) legislation and environmental controls. The total general equilibrium effects of such diverse issues can be a complex product of many different changes. Here, we show the results of a productivity improvement in air transport. The $20.6bn increase in GDP that results is spread across industries, with air transport itself increasing in size to account for an extra $2bn in GDP, industries that use air transport such as 'all other commodities' also increasing.

Most sectors that have a reduced GDP contribution are other transport industries, which compete with air transport. The Nottingham Tourism, Policy and Forecasting models apply tourism within a general equilibrium setting. They are an innovative and significant means of combining tourism satellite accounts, input-output tables and economic modelling. They expand on the TSA's measurement of tourism's economic size to provide estimates of tourism's economic impact, including many effects that are not captured in input-output models. TPF models also provide an important tool for policy analysis, enabling the complex interactions in the economy that result from policy actions to be traced through a general equilibrium framework and assessed. The ability to have quantitative estimates of the effects of policy is of vital importance to policy makers.

TPF models can also be used as a basis for forecasting the levels and expenditures of tourists, taking relatively stable and predictable long-term trends in tourism source and destination countries to provide a method of robust long-term forecasting. The results presented here for the USA Tourism, Policy and Forecasting model provide an example of the TPF model's capabilities. The impact of tourism when including induced income effects and resource reallocation effects is dramatically different to the standard input-output results. In particular, the IO models overestimate the total GDP effect, underestimate the total effect on tourism sectors and completely miss the negative effects on non-tourism sectors. The results of the policy analysis using the TPF model are that most tourism sectors are effectively taxed at higher than the national average level.

In sectors such as hotels and transport sectors indirect taxation imposes lower welfare losses on the economy than in other sectors. This implies that the most urgent sectors for tax reductions (*i.e.* those where welfare distortions are disproportionately high relative to tax revenues) are auto and truck rental, retail, eating and drinking, recreation and entertainment, participant sports, and parking, automotive repair and highway tolls. We also report the results of a 'what-if' scenario that shows the effect of improved productivity in the air transport sector. The results show that increases in GDP are spread across the economy in sectors that use air transport. Competing transport sectors may contract as a result. The USA TPF model is intended to give an indication of the potential applications that TPF modelling has.

While the sector classification for this model is small to match the U.S. TSA as closely as possible, a full 494-sector model is also in operation. For the U.S., the model can be extended in various directions: tourism demand data on domestic tourism by state would enable the TPF model to include state effects. Otherwise, the model can be expanded to include different skill categories of labour and different households groups according to geographical location, income category, or other classification. This would be able to show how these different household groups are affected by both an expansion in tourism and by policies. Other possible ways of expanding this model are to incorporate similar data from other countries: a model of North America would, for example, include Canada and Mexico.

This would incorporate cross-border effects, to assess the effects that a tax on a tourism sector in the U.S. has on the economies of Canada and Mexico. As well as these extensions the U.S. TPF model, it is of course possible to build similar models for any country where a TSA and input-output table exist, and these can also incorporate regional differences, household distributions and different types of labour as well as incorporating more than one country. The underlying methodology of TPF models is well suited to developing countries, for which computable general equilibrium modelling has long been used.

THE IMPORTANCE OF TOURISM

Tourism can also be one of the most effective drivers for the development of regional economies. These patterns apply to both developed and emerging economies. Travel and Tourism is the world's largest industry and creator of jobs across national and regional economies. WTTC/WEFA research show that in 2000, Travel and Tourism will generate, directly and indirectly, 11.7% of GDP and nearly 200 million jobs in the world-wide economy. These are forecasted to total 11.7% and 255 million respectively in 2010. Jobs generated by Travel and Tourism are spread across the economy—in retail, construction, manufacturing and telecommunications, as well as directly in Travel and Tourism companies. These jobs employ a large proportion of women, minorities and young people; are predominantly in small and medium sized companies; and offer good training and transferability.

CONTRIBUTING TO SUSTAINABLE DEVELOPMENT

The 1992 United Nations Conference on Environment and Development (UNCED), the Rio Earth Summit, identified Travel and Tourism as one of the key sectors of the economy which could make a positive contribution to achieving sustainable development. The Earth Summit lead to the adoption of Agenda 21, a comprehensive programme of action adopted by 182 governments to provide a global blueprint for achieving sustainable development. Travel and Tourism is the first industry sector to have launched an industry-specific action plan based on Agenda 21.

Travel and Tourism is able to contribute to development which is economically, ecologically and socially sustainable, because it:

- Has less impact on natural resources and the environment than most other industries;
- Is based on enjoyment and appreciation of local culture, built heritage, and natural environment, as such that the industry has a direct and powerful motivation to protect these assets;
- Can play a positive part in increasing consumer commitment to sustainable development principles through its unparalleled consumer distribution channels; and
- Provides an economic incentive to conserve natural

environments and habitats which might otherwise be allocated to more environmentally damaging land uses, thereby, helping to maintain bio-diversity.

There are numerous good examples of where Travel and Tourism is acting as a catalyst for conservation and improvement of the environment and maintenance of local diversity and culture. (Some of these are set out in Section B of this paper and a fuller illustration of the range of industry action can be found on the World Travel and Tourism Council's. Of course, there are also examples where development has not been sustainable.

PROVIDING INFRASTRUCTURE

To a greater degree than most activities, Travel and Tourism depends on a wide range of infrastructure services—airports, air navigation, roads, railheads and ports, as well as basic infrastructure services required by hotels, restaurants, shops, and recreation facilities (*e.g.* telecommunications and utilities).

It is the combination of tourism and good infrastructure that underpins the economic, environmental and social benefits. It is important to balance any decision to develop an area for tourism against the need to preserve fragile or threatened environments and cultures.

However, once a decision has been taken where an area is appropriate for new tourism development, or that an existing tourist site should be developed further, then good infrastructure will be essential to sustain the quality, economic viability and growth of Travel and Tourism. Good infrastructure will also be a key factor in the industry's ability to manage visitor flows in ways that do not affect the natural or built heritage, nor counteract against local interests.

CHALLENGE FOR THE FUTURE

Travel and Tourism creates jobs and wealth and has tremendous potential to contribute to economically, environmentally and socially sustainable development in both developed countries and emerging nations. It has a comparative advantage in that its start up and running costs can be low compared to many other forms of industry development. It is also often one of the few realistic options for development in many areas. Therefore, there is a strong likelihood that the Travel and Tourism industry will continue to grow globally over the short to medium term.

Of course, if Travel and Tourism is managed badly, it can have a detrimental effect—it can damage fragile environments and destroy local cultures. The challenge is to manage the future growth of the industry so as to minimise its negative impacts on the environment and host communities whilst maximising the benefits it brings in terms of jobs, wealth and support for local culture and industry, and protection of the built and natural environment.

INDUSTRY INITIATIVES

Travel and Tourism takes many different forms—from a trip only a few hours away from home to long distance travel overseas. A common belief is that most Travel and Tourism involves large numbers of visitors from developed countries travelling by air to destinations in emerging countries. In fact, in most countries, the domestic tourism market is larger than the inbound market.

Of course, the social and cultural impact of inbound visitors is often greater than that of domestic tourists. Whether tourism is domestic or international, it involves visiting a destination away from the area in which one lives and using the services available in that destination. Therefore, tourists' requirements are for travel services to reach their destinations and once there, for services such as shelter, water, food, sanitation and entertainment.

What makes tourism special is that, many of these different products and services are often supplied by different operators: usually small or medium sized businesses in local ownership. This makes tourism a highly fragmented and diverse industry and so co-ordinated, industry-wide action is difficult to achieve. The influence of Travel and Tourism's demand also extends far beyond traditional tourism companies, into upstream suppliers like aircraft manufacturers or food producers and into the downstream service providers for travellers, like retail shops. Despite the difficulties caused by fragmentation and lengthy supply chains, there has been a steady growth in environmental good practice across the industry in recent years.

There are examples of airlines and airports reducing pollution and noise impacts; cruise liners practising marine conservation; hotels implementing energy consumption and waste disposal programmes; car rental companies investing in increasingly fuel efficient fleets and railways sound proofing to dampen noise. The result is that there are a number of excellent initiatives in place designed to improve the environmental management of Travel and Tourism businesses. Of course, more needs to be done. WTTC with 105 members is the global business leaders' forum for the Travel and Tourism industry. The WTTC have set in place an extensive strategy to promote a culture of sustainable development and have put in place a three-tiered structure for its achievement. This involves:

In 1996 the WTTC, the World Tourism Organization and the Earth Council, joined together to launch an action plan entitled "Agenda 21 for the Travel and Tourism Industry: Towards Environmentally Sustainable Development"—a sectional sustainable development programme based on the results of the Rio Earth Summit in 1992. Since the launch of the document, the three organisations have begun a series of regional seminars to increase awareness of the conclusions, and to adapt the programme for local implementation. The programme has held regional seminars in London and Jakarta in 1997 and Victoria Falls and Dominica in 1998.

WTTC has recently introduced a major addition to the programme—the "Alliance for Sustainable Tourism", which invites public and private sector Travel and Tourism organisations to record their Agenda 21 based activities on a central web site and commit to cooperation with all other partners. In order to develop the programme from global principles to community based action, WTTC is also discussing with the International Council for Local Environment

Initiatives (ICLEI) on how the principles of "Agenda 21 for Travel and Tourism" can be built into Local Agenda 21 programmes. Furthermore, WTTC is considering pilot projects in 5 cities around the world to serve as models for other destinations.

In 1994, WTTC initiated the "GREEN GLOBE", an Agenda 21 based industry improvement programme, which provides guidance material and a certification process linked to both ISO standards and Agenda 21 principles. There are now 500 "GREEN GLOBE "members in 100 countries dedicated to improving environmental practice. The first certification has commenced with hotels groups in Jamaica and Manchester (UK). "GREEN GLOBE" has also developed a specific Destination Programme, which provides a methodology for Travel and Tourism destinations to implement sustainable development. The ultimate aim is that "GREEN GLOBE" will become the primary global standard of environmental commitment by the global Travel and Tourism industry and will be recognised by the public as such.

Currently, "GREEN GLOBE" has the support of over 20 international industry organisations representing thousands of businesses world-wide and the support of the World Tourism Organization, the United Nations Environment Programme and the Earth Council. WTTC have also developed "ECoNETT", a web-site containing advice and data on good practice and sources of help and advice. "ECoNETT" is increasingly recognised as a focal point for environmental information, good practice, new techniques and technologies. The International Hotel and Restaurant Association (IHandRA), based in Paris, represents over 700,000 establishments in more than 150 countries.

Its membership comprises some 50 national and international hotel and restaurant chains, over 110 national hotel and restaurant associations, independent hotel operators and restaurateurs, industry suppliers and 130 hotel schools. The IH&RA has offices in Asia-Pacific and Latin America. It is also the voice of the world's hotels and restaurants and plays a global role in representing, protecting, promoting and informing the industry to enable its members to achieve their business objectives.

The IH&RA has:

- Raised environmental awareness and developed programmes through joint workshops with national hotel associations and regularly encourages them to develop their own environmental awareness programmes;
- Established an annual Environmental Award sponsored by American Express and judged by the United Nations Environment Programme (UNEP) that recognises efforts by independent and chain hotels to "green" the industry;
- Published advice including practical publications such as the "Environmental Action Pack for Hotels" with the International Hotel Environment Initiative and UNEP and "Environmental Good Practice in Hotels" with UNEP;
- Supported regional initiatives such as the Caribbean Action for Sustainable Tourism; and
- Joined forces with UNEP and the International Hotel School Directors' Association to develop an "Environmental Teaching Resource Package for Hospitality Educational Institutes".

CORPORATE INITIATIVES

The International Hotel Environment Initiative (IHEI), based in London, England, is a programme of The Prince of Wales Business Leaders Forum. Founded in 1992 by a consortium of chief executives from 10 multinational hotel groups, IHEI is an educational charity designed to encourage continuous improvement in the environmental performance of the global hotel industry.

It does this through:

- Raising environmental awareness in the hotel industry by promoting good practice internationally;
- Developing hotel-specific guidance, enabling hotels of all sizes to implement environmental programmes; and

- Multiplying the reach and impact of IHEI by working with partners, including hotel associations, governments, NGOs, tourism bodies and businesses.

IHEI is a catalyst and conduit for hotels to pool their resources and to share experience via a non- competitive platform. In 5 years it has evolved into an organisation with global impact. IHEI has worked in 111 countries, stimulating and assisting with the establishment of local initiatives such as New Zealand's "Environmental Hotels of Auckland, the Asia Pacific Hotel Environment Initiative" and the Caribbean Action for Sustainable Tourism.

Member hotels now represent over 1 million guest rooms and more than 8,000 hotels on 5 continents. The Cooperative Research Centre for Sustainable Tourism, based in Australia, was established in 1997 to enhance the strategic knowledge available to the Travel and Tourism industry through:

- Long-term high-quality scientific and technological research which contributes to the development of an internationally competitive tourism industry;
- Strengthening the links between research and its commercial and other applications;
- Promoting cooperative research; and
- Stimulating education and training, particularly in graduate programmes, through active involvement of researchers from outside the higher education system in educational activities, and of graduate students in major research programmes.

COMPANY INITIATIVES

The number of initiatives undertaken by individual companies is large. Just two examples from this are as follows:

The Kandalama hotel in Sri Lanka has been a recipient of the "GREEN GLOBE" award, 3 years in a row, for its commitment to environmental excellence.

The hotel has undertaken measures in the following areas to ensure that its operations are more sustainable:

- Cultural and social—hotel employment, providing community infrastructure and development;

- Natural environment—soil erosion measures and planting forests;
- Pollution—sewage, solid waste and noise pollution reduction programmes; and
- Environmental communication—construction of an Eco Park where all waste is treated within the park, a dry debris sorting centre, a lecture room to promote environmental awareness and a sustainable development library.

Canadian Pacific Hotels, the largest hotel conglomerate in Canada, has developed an environmental programme, which is recognised as the most comprehensive in the North American hotel industry. Based on the results of a survey, employee suggestions and the recommendations of a professional environmental consultant, Canadian Pacific Hotels developed a list of 16 goals to be attained by all hotels.

In addition to individual projects implemented at each of the 26 hotels, the goals set for the chain as a whole were ambitious:

- To reduce the amount of waste sent to landfill by 50% across the chain, by launching an extensive recycling programme;
- To redesign purchasing policies to ensure that waste is reduced at source, and supplies used in the hotels are nature friendly.

INTER-REGIONAL LEVEL

The Caribbean Action for Sustainable Tourism (CAST) is an alliance for sustainable growth developed by the Caribbean Hoteliers Association with the support of the WTTC, the IHEI and the Caribbean Tourism Organisation. CAST has developed workshops, training courses and guidance material for its members on a wide range of environmental issues, including:

- Setting up environmental management systems;
- Energy efficiency;
- Renewable energy; and
- Waste water management.

AGENTS AND PARTNERSHIPS FOR CHANGE

The public sectors, particularly national and local

government, have an important role to play by setting the agenda and providing the framework in which action should take place. The regulatory environment also plays an important role in creating the conditions suitable for sustainable tourism. Self-regulation involving the agreement and cooperation of industry is always likely to be the most effective solution. Therefore, the role of trade associations and industry organisations in distributing information among their members and encouraging participation is essential.

The major partnerships to be formed are between:

- Industry and the public sector—to ensure consistency with the framework;
- Industry and the voluntary sector—to tap into the enormous resources of expertise and goodwill that this sector is able to generate; and
- Industry and the public—both travellers themselves and the people who live in the places they visit to develop more sustainable forms of tourism.

AREAS FOR FURTHER ACTION

The industry is already doing much to improve its performance in terms of sustainable development. The challenge for the new millennium is to move from the existing ad hoc approach to a more systematic one.

To do this will involve a partnership between industry and national governments to deliver the following:

- *Governments*:
  - Integration of travel and tourism policy into broader government policies, especially the environment;
  - Incentives for the Travel and Tourism industry, backed up where necessary by effective regulation.
- *Public/Private partnership*:
  - Infrastructure planned and developed with a long-term view and within a reference framework based on Agenda 21;
  - Indicators and environmental impact assessment

tools to enable effective local management and appropriate development.

- *International bodies*:
  - Co-ordination at an international level of environmental action undertaken by all sectors of the Travel and Tourism industry;
  - Review of existing voluntary initiatives to improve the quality of reporting, their transparency and credibility, and the assessment of their contribution to sustainability.
- *Companies*:
  - Commitment to place sustainable development issues at the core of the management structure;
  - Innovation of process and application through new technology;
  - Commitment to education and environmental training of staff.

INFLUENCING CONSUMER BEHAVIOUR TO PROMOTE SUSTAINABLE TOURISM

Problems

At the 1998 World Travel Market, WTTC hosted, as a part of its Environmental Awareness Day, a seminar entitled "Does the Consumer Care?" At this event, MORI presented the latest findings from their Business and the Environment survey—an annual UK survey devoted to public attitudes to the environment.

The survey is now in its tenth year and illustrates the challenge facing the Travel and Tourism industry in influencing consumer behaviour to promote sustainable tourism. According to this survey, Travel and Tourism is now more associated with environmental damage than it has been in the past. Despite this decline in perception, the industry's economic success is not dependent on its green record—public sensitivity to environmental problems on holiday/business trips has not increased and is no more of a deterrent to repeat travel than it was previously. There is a downward trend in the public's willingness to pay extra for environmental protection and environmentally friendly products, including "green" Travel and Tourism. Awareness of companies making environmental commitments is only marginally up.

Therefore, the challenge is to persuade the consumer that it is in their interests to adopt and promote a sustainable approach in their activities and purchasing decisions. Education programmes and the development and widespread acceptance of codes of conduct are useful tools in achieving this step. Once this message has been conveyed, it is then important to back this up with the necessary information to enable consumers to make informed choices. It is here that "ecolabels" and award programmes have value.

EDUCATION PROGRAMMES

The Foundation for Environmental Education in Europe (FEEE) seeks to promote environmental education by carrying out campaigns and improving awareness of the importance of environmental education. It is composed of a network of international organisations. The FEEE (headquarters in Denmark) runs three major campaigns in Europe for providing safe and clean beaches and marinas. The award itself is given annually to beaches and marinas that satisfy a number of essential criteria in three separate areas: water quality; beach management and safety; and environmental information and education.

"GREEN GLOBE"'s Dodo Campaign, is based on a cartoon character, who features in 65 Travel and Tourism videos. Dodo explains and promotes the actions that visitors can take to reduce the impacts of their travels. The videos are aimed at children and are designed to be fun, whilst conveying important messages about sustainable Travel and Tourism. The aim is to have these videos shown on in flight and in-room television channels to raise awareness and influence consumer behaviour.

CODES OF CONDUCT

Codes of conduct are also used to try and influence

consumer behaviour. For example, "Guidelines for Responsible Environmental Tourism" are prepared and distributed by the American Society of Travel Agents to all customers who book holidays through their members' branches. The Guidelines aim to "encourage the growth of peaceful tourism and environmentally responsible travel" and include 10 recommendations to encourage tourists to act responsibly and show respect for their hosts and the environment of their destinations.

The Pacific Asia Tourism Association (PATA) is an industrial association, which promotes the Pacific Asia area's Travel and Tourism destinations, products and services. PATA also serves as a central resource of information and research, travel industry education and training, as well as quality product development with sensitivity for culture, heritage and environment. In 1992, PATA introduced its "Code for Environmentally Responsible Tourism" to strengthen the principles of preservation in the region.

Businesses, organisations and individuals wishing to affirm their support for the PATA Code are encouraged to participate in the PATA Green Leaf programme. The Africa Travel Association has produced "Responsible Traveller Guidelines"; the Japanese Association of Travel Agents has produced the "Declaration of Earth Friendly Travellers" and there are many more examples of industry codes aimed at educating and influencing their customers.

ECO LABELLING

There are numerous examples of industry sponsored labelling schemes, whose aim is to recognise good industry practice and influence consumer behaviour into purchasing the labelled products. For example, the "Green Key, Denmark" certificate operated by the Hotel, Restaurant and Leisure Industry Association (HORESTA) has 56 criteria that includes environmental information, water and energy consumption and waste management. Special features also include ecological food products, outdoor areas, non-smoking rooms, and adaptations for access by disabled persons. There are a number of industries that runs and sponsors award programmes to highlight and promote examples of good practice. For example, British Airways has run the "Tourism for Tomorrow" awards since 1992 to encourage action to protect the environment. The awards are directed at tour operators, hotels, national parks and heritage sites, and other activities associated with tourism. By selecting projects showing best practice in their field as role models, others are encouraged to follow suit and consider the environment in the everyday running of their tourism business.

The awards are run annually, with a winner selected from each of five regions and an overall winner. In addition, two special awards are made for mass tourism destinations. The awards are run in association with the British Tourist Authority, the Association of British Travel Agents, the Pacific Asia Travel Association and the American Society of Travel Agents. Entries to the awards have been increases every year. American Express also sponsors a variety of environmental awards for international tourism organisations.

Agents and Partnerships for Change

- A broad based approach is called for which requires Travel and Tourism to work with: national governments to raise the profile of environmental and social issues within the education system;
- NGOs to raise awareness of tourism issues in their work and activities and provide feedback to the Travel and Tourism industry;
- Development organisations to communicate with host communities to understand their needs and requirements;
- Local authorities to engage local people through the inclusion of tourism issues in Local Agenda21 plans;
- National and international trade associations, labour representative organisations and training providers to increase awareness and training of staff in environmental and social issues;
- Travel and Tourism publications (such as travel guides);

- Travel and Tourism journalists to raise the profile of reporting environmental and social impacts of tourism among consumers and tourism businesses;
- The Internet as a source of information for potential travellers.

AREAS FOR FURTHER ACTION

The WTTC/MORI data shows the scale of the task still remaining. The industry has developed a number of initiatives to influence consumer behaviour. However, if consumers do not understand or are not aware of the issues involved and do not demand more sustainable products then, in the long term, it will not be in the industry's interests to move in that direction. The priority for future action, therefore, should be to raise awareness among travellers of the issues associated with tourism and the impact their activities can have on local destinations and cultures.

BROAD-BASED SUSTAINABLE DEVELOPMENT THROUGH TOURISM

The Travel and Tourism industry has a vested interest in protecting the natural and cultural resources that are the core of its business. Travel and Tourism has less impacts on natural resources and the environment than other sectors and it has already done much to address the issues arising from its activities.

There are examples, however, from around the world where the impact of Travel and Tourism has been damaging to the local environment and people.

Some of the factors which contributes to the harmful impact of tourism are:

- A lack of awareness on the part of those making decisions about tourism development of the social, economic and environmental balance to be pursued in achieving sustainable development;
- A lack of commitment by tourism operators and travellers to contribute to the maintenance of the local environment and culture of the host destination;

- A weak institutional framework with inadequate controls can lead to tourism development which is both inappropriate and intrusive;
- Unfairly traded tourism, whereby local communities are unable to share in its benefits;
- Large flows of visitors in remote or sensitive locations can place considerable strains on local resources (particularly water) and supply systems. Travellers' expectations of the goods and services, which should be available, can lead to these items or services, being imported from outside or local supply chains, being distorted to meet demands; and
- Tourism can change a destination's cultural make-up and, if poorly developed, can increase crime, prostitution and other social problems.

In order for tourism to realise its potential to achieve broad-based sustainable development, an effective partnership between Government and all sectors of the industry will be required. The following illustrates what is being done:

INTERNATIONAL COOPERATION

IH&RA and the United Nations Organisation for Education, Science and Culture (UNESCO) have signed a cooperation agreement to encourage world-wide hotel chains to sponsor UNESCO cultural heritage sites and attract tourism to them via their marketing campaigns.

NATIONAL GOVERNMENTS

In India, the government is pump priming local "eco-tourism" activities, which are primarily driven by local women. In Mexico, the government is kick starting village development for "eco-tourism" lodges in the Chiapas region involving the whole community. In England, the government has recently held a national consultation on sustainable tourism and, as a result, is developing a new strategy for tourism, which incorporates the principles of sustainable development as a core component. The Caribbean Tourism Organisation has developed a comprehensive strategy to develop "eco-tourism" in the Caribbean region. This strategy is closely integrated with the goals of the Association for Caribbean States (ACE) for a green Caribbean.

"GREEN GLOBE" has developed a specific "Destinations" programme to recognise those tourist destinations where there is a concerted effort by all those involved in the local tourism industry to improve the quality of the environment. The Destinations process provides a framework to guide tourist locations towards achieving sustainable development based on the principles of Agenda 21. The Destinations programmes are tailor made to reflect local circumstances, such as the level of environmental awareness, action taken to date and available resources. Each programme is based on achieving progressive environmental improvements.

Targets are set within a realistic timetable and are developed by a steering group made up of key partners. The island of Jersey has become the first "GREEN GLOBE" Destination. Vilamoura in Portugal, Dominica in the Caribbean and 3 destinations in the Philippines have also entered the Destination programme.

For example, in 1996 Luso tour SA, a tourism development company, enacted a management plan for Vilamoura whereby employees are given responsibility for individual environmental tasks. The company has invested money into rehabilitating the surrounding natural environment, which includes pine forests and a lake that has significance to local wetland areas. Guests are provided with a copy of the environmental policy and are encouraged to participate in the scheme through specialised brochures.

The campaign includes recycling; treating diseased pine areas; regular cleaning of the beaches and marinas; development of a sewage treatment plant and new buildings in the resort are designed to minimise visual and environmental impacts. For its work in Vilamoura, Lusotour SA is also a winner of the British Airways Tourism for Tomorrow Awards.

The "Africa tourism" brand has been developed by the Open Africa Foundation to encourage products, which embraces sustainable ecological, economic and social development based on Africa's unique cultural, natural and wildlife heritage. "Open Africa" is also developing a continuous network of "Africa tourism" routes from the Cape to Cairo, known as the "African Dream". The Dream helps to create awareness of the many rural and environmental projects, which exist throughout Africa. "Team Africa", a transcontinental alliance of governments, corporations, institutions, professionals and individuals, provides leadership and motivation in the development of the "African Dream".

Host Communities

"Whale Watch Kaikoura" is an initiative of local Maori people from a small town on the East Coast of New Zealand's South Island. Within a kilometre of the Kaikoura shore is an area ideal for whales, where visitors are guaranteed to see them all year round. The Whale Watch began 11 years ago and is now a booming tourist destination, run by indigenous people with a strong sense of heritage and a view of the future based on strong principles of sustainability.

Jordan Tourism Investments, has revitalised the traditional village of Taybeh, in Jordan, into a cultural tourist resort, with the help and agreement of villagers. With many of the younger generation moving to the cities, the village was losing its character. By restoring its 19th century buildings and reviving old crafts, the village is now thriving again. The village lies 9km south east of the historic city of Petra. Opened in July 1994, the village now accommodates around 60,000 guests each year.

Uluru and Kakadu National Parks are both owned by indigenous Australians, the local Aboriginal communities, and jointly run with the National Parks and Wildlife Service. They are both major tourism destinations and involve indigenous participation in planning, management, and ownership of tourism infrastructure, as well as interpretation for visitors. They bring significant economic, social and cultural benefits to the local indigenous communities. The Conservation Corporation in Africa has established a series of high quality game parks in which local communities are major stakeholders and beneficiaries of tourism. This initiative is also helping to re-invigorate local crafts.

AGENTS AND PARTNERSHIPS

The challenge facing the tourism industry in moving towards a more sustainable future is set out in "Agenda 21 for the Travel and Tourism Industry". To achieve the goals set out in this document will require a partnership between government departments, national tourism authorities, international and national trade organisations and Travel and Tourism companies.

Working together in close cooperation such partnerships should aim to deliver the following:

- Close cooperation between the public and private sectors to deliver a regulatory regime, which encourages voluntary action but supplement, where necessary, with regulation in areas such as land-use and waste management.
- Agreed common standards and tools to enable the measurement of progress towards achieving sustainable development.
- Certification criteria developed and more widely applied to industry initiatives.
- A commitment to the controlled expansion, where appropriate, of infrastructure.
- Environmental taxes, where applied, should be fair and non-discriminatory. They should be carefully thought out to minimise their impact on economic development, and revenues should be allocated to Travel and Tourism associated environment improvement programmes.
- International, national and local funding bodies should include sustainable development as apart of their criteria, so that in time, all funding would be dependent on sound environmental practice.
- Contemporary research into sustainable tourism needs to be funded and developed. Issues requiring

attention include design, carrying capacity, tour operator activities, environmental reporting, auditing and environmental impact assessments.

- Environmental education and training should be increased, particularly in schools, for future hotel and tourism staff.
- Greater investment and commitment to the use of new technology.

COASTAL IMPACT OF TOURISM

Tourism provides an essential lifeline for many coastal communities. Faced with the prospect of increasing financial hardship, more and more coastal communities have turned to tourism as a means of generating income and survival. Tourism's impact on the coastal zone has, therefore, been largely positive. Of course, as in any area, if Tourism is not properly managed and developed, it can be harmful.

Impacts arise from the construction of infrastructure (hotels, marinas, transport, waste treatment facilities, groynes etc.) and from recreation (golf courses, water sports, theme parks etc). Coastal communities are now faced with tourism on a considerable scale, and the host to guest ratio can be very high in such areas. At the same time, coastal communities must try to maintain the resort's attraction as tourist demands change, sometimes quite rapidly.

With coastal regions being primary tourist destinations, sensitive marine and coastal environments can suffer dramatically. For example, as a result of large-scale sea-front tourist development, considerable beach and dune erosion can occur.

Tourism also impacts on environmental quality in the following ways:

- Ribbon development, infrastructure requirements, particularly transport links;
- The treatment and disposal of solid and/or liquid wastes, particularly during peak tourist seasons, may be inadequate or at worst non-existent; and
- Water is often consumed excessively, not only for

drinking but for showers, laundry, swimming pools, maintenance of golf courses etc. This can affect the quantity and quality of fresh water available to indigenous coastal populations.

Recreational activities can also have a significant impact on the coastal zone:

- Golf course's impact can be considerable, with those situated directly on coastal habitats(especially sand dunes) in particular;
- Erosion of reefs and coral from divers and swimmers;
- Pollution from boats and jets skis; and
- Noise from motor boats and jet skis, cars and buses, nightlife and other activities.

The development of a sustainable tourism industry in the coastal zone offers numerous opportunities. Opportunities includes, those for nature conservation—which, given the increasing interest in high quality natural and cultural experiences, can help to reverse the decline in market share of many coastal destinations. Tourism also provides important opportunities for strengthening local industries. Where industries are in decline, tourism ventures can help supplement declining income.

The following examples illustrate what can be done to make the most of the opportunities offered by tourism in the coastal zone:

Calvia is a Municipality on the Mediterranean coast that has undertaken an Agenda 21 project to assist the sustainable development of its tourism sector, in order to counter the negative impact of short-term tourism development since the 1960s. The local council has now implemented a transferable policy aimed at modernising, improving and diversifying the local tourist industry, involving all stakeholders, including the local population.

A Project Plan was enacted, and achievements so far include:

- Indigenous development, based on the sustainable use of available resources;
- High quality services and an appropriate bed night capacity;

- A ban on new development on 1,700 acres;
- Active participation of the residents in community life;
- Environmental management of municipality buildings, waste recycling, reduction in spending on electricity, and use of environmentally friendly materials for office use.

Quicksilver Tours, Queensland, Australia, is owned by one of the largest tourism operators to the Great Barrier Reef. Quicksilver have five large catamarans, which take about 1,000 tourists a day to dive on the reef. They have their own reef site with fixed diving platforms. They employ a team of biologists, both for environmental management and assessment as well as widespread environmental interpretation. Recent assessment of the reef, in the vicinity of the operation, shows that it is being maintained in pristine condition.

Kingfisher Bay Resort is found at Fraser Island, Queensland. It is a large five star "ecotourism" resort built in a beautiful, but fragile environment off the Queensland coast. Its concept, design, construction and management were conceived using the latest ecologically sustainable principles. It is a state-of-the-art "ecotourism" resort, which has won Australia's top tourism awards, and its economic and environmental success has influenced new coastal tourism developments.

Maho Bay's camps and studios in the US Virgin Islands have based their product on a commitment to minimise impact on the environment, conserve natural resources, engage in active and passive environmental education of their guests, and contribute to the local economy. Specific initiatives introduced at Maho Bay include the following: use of new technology; purchasing policies; waste management; environmental education; energy and water conservation; and support for local communities and culture. These initiatives show an appreciation of the need for alternative solutions to issues such as packaging and waste disposal through landfill. These are issues, which as the industry grows, will be increasingly important for the Travel and Tourism industry as a whole to address. The agents, partnerships for change and areas for further action in relation to tourism in the coastal zone are similar to the development of broad based sustainable tourism in general. A number of issues do, of course, have particular importance for the coastal zone.

Above all, the key to success is better participation at destination level among all the stakeholders concerned. In the case of the coastal zone, there are a number of additional organisations with an interest in coastal policy, marine conservation, shipping etc., which needs to be identified and included in partnerships for the coastal zone. Successful planning for tourism is very important for the future of the industry in coastal regions, because a significant percentage of tourism occurs within the geographical parameters of the definition of a coastal zone. Concerted support from all countries involved (and the industries within them) is vital to protect the shared natural resources that coastal zones represent.

Historically, the influence most hoteliers have on the environmental impact of their business is limited to working within existing buildings, or after a new site has been completed. In April 1998, the IHEI convened a group of hoteliers, tour operators, architectural firms and sustainable development specialists with the goal of creating a partnership to be called the "Sitting and Design Programme". The new initiative's mission will be to define responsible planning and design specifications that will cause minimal environmental damage at new sites. Particular attention will be paid to sites located within ecologically sensitive areas and upon waterfronts. The "Siting and Design Programme" will strive to reach hotel owners, investors and developers to bring these issues to the attention of the entire industry. Linkages with government authorities that uphold responsible development standards would complete the partnership.

Travel and Tourism has a number of advantages over other industry sectors:

- It creates jobs and wealth whilst;

- At the same time, it can contribute to sustainable development;
- It tends to have low start-up costs;
- Is a viable option in a wide range of areas and regions;
- Is likely to continue to grow for the foreseeable future; and
- The industry is, in a large part, aware of the need to protect the resource on which it is based—local culture and built and natural environment—and it is committed to these resources' preservation and enhancement.

The industry is, therefore, making a concerted effort to build up programmes for sustainable development. However, it cannot do this alone. If Travel and Tourism is to continue to flourish and to contribute to sustainable development, it needs help from national Governments. This assistance is needed in two forms:—both positive encouragement for sustainable tourism initiatives and an understanding that policy decisions in other areas can effect Travel and Tourism. In practical terms, what this means is the following:

The first point of action needed from Governments is to incorporate Agenda 21 principles into tourism policies at international and national level, and to promote their inclusion in regional and local tourism strategies. By providing such a lead and establishing a coherent global framework based on Agenda 21, national governments will make a vital contribution to developing a more sustainable tourism industry. Governments should also recognise that Travel and Tourism is a core service sector which should always be considered when looking at policies to expand trade, increase employment, modernise infrastructure and encourage investment—at both domestic and international level. It should also be included in national statistics with its economic impact calculated by means of a national tourism satellite account.

Governments should also consider helping Travel and Tourism by seeking to minimise regulatory impediments and by offering appropriate investment incentives. By supporting tourism and allowing it to compete in open and fair markets, tourism's benefits can be more easily secured. Finally, governments can address some of the fundamental barriers to tourism growth by looking at how to expand and modernise infrastructure, to apply taxes fairly and to invest in human resource development. If the programme of action outlined above can be undertaken by national governments in cooperation with continued industry commitments and initiatives for sustainable tourism then we can look to a brighter future.

4

Travel Law

COUPONS AND CREDITS

In the United States both state and federal courts have procedures permitting the aggregation of similar claims into a class action where the named plaintiff prosecutes a claim on behalf of hundreds or thousands of absent class members. Australia and the Canadian Provinces of Quebec, Ontario and British Columbia have class action procedures similar to those in the United States.

BROAD SPECTRUM OF CLAIMS

Travel class actions have been brought against:

- Airlines for physical injuries 60,000 flight attendants injured from second hand smoke in passenger cabins, flight delays 8,000 passengers delayed and many stranded for 8 hours in aircraft waiting on runways during snowstorm, cancellations 2,000 passengers stranded when tour operator goes out of business, overbooking, discrimination, misrepresented cargo rates, misrepresenting an air carrier's liability for lost jewelry, price fixing nine domestic airlines fix prices for air transportation between city pairs by signaling price changes on CRS, three airlines conspire to fix and stabilize prices on North Atlantic routes, price overcharges consumers challenge airline's 25% cancellation fee, improper collection of taxes airline collects federal excise tax from passengers during period when taxes were not authorized by Congress, imposing unreasonable penalties for replacing lost tickets, mismanaging consumer funds for the payment of charter tours, and failing to deliver advertised itineraries and hotel accommodations.

- Cruiseships for physical injuries contaminated food and water, vomiting and diarrhea, Legionnaires' disease, respiratory attacks, delays, port-skipping and itinerary changes, discomfort aboard ship QEII sailed before major refitting work on cabins and other facilities was completed, malfunctioning toilet flushing systems, breakdown of air conditioning system and lack of fresh water, misrepresentations capability of ship to meet scheduled itinerary, availability of promised services, facilities and activities aboard ship, deceptive port charges " The gravamen of plaintiff's complaint is that...each passenger is required to pay an amount referred to as a` port and handling charge`...often exceeds $150 per passenger...Cunard intentionally misleads passengers into believing that these port charges are paid to port authorities Cunard does not disclose that only a small percentage of the separate port charge is actually turned over to port authorities...the substantial balance is pocketed by Cunard ", lost, damaged or stolen baggage loss resulting from fire on board ship and bumping some passengers " bumped" from QEI.
- Railroads, Buses and Rental Car Companies for
  - Physical injuries,
  - Misrepresenting the nature, sponsorship and licensing of interstate ski tour services, price overcharges rental car company imposed $1.00 surcharge on customers' bills, taxi company uses " fast metres ", unconscionable replacement gasoline charges,
  - Age discrimination rental car companies refused to rent cars to persons under the age of 2539,
  - Price fixing insurance tie-in and fleet purchase price fixing conspiracy,

- Failure to deliver insurance coverage, rental cars as part of package tour.

- Hotels, Resorts and Time Shares for
  - Physical injuries failing skywalks, food poisoning, gastrointestinal disorders, " crater lake crud ",
  - Overbooking hotels on tours to England and Germany overbooked and consumers sent to inferior hotels, misrepresentations of major renovations at hotel and the availability of Glatt Kosher food, of the quality of the services, of the availability of accommodations in Munich, Germany, of the availability of numerous free sports activities and proximity to the beach,
  - Price overcharging and price fixing [overcharges for telephone calls, room rate overcharges, overcharges for out of state residents,
  - Time share " bait and switch "schemes and other frauds.
- Entertainment Suppliers and Vacation Clubs for fraud and misrepresentation season ticket holders sue football team that relocates, season ticket holders sue hockey team that goes out of business, season ticket holders sue basketball team when star player is traded, campground facilities and services inadequate.
- Tour Operators for
  - Physical injuries bus accident, gastrointestinal disorders,
  - Flight delays and cancellations,
  - Hotel "bait and switch "schemes,
  - Misrepresentations available hotels and itineraries, Glatt kosher food, services, facilities and proximity to the beach
  - Mismanagement and theft of consumer deposits.

How To Settle Travel Class Actions

At some point after the class action is commenced the parties will, typically, begin settlement discussions.

Ideally, the class members should receive compensation of:

- Travel services not delivered,
- Out of pocket expenses incurred
- The discomfort endured, discounted by the difficulty of proving the case and the ability of plaintiffs and defendants to finance continued litigation.

Cash Settlements are the Best

When possible travel class actions should be settled with a cash payment to each class member. For example, in Neilan v. Value Vacations, Inc in excess of $1.5 million was tendered by the defendants for distribution to class members who filed claims and the payment of attorneys' fees and costs. The distribution formula provided for various payments depending upon each class members' circumstances.

In Charleston-Coad v. Cunard Line Limited cruise passengers were offered cash and credits towards the purchase of a future cruise. And in Irving Trust Company v. Nationwide Leisure Corporation class members were offered specific sums of money for being accommodated at an inferior hotel in London, England or Munich, Germany [$50.00] or having suffered through a flight delay during a snowstorm $35.00.

Issuing Coupons for the Purchase of Travel Services

There are occasions when it may be appropriate for the court to approve a non-cash settlement which provides for the distribution of coupons or credits for the purchase of travel services from the defendants. For example, In Re Domestic Air Transportation Antitrust Litigation, In re North Atlantic Air Travel Antitrust Litigation, Pickett v. Holland America Line-Westours, Charleston-Coad v. Cunard Line Limited and Geelan v. Pan American World Airways, Inc. class claims were resolved, in whole or in part, with the issuance of coupons or credits for the purchase of future travel services from the defendants. The reasons for allowing these types of settlements include recovery of de minimus damages which would make the cost of distribution of each individual's cash award higher than that individual's claims, and the inability to identify class members. Another reason that may be acceptable to a court is the defendant's inability to afford to pay a cash recovery to the class. In this instance, as a threshold issue, the court should require that the defendant affirmatively establish its financial inability to pay cash. Without such a showing, a non-cash settlement on the grounds of "poverty " should not be approved. In all cases, non-cash settlements must be carefully examined by the court for adequacy since such settlements are generally worth less to consumers than cash and may benefit the defendant and class attorneys more than they benefit class members. Yet these settlements are justified because they solve manageability problems and require a defendant to disgorge improperly obtained monies.

Transferability

Typically, non-cash settlements such as coupons will require the class member to make a purchase of specific travel services which the consumer may not want. As a result, a settlement that relies on the distribution of coupons should provide that the distributed paper be convertible to cash either by redemption of or allowing them to be transferable to others. In one instance, to assist class members to convert their certificates to cash, the defendants agreed to "establish a clearinghouse for the purpose of helping those certificate holders desiring to find buyers ". The court approved the settlement stating "that there will be a lively market for certificates ".

A non-cash settlement may be acceptable if the coupons are convertible into cash albeit at a discount. In any event, without a feature allowing the conversion of coupons into cash by making them transferable or otherwise, the court should reject a non-cash settlement.

Redemption Rate

The most attractive feature for defendants of a non-cash coupon settlement is that, for a variety of reasons, not all of the issued coupons will be redeemed and used by class members. In fact, the average redemption rates on food and beverage coupons, have consistently been between 2% and 6%77. In evaluating the merit of a non-cash settlement, the only proper means of measuring true value is by estimating the actual redemption rate of the offered coupon. Unfortunately, in approving non-cash settlements most courts have neglected to require post settlement tracking of how many class members actually redeem the coupons.

In one of the few cases for which this data was available, the claim rate was only 0.54%79, and the subsequent coupon redemption rate was even lower. Such a low redemption rate makes a mockery of the concept that class members should receive value for settling their claims. This is especially true when class attorneys are paid in cash while the class receives coupons of dubious value. To prevent this emasculation of the settlement concept the court should require that be 100% redemption of the offered coupons. This means not only that the coupons must be transferable and cash convertible, but the defendant must continue to issue coupons until the agreed upon cash face value of the settlement is reached.

Time of Redemption

The time of redemption is an important factor in measuring the actual value of coupons. If the retailer is aware that the consumer intends to use a coupon he may increase the sale price to compensate for the reduced payment. This potential problem was circumvented in Branch v. Crabtree, a consumer class action alleging misrepresentations in the sale of Hyundai motor vehicles. A proposed settlement provided for the issuance of $1,000 certificates towards the purchase of a new or used car. The certificates could be withheld by the consumer until he or she had negotiated the best price. At that point the certificate could be produced for a further reduction in the vehicle price.

The Problem of Attorneys Fees

Non-cash settlements must be carefully reviewed by the courts, not the least reason being that there is an opportunity for substantial self-dealing on the part of class counsel.

Considering the low redemption rate of coupon settlements, defendants may be willing to pay inordinately high cash fees to class counsel in return for support in promoting a non-cash settlement in which the class receives near worthless coupons. Certainly, fee awards should not be based on a percentage of an estimated settlement value which itself is based upon an estimated redemption rate.

To prevent this opportunity for abuse, the court should require that class counsel accept all or a substantial portion of his fee in the same non-cash consideration being offered in settlement or fees should be based upon the actual recovery to the class. The rationale for requiring class counsel to share and share alike with class members is that this ensures value for the non-cash component on the theory that class counsel would not accept as a fee something that is relatively worthless. The settlement of travel class actions with the issuance of coupons or credits for the purchase of travel services from the defendants can be good for business and good for the consumer. Such settlements, however, must be carefully designed so that consumers actually receive something of value in return for releasing their claims against defendants.

Having regard to the Treaty establishing the European Community, and in particular Article 80(2) thereof, Having regard to the proposal from the Commission, Having regard to the opinion of the European Economic and Social Committee, After consulting the Committee of the Regions, Acting in accordance with the procedure laid down in Article 251 of the Treaty, in the light of the joint text approved by the *Conciliation Committee on 1 December 2003, Whereas*:

- Action by the Community in the field of air transport should aim, among other things, at ensuring a high level of protection for passengers. Moreover, full account should be taken of the requirements of consumer protection in general.
- Denied boarding and cancellation or long delay of flights cause serious trouble and inconvenience to passengers.
- While Council Regulation (EEC) No 295/91 of 4

February 1991 establishing common rules for a denied boarding compensation system in scheduled air transport created basic protection for passengers, the number of passengers denied boarding against their will remains too high, as does that affected by cancellations without prior warning and that affected by long delays.

- The Community should therefore raise the standards of protection set by that Regulation both to strengthen the rights of passengers and to ensure that air carriers operate under harmonised conditions in a liberalised market.
- Since the distinction between scheduled and non-scheduled air services is weakening, such protection should apply to passengers not only on scheduled but also on non-scheduled flights, including those forming part of package tours.
- The protection accorded to passengers departing from an airport located in a Member State should be extended to those leaving an airport located in a third country for one situated in a Member State, when a Community carrier operates the flight.
- In order to ensure the effective application of this Regulation, the obligations that it creates should rest with the operating air carrier who performs or intends to perform a flight, whether with owned aircraft, under dry or wet lease, or on any other basis.
- This Regulation should not restrict the rights of the operating air carrier to seek compensation from any person, including third parties, in accordance with the law applicable.
- The number of passengers denied boarding against their will should be reduced by requiring air carriers to call for volunteers to surrender their reservations, in exchange for benefits, instead of denying passengers boarding, and by fully compensating those finally denied boarding.
- Passengers denied boarding against their will should

be able either to cancel their flights, with reimbursement of their tickets, or to continue them under satisfactory conditions, and should be adequately cared for while awaiting a later flight.

- Volunteers should also be able to cancel their flights, with reimbursement of their tickets, or continue them under satisfactory conditions, since they face difficulties of travel similar to those experienced by passengers denied boarding against their will.
- The trouble and inconvenience to passengers caused by cancellation of flights should also be reduced. This should be achieved by inducing carriers to inform passengers of cancellations before the scheduled time of departure and in addition to offer them reasonable rerouting, so that the passengers can make other arrangements. Air carriers should compensate passengers if they fail to do this, except when the cancellation occurs in extraordinary circumstances which could not have been avoided even if all reasonable measures had been taken.
- Passengers whose flights are cancelled should be able either to obtain reimbursement of their tickets or to obtain re-routing under satisfactory conditions, and should be adequately cared for while awaiting a later flight.
- As under the Montreal Convention, obligations on operating air carriers should be limited or excluded in cases where an event has been caused by extraordinary circumstances which could not have been avoided even if all reasonable measures had been taken. Such circumstances may, in particular, occur in cases of political instability, meteorological conditions incompatible with the operation of the flight concerned, security risks, unexpected flight safety shortcomings and strikes that affect the operation of an operating air carrier.
- Extraordinary circumstances should be deemed to exist where the impact of an air traffic management

decision in relation to a particular aircraft on a particular day gives rise to a long delay, an overnight delay, or the cancellation of one or more flights by that aircraft, even though all reasonable measures had been taken by the air carrier concerned to avoid the delays or cancellations.

- In cases where a package tour is cancelled for reasons other than the flight being cancelled, this Regulation should not apply.
- Passengers whose flights are delayed for a specified time should be adequately cared for and should be able to cancel their flights with reimbursement of their tickets or to continue them under satisfactory conditions.
- Care for passengers awaiting an alternative or a delayed flight may be limited or declined if the provision of the care would itself cause further delay.
- Operating air carriers should meet the special needs of persons with reduced mobility and any persons accompanying them.
- Passengers should be fully informed of their rights in the event of denied boarding and of cancellation or long delay of flights, so that they can effectively exercise their rights.
- Member States should lay down rules on sanctions applicable to infringements of the provisions of this Regulation and ensure that these sanctions are applied. The sanctions should be effective, proportionate and dissuasive.
- Member States should ensure and supervise general compliance by their air carriers with this Regulation and designate an appropriate body to carry out such enforcement tasks. The supervision should not affect the rights of passengers and air carriers to seek legal redress from courts under procedures of national law.
- The Commission should analyse the application of this Regulation and should assess in particular the opportunity of extending its scope to all passengers

having a contract with a tour operator or with a Community carrier, when departing from a third country airport to an airport in a Member State.

- Arrangements for greater cooperation over the use of Gibraltar airport were agreed in London on 2 December 1987 by the Kingdom of Spain and the United Kingdom in a joint declaration by the Ministers of Foreign Affairs of the two countries. Such arrangements have yet to enter into operation.
- Regulation (EEC) No 295/91 should accordingly be repealed.

Subject

- This Regulation establishes, under the conditions specified herein, minimum rights for passengers when:
  - They are denied boarding against their will;
  - Their flight is cancelled;
  - Their flight is delayed.
- Application of this Regulation to Gibraltar airport is understood to be without prejudice to the respective legal positions of the Kingdom of Spain and the United Kingdom with regard to the dispute over sovereignty over the territory in which the airport is situated.
- Application of this Regulation to Gibraltar airport shall be suspended until the arrangements in the Joint Declaration made by the Foreign Ministers of the Kingdom of Spain and the United Kingdom on 2 December 1987 enter into operation. The Governments of Spain and the United Kingdom will inform the Council of such date of entry into operation.

For the purposes of this Regulation:

- 'Air carrier' means an air transport undertaking with a valid operating licence;
- 'Operating air carrier' means an air carrier that performs or intends to perform a flight under a

contract with a passenger or on behalf of another person, legal or natural, having a contract with that passenger;

- 'Community carrier' means an air carrier with a valid operating licence granted by a Member State in accordance with the provisions of Council Regulation (EEC) No 2407/92 of 23 July 1992 on licensing of air carriers;
- 'Tour operator' means, with the exception of an air carrier, an organiser within the meaning of Article 2, point 2, of Council Directive 90/314/EEC of 13 June 1990 on package travel, package holidays and package tours;
- 'Package' means those services defined in Article 2, point 1, of Directive 90/314/EEC;
- 'Ticket' means a valid document giving entitlement to transport, or something equivalent in paperless form, including electronic form, issued or authorised by the air carrier or its authorised agent;
- 'Reservation' means the fact that the passenger has a ticket, or other proof, which indicates that the reservation has been accepted and registered by the air carrier or tour operator;
- 'Final destination' means the destination on the ticket presented at the check-in counter or, in the case of directly connecting flights, the destination of the last flight; alternative connecting flights available shall not be taken into account if the original planned arrival time is respected;
- 'Person with reduced mobility' means any person whose mobility is reduced when using transport because of any physical disability (sensory or locomotory, permanent or temporary), intellectual impairment, age or any other cause of disability, and whose situation needs special attention and adaptation to the person's needs of the services made available to all passengers;

- 'Denied boarding' means a refusal to carry passengers on a flight, although they have presented themselves for boarding under the conditions laid down in Article 3(2), except where there are reasonable grounds to deny them boarding, such as reasons of health, safety or security, or inadequate travel documentation;
- 'Volunteer' means a person who has presented himself for boarding under the conditions laid down in Article 3(2) and responds positively to the air carrier's call for passengers prepared to surrender their reservation in exchange for benefits.
- 'Cancellation' means the non-operation of a flight which was previously planned and on which at least one place was reserved.

Scope

- *This Regsulation shall apply*:
  - To passengers departing from an airport located in the territory of a Member State to which the Treaty applies;
  - To passengers departing from an airport located in a third country to an airport situated in the territory of a Member State to which the Treaty applies, unless they received benefits or compensation and were given assistance in that third country, if the operating air carrier of the flight concerned is a Community carrier. 2. Paragraph 1 shall apply on the condition that passengers:
  - Have a confirmed reservation on the flight concerned anad, except in the case of cancellation referred to in Article 5, present themselves for check-in,—as stipulated and at the time indicated in advance and in writing (including by electronic means) by the air carrier, the tour operator or an authorised travel agent, or, if no

time is indicated,—not later than 45 minutes before the published departure time; or

- Have been transferred by an air carrier or tour operator from the flight for which they held a reservation to another flight, irrespective of the reason.

- This Regulation shall not apply to passengers travelling free of charge or at a reduced fare not available directly or indirectly to the public. However, it shall apply to passengers having tickets issued under a frequent flyer programme or other commercial programme by an air carrier or tour operator.
- This Regulation shall only apply to passengers transported by motorised fixed wing aircraft.
- This Regulation shall apply to any operating air carrier providing transport to passengers covered by paragraphs 1 and 2. Where an operating air carrier which has no contract with the passenger performs obligations under this Regulation, it shall be regarded as doing so on behalf of the person having a contract with that passenger.
- This Regulation shall not affect the rights of passengers under Directive 90/314/EEC. This Regulation shall not apply in cases where a package tour is cancelled for reasons other than cancellation of the flight.

Denied Boarding

- When an operating air carrier reasonably expects to deny boarding on a flight, it shall first call for volunteers to surrender their reservations in exchange for benefits under conditions to be agreed between the passenger concerned and the operating air carrier. Volunteers shall be assisted in accordance with Article 8, such assistance being additional to the benefits mentioned in this paragraph.
- If an insufficient number of volunteers comes forward to allow the remaining passengers with

reservations to board the flight, the operating air carrier may then deny boarding to passengers against their will.

- If boarding is denied to passengers against their will, the operating air carrier shall immediately compensate them in accordance with Article 7 and assist them in accordance with Articles 8 and 9.

Cancellation

In case of cancellation of a flight, the passengers concerned shall:

a. Be offered assistance by the operating air carrier in accordance with Article 8;

b. Be offered assistance by the operating air carrier in accordance with Article 9(1)(a) and 9(2), as well as, in event of rerouting when the reasonably expected time of departure of the new flight is at least the day after the departure as it was planned for the cancelled flight, the assistance specified in Article 9(1)(b) and 9(1)(c);

c. Have the right to compensation by the operating air carrier in accordance with Article 7, unless:

    i. They are informed of the cancellation at least two weeks before the scheduled time of departure;

    ii. They are informed of the cancellation between two weeks and seven days before the scheduled time of departure and are offered re-routing, allowing them to depart no more than two hours before the scheduled time of departure and to reach their final destination less than four hours after the scheduled time of arrival;

    iii. They are informed of the cancellation less than seven days before the scheduled time of departure and are offered re-routing, allowing them to depart no more than one hour before the scheduled time of departure and to reach their final destination less than two hours after the scheduled time of arrival.

When passengers are informed of the cancellation, an explanation shall be given concerning possible alternative transport. An operating air carrier shall not be obliged to pay compensation in accordance with Article 7, if it can prove that the cancellation is caused by extraordinary circumstances which could not have been avoided even if all reasonable measures had been taken. The burden of proof concerning the questions as to whether and when the passenger has been informed of the cancellation of the flight shall rest with the operating air carrier.

Delay

When an operating air carrier reasonably expects a flight to be delayed beyond its scheduled time of departure:

a. For two hours or more in the case of flights of 1 500 kilometres or less;
b. For three hours or more in the case of all intra-Community flights of more than 1 500 kilometres and of all other flights between 1 500 and 3 500 kilometres;
c. For four hours or more in the case of all flights not falling under (a) or (b), passengers shall be offered by the operating air carrier:
    i. The assistance specified in Article 9(1)(a) and 9(2); and
    ii. When the reasonably expected time of departure is at least the day after the time of departure previously announced, the assistance specified in Article 9(1)(b) and 9(1)(c);
    iii. When the delay is at least five hours, the assistance specified in Article 8(1)(a).

In any event, the assistance shall be offered within the time limits set out above with respect to each distance bracket. L 46/4 EN Official Journal of the European Union 17.2.2004

Right to Compensation

Where reference is made to this Article, passengers shall receive compensation amounting to:

a. EUR 250 for all flights of 1 500 kilometres or less;
b. EUR 400 for all intra-Community flights of more than

1 500 kilometres, and for all other flights between 1 500 and 3 500 kilometres;

c. EUR 600 for all flights not falling under (a) or (b). In determining the distance, the basis shall be the last destination at which the denial of boarding or cancellation will delay the passenger's arrival after the scheduled time.

When passengers are offered re-routing to their final destination on an alternative flight pursuant to Article 8, the arrival time of which does not exceed the scheduled arrival time of the flight originally booked

a. By two hours, in respect of all flights of 1 500 kilometres or less;
b. By three hours, in respect of all intra-Community flights of more than 1 500 kilometres and for all other flights between 1 500 and 3 500 kilometres;
c. By four hours, in respect of all flights not falling under (a) or (b), the operating air carrier may reduce the compensation provided for in paragraph 1 by 50%.

The compensation referred to in paragraph 1 shall be paid in cash, by electronic bank transfer, bank orders or bank cheques or, with the signed agreement of the passenger, in travel vouchers and/or other services. The distances given in paragraphs 1 and 2 shall be measured by the great circle route method.

Right to Reimbursement or Re-routing

Where reference is made to this Article, passengers shall be offered the choice between:

a. Reimbursement within seven days, by the means provided for in Article 7(3), of the full cost of the ticket at the price at which it was bought, for the part or parts of the journey not made, and for the part or parts already made if the flight is no longer serving any purpose in relation to the passenger's original travel plan, together with, when relevant,—a return flight to the first point of departure, at the earliest opportunity;

b. Re-routing, under comparable transport conditions, to their final destination at the earliest opportunity;
c. Re-routing, under comparable transport conditions, to their final destination at a later date at the passenger's convenience, subject to availability of seats.

Paragraph 1(a) shall also apply to passengers whose flights form part of a package, except for the right to reimbursement where such right arises under Directive 90/314/EEC.

When, in the case where a town, city or region is served by several airports, an operating air carrier offers a passenger a flight to an airport alternative to that for which the booking was made, the operating air carrier shall bear the cost of transferring the passenger from that alternative airport either to that for which the booking was made, or to another close-by destination agreed with the passenger.

Right to Care

Where reference is made to this Article, passengers shall be offered free of charge:

- Meals and refreshments in a reasonable relation to the waiting time;
- Hotel accommodation in cases—where a stay of one or more nights becomes necessary, or—where a stay additional to that intended by the passenger becomes necessary;
- Transport between the airport and place of accommodation (hotel or other).

In addition, passengers shall be offered free of charge two telephone calls, telex or fax messages, or e-mails. In applying this Article, the operating air carrier shall pay particular attention to the needs of persons with reduced mobility and any persons accompanying them, as well as to the needs of unaccompanied children.

Upgrading and Downgrading

If an operating air carrier places a passenger in a class higher than that for which the ticket was purchased, it may not request any supplementary payment. If an operating air carrier places a passenger in a class lower than that for which the ticket was purchased, it shall within seven days, by the means provided for in Article 7(3), reimburse,

a. 30% of the price of the ticket for all flights of 1 500 kilometres or less, or 17.2.2004 EN Official Journal of the European Union L 46/5
b. 50% of the price of the ticket for all intra-Community flights of more than 1 500 kilometres, except flights between the European territory of the Member States and the French overseas departments, and for all other flights between 1 500 and 3 500 kilometres,
c. 75% of the price of the ticket for all flights not falling under (a) or (b), including flights between the European territory of the Member States and the French overseas departments.

Persons with Reduced Mobility or Special Needs

Operating air carriers shall give priority to carrying persons with reduced mobility and any persons or certified service dogs accompanying them, as well as unaccompanied children. In cases of denied boarding, cancellation and delays of any length, persons with reduced mobility and any persons accompanying them, as well as unaccompanied children, shall have the right to care in accordance with Article 9 as soon as possible.

Further Compensation

This Regulation shall apply without prejudice to a passenger's rights to further compensation. The compensation granted under this Regulation may be deducted from such compensation. Without prejudice to relevant principles and rules of national law, including case-law, paragraph 1 shall not apply to passengers who have voluntarily surrendered a reservation under Article 4(1).

Right of Redress

In cases where an operating air carrier pays compensation or meets the other obligations incumbent on it under this

Regulation, no provision of this Regulation may be interpreted as restricting its right to seek compensation from any person, including third parties, in accordance with the law applicable. In particular, this Regulation shall in no way restrict the operating air carrier's right to seek reimbursement from a tour operator or another person with whom the operating air carrier has a contract.

Similarly, no provision of this Regulation may be interpreted as restricting the right of a tour operator or a third party, other than a passenger, with whom an operating air carrier has a contract, to seek reimbursement or compensation from the operating air carrier in accordance with applicable relevant laws.

Obligation to Inform Passengers of their Rights

The operating air carrier shall ensure that at check-in a clearly legible notice containing the following text is displayed in a manner clearly visible to passengers: 'If you are denied boarding or if your flight is cancelled or delayed for at least two hours, ask at the check-in counter or boarding gate for the text stating your rights, particularly with regard to compensation and assistance'.

An operating air carrier denying boarding or cancelling a flight shall provide each passenger affected with a written notice setting out the rules for compensation and assistance in line with this Regulation. It shall also provide each passenger affected by a delay of at least two hours with an equivalent notice. The contact details of the national designated body referred to in Article 16 shall also be given to the passenger in written form. In respect of blind and visually impaired persons, the provisions of this Article shall be applied using appropriate alternative means.

Exclusion of Waiver

Obligations vis-à-vis passengers pursuant to this Regulation may not be limited or waived, notably by a derogation or restrictive clause in the contract of carriage. If, nevertheless, such a derogation or restrictive clause is applied in respect of a passenger, or if the passenger is not correctly informed of his rights and for that reason has accepted compensation which is inferior to that provided for in this Regulation, the passenger shall still be entitled to take the necessary proceedings before the competent courts or bodies in order to obtain additional compensation.

Infringements

Each Member State shall designate a body responsible for the enforcement of this Regulation as regards flights from airports situated on its territory and flights from a third country to such airports. Where appropriate, this body shall take the measures necessary to ensure that the rights of passengers are respected.

The Member States shall inform the Commission of the body that has been designated in accordance with this paragraph. L 46/6 EN Official Journal of the European Union 17.2.2004 Without prejudice to Article 12, each passenger may complain to any body designated under paragraph 1, or to any other competent body designated by a Member State, about an alleged infringement of this Regulation at any airport situated on the territory of a Member State or concerning any flight from a third country to an airport situated on that territory.

The sanctions laid down by Member States for infringements of this Regulation shall be effective, proportionate and dissuasive.

The Commission shall report to the European Parliament and the Council by 1 January 2007 on the operation and the results of this Regulation, in particular regarding:—the incidence of denied boarding and of cancellation of flights,—the possible extension of the scope of this Regulation to passengers having a contract with a Community carrier or holding a flight reservation which forms part of a 'package tour' to which Directive 90/314/EEC applies and who depart from a third-country airport to an airport in a Member State, on flights not operated by Community air carriers,—the possible revision of the amounts of compensation referred to in Article 7(1). The report shall be accompanied where necessary by legislative proposals.

Selecting a Good Travel Agent

Selecting a good travel agent is a risky business. Very few States require travel agents to be licensed, tested annually for competence and proficiency or financially responsible, *e.g.*, maintaining insurance and surety bonds for the benefit of consumers, escrowing consumer deposits and funding consumer compensation funds. Nonetheless, there are certain things to look for when selecting a reliable travel agent. "There are good travel agents and there are bad travel agents. The good ones find airfares and cruises priced below advertised rates, negotiate free upgrades, find rooms in ` full ` hotels, understand and tell you about travel insurance, and, when things go wrong, either fight for you or try to make it up to you. The bad ones don't do any of this...Word of mouth is a good way to find a reliable agent.

But if you're looking for one on your own, consider the following:

- How experienced is the agent?,
- How knowledgeable is the agent about your destination? How often has he or she traveled to a place or sent other clients there?
- Does the agent ask about your needs, desires and travel habits?
- Is the agent certified by the Institute of Certified Travel Agents?
- Is the agent skilled at using the computer reservations systems?
- Does the agency belong to a consortium? Small, independent agencies join consortiums in order to offer competitive rates on travel opportunities.
- Does the agency use a consolidator who sells discounted airline tickets, usually at rates below those advertised to the public?
- Does the agency have a 24-hour phone line?
- Does the agency protect client's deposits? Does it put them in an escrow account or post a bond? "

The Legal Status of Travel Agents

Travel agents are agents of the consumer and have been declared to be fiduciaries with a high standard of care in several States including Arizona Maurer v. Cervenik-Anderson Travel, Inc. (teenager on student tour is crushed by steel wheels of tour operator's Party Train traveling to Mazatlan, Mexico), California McCollum v. Friendly Hills Travel Centre (tourist injured while water skiing at resort), District of Columbia, Illinois. McCoy v. MTI Vacations, Inc. (travel agent failed to notify consumer of flight changes); Louisiana Philippe v. Lloyd's Aero Boliviano (tourist suffers cerebral hemorrhage on chartered aircraft in Bolivia); New Jersey Rodriquez v. Cardona Travel Bureau (charter air carrier goes bust and defaults in delivery of flight); New York Pelegrini v. Landmark Travel Group (consumer misinformed by travel agent that tour vouchers refundable); Ohio Grigsby v. O.K. Travel (tour operator defaults in delivery of tour); Oklahoma Douglas v. Steele (tour operator defaults in delivery of tour); and Pennsylvania Touhey v. Trans National Travel (accommodations and facilities at hotel misrepresented.

The virtue of being a fiduciary is that the travel agent's duties and obligations to the consumer are independent from the travel agent's relationship with airlines, cruise lines, hotels or tour operators. What should consumers reasonably expect from their travel agents?

Duty to Make and Confirm Reservations

After selecting specific travel services the consumer expects the travel agent to contact the supplier or tour operator and make reservations. This function may be accomplished by computer, telephone or in writing. A failure to make the agreed upon reservations renders the travel agent liable for the consumer's damages Slade v. Cheung and Risser Enterprises (travel agent liable for consumer's lost deposit for failing to contact insolvent cruise company and establish availability of cruise); Reservations Desk v. ALIA (failure to confirm airline reservations); Carro v. Parente World Travel Centre (travel agent responsible for making airline reservations); Lathigra v. British Airways (passengers stranded in Nairobi for five days because airline reconfirmed reservations on discontinued flight); Rosen v. DePorter-Butterworth Tours (failure to inform consumer of itinerary change); Van Rossem v. Penney Travel Service (failure to confirm hotel accommodations); Zobler v. Windward Travel Centre (failure to deliver tickets for honeymoon trip); Fuller v. Healey Transportation (failure to send consumers to proper airport for flight).

Independent Duty to Verify Reservations

Travel agents may find it convenient to rely upon various sources of information in confirming reservations. For example, the travel agent may rely upon wholesalers or tour operators Bucholtz v. Sirotkin Travel Service (travel agent relied upon wholesaler to make reservations at selected Las Vegas hotel) or computers Bhattal v. Grand Hyatt-New York (computer error results in guest's baggage being sent to Saudi Arabia) to verify that reservations have been made. Such reliance may be insufficient, however, since travel agents should be prepared to contact suppliers such as air carriers, cruise lines and hotels, directly, and independently verify that the purchased travel services will, in fact, be delivered [Prechtl v. Travel House of Garden City (travel agent should have contacted air carrier instead of relying on computer to make reservations on a flight which air carrier had discontinued); Trip Tours, Ltd. v. Zamani (travel agent should have contacted air carrier instead of relying on an irresponsible tour operator to make airline reservations that never materialized); Touhey v. Trans National Travel (travel agent failed to independently verify conditions at half finished hotel; $25,000 in special damages awarded against travel agent).

Failure to Disclose Identity of Supplier

In recommending specific travel services the travel agent must disclose the identity of the supplier or tour operator responsible for delivering the services. If the travel agent fails to make such a disclosure then the travel agent may be held responsible for the supplier's or tour operator's default Spiro v. Delmar Travel Bureau (travel agent will be held liable for defaults of tour operator if it fails to disclose tour operator's identity); Van Rossem v. Penney Travel Service (inferior hotel accommodations substituted during honeymoon vacation in Jamaica; travel agent liable for failing to disclose identity of tour operator).

Vouching for the Reliability of Suppliers

In recommending suppliers and tour operators the travel agent may vouch for or warranty the performance of a specific airline, cruise line, hotel or tour operator. In doing so the travel agent may be held liable for the supplier's or tour operator's default under a variety of legal theories including

- Assumed duty [Hernandez v. Rapid Bus Company (passenger rapes passenger; bus company liable for assuming duty to provide safe transportation); Cohen v. Heritage Motor Tours (tourist slips and falls on slippery rocks crossing stream during tour of Canadian Rockies; tour operator and tour guide may have assumed duty to determine whether stones were safe to use as a path),
- Breach of warranty Glenview Park District v. Melhus (canoeist who drowned during trip down river was promised that canoeing would " be perfectly safe "); Pau v. Yosemite Park and Curry Company (bicycle accident; express warranty of safety claim based on promises of safe trails and " safe and enjoyable cycling areas "); Chan v. Society Expeditions (tourists being transported from cruise ship to shore excursion drown when Zodiac raft overturns; brochures " advertised the Zodiac's versatility and safety in the hands of (tour operator's) `highly skilled boatman');
- Negligent or fraudulent misrepresentation Maurer v. Cerkvenik-Anderson Travel, Inc. (student on tour falls to death under steel wheels of Party Train to Mazatlan, Mexico; negligent failure to reveal three prior deaths of students on same train); Pelegrini v.

Landmark Travel Group (travel agent misrepresents refundability of tour vouchers as being refundable); Marcus v. Zenith Travel (tourists stranded in Japan when tour operator defaults; travel agent negligently misrepresented that tour operator was financial stable); Gelfand v. Action Travel Centre (travel agent negligently misrepresented cruise ship's ability to deal with tourist's physical condition);

- Breach of implied warranty of habitability Touhey v. Trans National Travel (tourists vacation ruined because hotel under construction; travel agent contract carries with it an implied warranty of habitability of hotel accommodations; travel agent failed to make independent investigation of condition of hotel; $25,000 in special damages against travel agent); and
- Promissory estoppel Chow v. Trans World Airlines (passenger relies upon air carrier's false promises of priority seating on connecting foreign carrier and misses flight to Singapore); Keefe v. Bahama Cruise Line (reliance upon false promises resulted in delay in filing claim); Fogel v. Hertz International (rental car accident in Italy; liability of U.S. Hertz corporation may be based upon agency by estoppel).

Duty to Investigate Avtailability of Travel Services

Travel agents have ongoing duties to investigate the availability of the contracted for travel services, *e.g.*,

- Hotel closed, Barton v. Wonderful World of Travel (hotel closed; travel agent liable for failing to investigate conditions),
- Hotel under construction Josephs v. Fuller (hotel substandard; travel agent liable for failing to investigate conditions),
- Canceled charter flight, Rodriquez v. Cardona Travel Bureau (charter air carrier defaults; travel agent liable for failing to warn of risks of charters),
- Canceled scheduled flight Fix v. Travel Help (airline

goes bankrupt; travel agent liable for failing to investigate);

- Tour package not delivered Marcus v. Zenith Travel (travel agent liable for failing to reveal trade reports about financial instability of tour operator);
- Cruise ship impounded by a local sheriff Slade v. Cheung and Risser Enterprises (travel agent failed to contact cruise ship company directly and verify cruise availability),
- Tour operator changed the itinerary, Rosen v. DePorter-Butterworth Tours (travel agent failed to advise tourist of change in tour itinerary), and
- Hotel overbooking, Bucholtz v. Sirotkin Travel Service (Las Vegas hotel overbooks and walks customers; travel agent liable for failing to investigate reliability of tour wholesaler). The travel agent's duty to investigate continues even after the initial deposit is made Barton v. Wonderful World of Travel (travel agent required to keep in contact with hotel up to thirty days before departure).

Duty to Convey Needed Information

The most open ended duty of modern travel agents is to disclose any negative information which could have an adverse impact on the consumer's vacation or business trip. This duty is limited only by the actual availability of the information to the travel agent and to the consumer Stafford v. Intrav (travel agent has duty to disclose information unless " obvious and apparent " to the traveller)]; Markland v. Travel Travel Southfield (both travel agent and consumer knew of financial instability of Eastern Airlines prior to default)] and was the accident foreseeable and would the information have prevented the accident [Harvey v. American Airlines (vacation ruined because of inclement weather; no duty to warn of rainy weather); McCollum v. Friendly Hills Travel Centre (waterskiing accident at resort; no duty to warn of danger in the absence of information of prior accidents); Tucker v. Whitaker Travel, Ltd. (no duty to warn of risks of horseback riding); Connolly v. Samuelson (no duty to warn of dangers of walking on safari)].

- *Financial Instability:* Travel agents should investigate the financial stability of suppliers and tour operators and convey this information to the consumer [Marcus v. Zenith Travel (travel agent liable for failing to reveal reports in travel trade press about financial instability of tour operator); Spiro v. Delmar Travel Bureau (travel agent liable for defaults of bankrupt tour operator); Fix v. Travel Help (travel agent negligently misrepresents financial stability of bankrupt airline); Douglas v. Steele (travel agent liable for failing to reveal information regarding financial instability of tour operator)].
- *Inability:* To Deliver Services: Travel agents should investigate the willingness and ability of suppliers and tour operators to actually deliver contracted for travel services. Specifically, the travel agent should find out and inform the consumer if the hotel is closed [Barton v. Wonderful World of Travel (travel agent should have discovered that hotel was closed)] or under construction [Josephs v. Fuller (travel agent should have discovered that hotel was substandard)], or the cruise vessel has been impounded by the local sheriff [Slade v. Cheung and Risser Enterprises, Inc.], whether the cruise vessel can accommodate physically handicapped passengers [Gelfand v. Action Travel Centre (travel agent negligently misrepresents that cruise vessel could meet the needs of handicapped passenger)], whether the hotel has a policy of overbooking guests [Bucholtz v. Sirotkin Travel Service (travel agent should have investigated tour operator's track record in selling accommodations at hotels that overbooks guests)], or whether a specific flight has been canceled [Trip Tours, Inc. v. Zamani (charter tour operator fails to deliver flight; travel agent liable); Prechtl v. Travel House of Garden City (travel agent liable for failing to investigate

availability of flight)]. In addition, the travel agent should continue to investigate the ability of a supplier or tour operator to deliver even after the reservations are made [Marcus v. Zenith Travel (the travel agent learned of the tour operator's financial instability after the consumer's made their reservations but failed to reveal this negative information before full payment thus giving the consumers the opportunity to cancel with minimum losses)].

- *Need For Travel Documentation:* Without proper travel documents the purpose of the consumer's vacation or business trip may be defeated, *e.g.*, the traveller may be imprisoned or denied entry and forced to leave the destination country at great expense. Travel agents should investigate and inform consumers of the need for travel documentation [Compaigne Nationale Air France v. Castano (airline liable for failing to advise consumers of need for a visa to enter Spain); Levin v. Kasmir World Travel (travel agent liable for failing to advise consumer of need for a visa to enter China)].
- *Health And Safety Hazards:* The destination country may be suffering from a typhoid epidemic, have a high crime rate or be a violent environment because of war or revolution. Travel agents should contact the U.S. Centre for Disease Control [CDC] and obtain information about diseases and the need for medication and shots, the U.S. State Department and obtain any Travel Advisories warning of dangers and any other reasonably available source of information of health and safety hazards in the destination country [Glenview Park District v. Melhus (canoeist drowned during trip down river; sponsor should have investigate the water levels and determined imminent flood conditions); Loretti v. Holiday Inns (tourist assaulted and raped on beach in Bahamas; travel agent should investigate crime levels in destination);

Philippe v. Lloyd's Aero Boliviano (tourist suffered severe physical injuries because of a lack of oxygen during a flight in La Paz, Bolivia]; Maurer v. Cerkvenik-Anderson Travel (student falls to death under steel wheels of the Party Train to Mazatlan, Mexico; tour operator failed to reveal prior three deaths of students on the same train)].

- *Need For Travel Insurance:* Travel agents should advise consumers of the need for and availability of appropriate travel insurance [Rodriquez v. Cardona Travel Bureau (charter air carrier defaults; travel agent failed to advise of need for travel insurance); Markland v. Travel Southfield (travel agent not liable for default of tour operator; travel agent advised consumer to buy travel insurance)].
- *Itinerary Changes:* Travel agents should discover and warn consumers of any changes in flight schedules [McCoy v. MTI Vacations, Inc. (travel agent failed to notify consumers of flight changes); Vick v. National Airlines (failure to warn of schedule changes)] or tour itineraries [Rosen v. DePorter-Butterworth Tours, Inc. (failure to advise consumer of change in tour starting point)].
- *Restrictions:* On Tickets and Vouchers: Travel agents should discover and advise consumers of any restrictions on the use of tickets and vouchers [Das v. Royal Jordanian Airlines (travel agent failed to inform consumer that flight was wait listed); Burnap v. Tribeca Travel (travel agent failed to inform consumer of ticket restrictions); Pelegrini v. Landmark Travel Group (travel agent misrepresents refundability of tour vouchers)].

Recoverable Damages

The damages which a consumer may recover from a travel agent for breach of contract, negligence, fraud or violation of a Consumer Protection Statute will depend upon the nature of the injuries sustained. In non-physical injury cases recoverable should include the value of the components of the vacation not delivered, compensation for discomfort, annoyance and harassment and special damages for " loss of what was to have been a pleasant week " [Touhey v. Trans National Travel ($25,000 in special damages awarded)], or loss of " a refreshing, memorable vacation " [Vick v. National Airlines ($2,500 each for couple who suffered from missed flight)] or the " intangible pleasure of a 24 hour vacation day " [Semrod v. Mexicana Airlines88 ($3,000 awarded for loss of one vacation day)] or the loss of a planned vacation [Pelegrini v. Landmark Travel Group ($250 awarded for loss of planned vacation)].

CRUISE PASSENGER'S RIGHT AND REMEDIES

Modern cruise vessels are best viewed as floating hotels that transport their guests from exotic port to exotic port where the passengers stay a few hours for shopping, snorkeling, scuba diving, parasailing and touring. The cruise industry is growing rapidly with 6 million cruise passengers world wide in 1998, a 7.8% increase from the year before. The advertising for cruise vacations is seductive, indeed, with ships now being built that exceed 100,000 tons and accommodate over 3,000 passengers. The commitment of the cruise industry to the future is extraordinary with $10.5 billion invested in the construction of 35 new " mega " ships for delivery by 20023.

Common travel problems experienced by cruise passengers include physical injuries caused by:

- Slips, trips and falls [Bergonzine v. Maui Classic Cruises (350 lb. passenger on honeymoon cruise falls on gangplank); Rainey v. Paquet Cruises(fall on disco dance floor); Lee v. Regal Cruises (fall on melting ice cubes on stairway); Kunken v. Celebrity Cruises (ankle broken entering cabin);
- Drownings and other pool accidents [Carron v. Holland America Line (passenger in pool " propelled into a sharp statute...causing injury "); Brown v. New Commodore Cruise Line (passenger fractures ankle recklessly jumping into pool from one deck above)];
- Flying coconuts [McDonough v. Celebrity Cruises

(passenger struck in head with rum filled coconut [a speciality drink called the " Coco Loco "] dropped from a deck above];stray golf balls [Catalan v. Carnival Cruise Lines (passenger driving golf balls into sea strikes another passenger); discharging shot gun shells [Fay v. Oceanic Sun Line (skeet shooting passenger discharges shot gun shell into another passenger); and defective exercise equipment [Berman v. Royal Cruise Lines (passenger injured exercising on treadmill)];

- Legionnaires' disease [Freeman v. Celebrity Cruises, Inc. (exposure to bacteria causing Legionnaires' disease)] and other viruses [Mullen v. Treasure Chest Casino (respiratory disorder caused by improperly maintained air- conditioning and ventilating system)];
- Rapes [Morton v. De Oliveira (rape); Johnson v. Commodore Cruise Lines (rape of passenger and cover up on cruise); York v. Commodore Cruise Line (sexual assault); Travel Weekly, August 16, 1999 (" Cruising Holds Steady Despite Assault Reports...As reported, 108 allegations of sexual misconduct were included in a lawsuit filed in July by a former Carnival employee, who said she was raped by a Carnival officer...")] and assaults by crew members [Corna v. American Hawaii Cruises (crewman assaults passenger) and assaults by passengers [Colavito v. Carnival Cruise Lines, Inc. (assault by intoxicated passenger);];
- Malpractice by ship's doctor [Johnson v. Commodore Cruise Lines (passenger raped by crew member and misdiagnosed as having had heart attack; removed from ship and abandoned on shore); Gillmore v. Caribbean Cruise Line (ship not liable for medical malpractice)].
- Smoke inhalation [Travel Weekly, Sept. 27, 1999 (" Controversy surrounded Carnival Cruise Lines' Tropicale in the aftermath of a fire that left the ship drifting without power for almost 24 hours as a

tropical storm threatened "; Travel Weekly, March 1, 1999 (" Ecstasy Fire Prompts Closer Look At Safety On The Seas ")];

- Collisions [Travel Weekly, Aug. 30, 1999 ("Norwegian cancels sailings in wake of ship collision ")];
- Gastrointestinal disorders [Hernandez v. The Motor Vessel Skyward (contaminated food and water); Barbachym v. Costa Line (food poisoning); Williams v. Carnival Cruise Lines (seasickness; fear of seasickness)];
- Heart attacks [Bailey v. Carnival Cruise Lines, Inc. 27; Warren v. Ajax Navigation Corp. (passenger claimed malpractice by ship's doctor in treatment after heart attack)];
- Malfunctioning toilets [Kornberg v. Carnival Cruise Lines].

ACCIDENTS DURING SHORE EXCURSIONS

Prior to arriving at a port of call the cruise ship's staff will give lectures about the shopping to be expected and the availability of tours to include snorkeling and scuba dive areas, archaeological sites, catamaran rides, para-sailing, helicopter rides and so forth.

Cruise ships may generate substantial income from these tours, which are typically delivered by independent contractors not subject to the jurisdiction of U.S. courts and which may be uninsured, unlicenced and irresponsible [Winter v. I.C. Holidays, Inc.(tourists insured in bus accident; foreign bus company insolvent, uninsured and irresponsible; tour operator has duty to select responsible independent contractors)].

THREE ZONES OF DANGER

There are three zones in which accidents occur beyond the safety of the ship. First, accidents may occur while passengers are being transported from ship to shore [Chan v. Society Expeditions (inflatable raft ferrying passengers to shore capsizes); Favorito v. Pannell (engineer drives inflatable tender with 15 passengers into other vessels). Second, accidents may occur on the pier or areas immediately adjacent thereto [Gillmore v. Caribbean Cruise Line (passengers stabbed and robbed on pier); Sullivan v. Ajax Navigation Corp. (passenger injured on Mexican pier)]. Third, accidents may occur

- In the town [Petro v. Jada Yacht Charters (two passengers have fight in bar in town)];
- On local transportation [Dubret v. Holland America Line (bus accident during shore excursion); Paredes v. Princess Cruises (tour bus accident during ground tour in Egypt); DeRoche v. Commodore Cruise Line (motor scooter accident during shore excursion)];
- On a private beach [Berg v. Royal Caribbean Cruise (accident at private beach); Carlisle v. Ulysses Line (passengers ambushed, raped and robbed at private beach)];
- At a hotel owned by the cruise line [Rams v. Intrav, Inc. (passenger fell at hotel owned by cruise line during shore excursion)];
- Or while being transported to local ruins [Varey v. Canadian Helicopters Limited (cruise passengers drown when helicopter crashes on return to Cozumel, Mexico from tour of ruins in Chichen Itza) or touring a local site [Metzger v. Italian Line (accident during shore excursion)]. Accidents during shore excursions may involve
- Assaults, rapes, robberies and shootings [Gillmore v. Caribbean Cruise Line; Carlisle v. Ulysses Line; Travel Weekly, Jan. 9, 1997 (" A dozen passengers sailing on Holland America Line's Noordam were robbed at gunpoint at the Prospect Plantation In Ocho Rios, Jamaica ");
- Horseback riding [Colby v. Norwegian Cruise Lines (horse riding accident during shore excursion);
- Jet skis [In re Complaint of Royal Caribbean Cruises (passengers on jet skis collide)];
- Scuba diving [Tancredi v. Dive Makai Charters

(scuba accident during shore excursion); Courtney v. Pacific Adventures (scuba diver's leg becomes entangled in boat propeller)];

- Boat tours [United Shipping Co. v. Witmer (cruise passengers drown during boat tour in the Bahamas)];
- Traffic accidents [Young v. Players Lake Charles (intoxicated gamblers leave casino boat and have traffic accident)].
- Medical malpractice [DeRoche v. Commodore Cruise Line (passenger suffered injuries from motor scooter accident in Cozumel, Mexico and subsequent malpractice of Mexican doctors)].

OTHER COMMON COMPLAINTS

Besides physical injuries cruise passengers may have claims arising from:

- Cancellations [Slade v. Cheung and-Risser Enterprises (Great Lakes cruise line absconded with passenger payment; travel agent liable for failing to investigate financial responsibility); Ocean Cruise Lines, Inc. v. Abeta Travel Service],
- Flight delays [Harden v. American Airlines (passengers miss two days of cruise because of delayed air transportation)],
- Baggage loss [Mainzer v. Royal Olympic Cruises (cruise vessel losses one peace of passenger's baggage for four days)],
- Port skipping and unannounced itinerary changes [Casper v. Cunard Line (mechanical breakdown and scheduled itinerary changed); Bloom v. Cunard Line (two ports of call, Puerto Rico and Nassau, canceled)],
- Misrepresentations about
  - The existence of specific facilities [Boyles v. Cunard Line (cruise line misrepresented availability of " Spa at Sea " programme)],
  - The quality of the facilities [Vallery v. Bermuda Star Line ("The drapes were partly dirty and dingy...the headboards of the beds were broken

and the mattresses of the beds were concave...The stateroom...did not meet the quality as described in the brochure as being special, luxurious and beautiful nor was it exquisite..."); Gelfand v. Action Travel Centre (cruise vessel misrepresented as being new when only refurbished)], handicapped accessability [Bergonzine v. Maui Classic Charters (cruise line misrepresented that cruise was suitable for handicapped); Deck v. American Hawaii Cruises (passenger charges cruise line with violating American With Disabilities Act)],

- Discomfort [Charleston-Coad v. Cunard Line (QEII sailed before major refitting work on cabins and other facilities was complete; asbestos removal); Simon v. Cunard Line (lack of fresh water and malfunctioning air conditioning system)],
- Deceptive port charges [Cronin v. Cunard Line ("The gravamen of plaintiff's complaint is that in addition to Cunard's advertised all-inclusive fare, each passenger is required to pay an amount referred to as a ` port and handling charge `...but often exceeds $150 per passenger. Plaintiffs allege that Cunard intentionally misleads passengers into believing that these port charges are paid to port authorities and governmental agencies and that Cunard is a mere conduit for the collection of these fees.

In reality...Cunard does not disclose that only a small percentage of the separate port charge is actually turned over to port authorities or government agencies and the substantial balance is pocketed by Cunard.

Plaintiffs claim that Cunard's promotional materials deceptively portray the port charges as being a separate fee, beyond the control of Cunard, but are really designed to enhance Cunard's revenue while keeping the price of the fare competitive with other cruise lines"); Travel Weekly, April 12, 1999 ("Royal Caribbean International and Celebrity Cruises each notified hundreds of thousands of their past passengers that they may be eligible for benefits as part of voluntary agreements to settle class-action suits involving port charges")].

21ST CENTURY CRUISING, 19TH CENTURY RIGHTS

"The unpleasant reality is that the cruise vessel's responsibilities and your rights as an injured passenger are governed not by modern, consumer oriented common and statutory law, but by 19th century legal principals, the purpose of which is to insulate the maritime industry from the legitimate claims of passengers. The policy enunciated by the Second Circuit Court of Appeals 35 years ago in Schwartz v. S.S. Nassau, a case involving a passenger's physical injuries, applies equally today, " The purpose of [46 U.S.C. 183c]...' was to encourage shipbuilding and (its provisions)...should be liberally construed in the shipowner's favour `". Although recent years have seen the expansion of travel consumers' rights and remedies in actions against airlines, domestic hotels, international hotels, tour operators, travel agents, informal travel promoters and depository banks, there has been little, if any, change in the passengers' rights and remedies in actions against cruise lines." Cruise passengers are at a distinct disadvantage in prosecuting their claims.

TICKET PRINT SIZE AND LANGUAGE

A cruise passenger's rights are, to a large extent, defined by the terms and conditions set forth in the passenger ticket. Modern consumers expect the size of the print in consumer contracts to be large enough to be visible and readable. New York State, for example, requires consumer transaction contracts to be " printed...clear and legible [in print] eight points in depth or five and one-half points in depth for upper case type [to be admissible] in evidence in any trial ". Cruise passenger tickets, however, may be in any size type [Lerner v. Karageorgis Lines, Inc. (four-point type)]. The microscopic terms and conditions in passenger tickets are, clearly, meant to be unreadable and invisible. In fact, maritime law, which governs the rights and remedies of cruise passengers, preempts all State laws requiring consumer contracts to be in a given type size [Lerner v. Karageorgis Lines, Inc. (enforcement of time limitation provision in four-point type; maritime law preempts New York's statute requiring consumer contracts to be in ten-point type)]. In addition, the terms and conditions in passenger tickets are enforceable even though the passenger can neither read nor understand the language in which the tickets are printed [Paredes v. Princess Cruises (time limitations in passenger ticket in English language enforced even though passenger was unable to read English)].

TIME LIMITATIONS

Most States allow injured consumers, at least, 2½ years in which to commence physical injury lawsuits and up to 6 years for breach of contract and fraud claims. Maritime law, however, allows cruise lines to impose very short time limitations for the filing of claims and the commencement of lawsuits. For physical injuries occurring on cruise vessels that touch U.S. ports [Lerner v. Karageorgis Lines (46 U.S.C. 183b time limitations apply only to cruise vessels touching U.S. shores)] passengers may be required to file a claim within six months and commence a lawsuit within one year [Buriss v. Regency Maritime Corp (passenger's bunk crashed to floor; one year time limitation enforced)]. On occasion the Courts may decide not to enforce the one year time limitation [Dillon v. Admiral Cruises (trip and fall in ship's lounge; cruise line may be stopped from relying on one year time limitation); Rams v. Royal Caribbean Cruise Lines (one year time limitation does not apply to accidents during shore excursions); Berg v. Royal Caribbean Cruises (passenger mislead into not filing lawsuit within one year)].

For non-physical injury claims cruise lines may impose even shorter time limitation periods [Boyles v. Cunard Line (cruise vessel misrepresented availability of exercise facilities in "Spa at Sea "; six months time limitation to file lawsuit enforced); Cronin v. Cunard Line (deceptive port charges; six months' time limitation in which to commence lawsuit enforced)]. On occasion the Courts may decide not to enforce these particularly short time limitations [Johnson v. Commodore Cruise Line (passenger raped by crew member; claim for negligent infliction of emotional distress governed by Mississippi's 3 year statute of limitations; passenger ticket time limitations of 15 days to file claim and 6 months to sue for non-physical claims void)].

JURISDICTION

Most consumers purchase cruise vacations from their local retail travel agent. The cruise will depart from one of several domestic ports of call, *e.g.*, New York or Port of Miami, typically, where the cruise line is headquartered. Modern consumers expect to be able to file a complaint or commence a lawsuit over a defective good or service in their local courts. Such is not the rule, however, when it comes to complaints against cruise lines. To be able to sue a cruise company locally the consumer's court must have jurisdiction. Even though cruise companies may distribute brochures through and take orders from retail travel agents, such marketing activities are insufficient to serve as a basis for jurisdiction [Kaufman v. Ocean Spirit Shipping (dissemination of cruise brochures through travel agents and advertising in scuba magazine insufficient to support long arm jurisdiction)].

The "solicitation-plus doctrine" doctrine governs jurisdiction in travel cases with the "plus" equivalent to contract formation in the local forum [Afflerbach v. Cunard Line, Ltd (national advertising of cruise vacations and sales through travel agents insufficient for jurisdiction)]. With the possible exception of Internet sales through interactive web sites [Dickerson, The Internet, The " Solicitation Plus " Doctrine, And Jurisdiction Over Foreign Hotels and Other Travel Suppliers)] the Courts have, generally, held that contract formation does not take place at the consumer's location [Thompson v. Handa-Lopez (California corporation doing sufficient business in Texas through interactive web site allowing Texans to enter into contracts to play casino games)]. Some courts, however, have been willing to assume jurisdiction on little more than local advertising [Nowak v. Tak

How Inv. (guest drowns in Hong Kong hotel pool; being available for litigation in local forum is reasonable cost of doing business in the forum)].

FORUM SELECTION CLAUSES

The passenger ticket may contain a forum selection clause and a choice of law clause, both of which can have a negative impact upon the passenger's ability to prosecute his claim. A forum selection clause will require that all passenger lawsuits be brought in the local court where the cruise line is headquartered [Carnival Cruise Lines, Inc. v. Shute (a clause in the ticket provided that " It is agreed...that all disputes...shall be litigated...before a Court located in the State of Florida, U.S.A., to the exclusion of the Courts of any other state or country ")].

Forum selection clauses are, generally, enforceable if notice is adequate [Osborn v. Princess Tours (passenger must have " ample opportunity to examine... contents " of passenger ticket); Schaff v. Sun Line Cruises (forum selection clause (Athens, Greece) not enforced; ticket delivered too late to allow consumer to seek refund of $1,770 ticket price)] and they are reasonable and fair [Carnival Cruise Lines, Inc. v. Shute (forum selection clauses subject to judicial scrutiny for fundamental reasonableness)].

Stated, simply, it is less expensive and more convenient for injured passengers to be able hire an attorney and sue in a local court than being forced to travel to and prosecute their claim in Greece [Effron v. Sun Line Cruises], Peru [Affram Carriers, Inc. V. Moeykens], Naples, Italy [Hodes v. SNC Achille Lauro], the State of Washington [Carron v. Holland America Line-Westours, Inc.] and even Miami, Florida [Hicks v. Carnival Cruise Lines]. When faced with prosecuting a claim in a distant forum most passengers will be discouraged from doing so. This purpose of forum selection clauses and explains why cruise lines favour their use in passenger tickets.

CHOICE OF LAW CLAUSES

In addition to forum selection clauses, passenger tickets may also designate the law to be applied in resolving any dispute which may arise. The law selected may be that of the Bahamas [Kirman v. Compagnie Francaise (choice of Bahamian law clause enforced; cruise between Singapore and Australia)] or China [Jewel Seafoods Ltd. v. M/V Peace River (choice of Chinese law clause enforced)].

In determining whether choice of law clauses should be enforced, the courts may consider several factors including:

- The place of the wrongful act,
- The law of the flag,
- The allegiance of domicile of the injured passenger,
- The allegiance of the ship owner,
- The place of the contract,
- The inaccessibility of the foreign forum
- The law of the forum [Klinghoffer v. S.N.C. Achille Lauro].

Choice of law clauses are, generally, enforceable unless the passenger can demonstrate that " enforcement would be unreasonable and unjust ", " the clause was invalid for such reasons as fraud or overreaching " or " enforcement would contravene a strong public policy of the forum in which the suit is brought " [Milanovich v. Costa Crociere, SPA].

The law to be applied to an injured traveller's claim can have a dramatic impact on the likelihood of recovering proper damages. For example, in a wrongful death case involving a crash in China in which two Americans were killed, the court, relying on New York choice of law rules, decided to apply Chinese law which limited the maximum recoverable damages to $20,000 [Barkanic v. General Administration of Civil Aviation].

In another case, the traveller was seriously injured when she was thrown from a horse during a vacation in the Bahamas. She sued several Bahamian entities most responsible for her injuries. However, the application of the Foreign Sovereign Immunities Act meant that the foreign entities would be insulated from any liability [Tucker v. Whitaker Travel, Ltd]. In yet another instance, the traveller slipped and fell on an unlighted path while vacationing in Mexico. At issue was whether the court should apply Arizona or Mexican law to the issue of recoverable damages. The difference was dramatic.

Mexico allowed no more than twenty-five pesos per day in lost wage claims, while Arizona had no such limits. The court applied the more generous law of Arizona [Wendelken v. Superior Court]. Just the opposite happened in a case involving an accident on a water slide at a Mexican hotel in which the court applied Mexican damages law resulting in a severe limit on the plaintiff's pain and suffering damages[Feldman v. Acapulco Princess Hotel].

DISCLAIMERS OF LIABILITY

As a general rule, cruise vessels are common carriers and held to a relatively high standard of care [Kermarec v. Compagnie Generale Transatlantique]. The passenger ticket will contain a host of invisible clauses many of which seek to disclaim liability for a variety of problems that may arise during the cruise. As with consumer contracts on dry land instances of gross negligence and intentional misconduct can not be disclaimed by common carriers [Royal Ins. Co. v. Southwest Marine].

In addition, some Courts have held that disclaimers of simple negligence, particularly, regarding the health and safety of the passengers can not be disclaimed as well [Kornberg v. Carnival Cruise Lines (malfunctioning toilets)]. The Courts have been willing to enforce disclaimers of liability regarding accidents that occur during shore excursions [Dubret v. Holland America Line Westours (bus accident during shore excursion; disclaimer of liability enforced)]. Such a disclaimer may not be enforceable if the injured passenger relied upon representations, or warranties regarding safety [Bergonzine v. Maui Classic Charters (350 lb. handicapped passenger broke ankle because of inattention and lack of assistance by crew; misrepresentations in brochure that cruises were " suitable for handicapped individuals "; $42,500 in special damages awarded)], competence and reliability of on-shore suppliers of travel services.

LIMITATIONS ON RECOVERABLE DAMAGES

Cruise vessels that touch U.S. shores may not disclaim

liability for loss, death, damage or delay caused or contributed to by the vessel's negligence [46 U.S.C. 183c; Kornberg v. Carnival Cruise Lines (malfunctioning toilets; disclaimers not enforced)]. However, in 1996 the cruise industry was able to convince Congress to enact a provision permitting " provisions or limitations in contracts, agreements or ticket conditions of carriage with passengers which relieve...operator of a vessel from liability for infliction of emotional distress, mental suffering or psychological injury " [46 U.S.C. 183c(b)(1)]. Such a disclaimer does not apply to physical injuries, or those arising from being "at actual risk of physical injury "caused by the negligence or intentional misconduct of the cruise vessel or crew. Nor does such a disclaimer limit liability arising from "sexual harassment, sexual assault or rape ". In addition, a cruise vessel may invoke the Limitation of Vessel Owner's Liability Act which allows it to limit liability to the value of the vessel. In one case involving a passenger injured in a jet ski accident the Court would have allowed the cruise vessel to limit its liability for the collision to the value of the jet ski [Mashburn v. Royal Caribbean Cruises].

MEDICAL TREATMENT AND MALPRACTICE

The most disturbing aspect of cruise vacations is what happens when a passenger is sick or injured and needs the care of on board medical professionals. First, there are no uniform standards for medical care professionals or for the nature and quality of the medical equipment in the clinic and operating room. As noted in Consumer Reports Travel Letter "Many passengers would be surprised to discover that there are no international standards for medical care on passenger cruise ships—not even one requiring that a physician be on board.

Although most cruise ships generally do carry doctors, many of them are not US-trained or licensed to practice medicine in the States...No international agency regulates the infirmary facilities or equipment, or requires a standard of training for cruise-ship doctors...Bradley Feuer, DO, surveyed the medical facilities and staff qualifications of 11 cruise lines in 1996...Among the findings: 27% of nurses and doctors were not certified in advanced cardiac life support; 54% of doctors and 72% of nurses were not certified in advanced trauma life support. Nearly half the doctors—45%—weren't board certified in their areas of practice ".

Second, and even more worrisome, is the fact that cruise lines are, typically, not held liable for the medical malpractice committed by their on board doctors and nurses [Gillmore v. Caribbean Cruise Line (ship not liable for medical malpractice); Bonaventure v. Home Lines, Inc. (malpractice by ship's doctor; no jurisdiction; no liability)]. Some Courts, however, have been willing to find a cruise vessel liable for the medical malpractice of a ship's doctors [Fairley v.Royal Cruise Line (rejecting policy that cruise lines not liable for medical malpractice)]. "Such a policy encourages cruise lines to hire less than the best medical personnel and does a great disservice to passengers who mistakenly may believe that new, modern cruise ships have the best medical personnel and equipment available."

Cruise vacations can be wonderful experiences. However, potential cruise passengers are well advised to think carefully about their legal rights should they be injured and otherwise be dissatisfied with a cruise vacation.

THE AIRLINES PASSENGER'S RIGHT AND REMEDIES

While domestic airline "have a good product that is selling well" and this year the airline industry "will record more than 600 million domestic passenger ` enplanements" the quality and timeliness of domestic air transportation has decreased dramatically in recent years. " Virtually every independent measure of customer satisfaction has declined...The unfortunate truth is that flying on an airplane today...is as unpleasant for many passengers as it has ever been. ". Between 1998 and 1999 passenger complaints to the U.S. Department of Transportation rose from 9,608 to a staggering 20,4955. Last month 8,590 flights were canceled out of 307,116 scheduled.

A year ago it was 6,487 out of 299,132...weather, air traffic, mechanical difficulties, rules governing crew hours and hundreds of other causes, including human error, can upset schedules " And regarding flight delays " Only about three-quarters of planes arrive within 15 minutes of the scheduled time, and in bad months, about one flight in 40 is canceled altogether " What are your rights and remedies when your flight, domestic or international, is delayed or canceled?

TYPES OF FLIGHT DELAYS

A flight delay is any change from the promised time and date of departure or arrival. Flight delays include, of course,

- Cancellations [Obuzor v. Sabena Belgian World Airlines (canceled flight due to fog causes a 5 day delay in arrival in Lagos, Nigeria); Pakistan Arts v. Pakistan International Airlines (2 day delay in Karachi, Pakistan forces entertainers to cancel concert in New York City); In Re Arrow Air, Inc. (8,000 consumers stranded when tour operator and air carrier default; settlement of claims);] as well as flight delays caused by
- Mechanical malfunctions (flight diverted because of mechanical malfunction; passengers involuntarily held on tarmac for one hour and fifteen minutes and later confined to transit lounge for one hour and ten minutes without access to telephones); Arkin v. Trans International Airlines (tire blow out during takeoff); Burke v. Air France (engine trouble during flight; mental anguish damages recoverable); In re Eastern Airlines, Inc. Engine Failure (all three jet engines fail during flight; one engine restarted);
- Acts of God [De Vera v. Japan Airlines (flight delay caused by typhoon and volcanic eruption which forced closing of Manila airport); Johnson v. Northwest Orient Airlines (flight canceled because of bad weather); Klakis v. Nationwide Leisure Corp. (charter tour delayed 2 ½ days because of snowstorm)];
- Schedule Changes [(Robinson v. American Airlines (passenger misses flight because airline advances

departure time by ten minutes); Prechtl v. Travel House of Garden City (flight from Seattle to Hawaii canceled by airline which never informed travel agent who relied upon information in computer reservations system; passengers waited sleepless in Seattle for two days for flight to Hawaii)];

- Hijackings and bombings [Shah v. Pan American World Services, Inc. (hijacking in Karachi, Pakistan); In re Air Disaster at Lockerbie (bomb explodes on aircraft over Scotland); In re Flight Explosion on TQA Aircraft (bomb explodes on aircraft)];
- Noxious body odors [Mohideen v. American Airlines, Inc. (passenger and children removed from aircraft because of noxious body odors)];
- False imprisonment [Bayne v. Adventure Tours USA (passenger detained and baggage searched; claims of false imprisonment); Curley v. American Airlines, Inc. (passenger claims false imprisonment after being detained by authorities who were informed that passenger was smoking marihuana in lavatory); Rombom v. United Air Lines (rude and unprofessional conduct by stewards who spitefully had passenger falsely arrested)];
- Wrongful detention [Uwagbai v. Alitalia Airlines (passenger detained in airport lounge for 3 days because of forged travel documents); Singh v. Tarom Romanian Air Transport (passenger removed from aircraft and detained for 6 days); Donkor v. British Airways, Corp. (passenger detained and deported from England); Macintosh v. Interface Group (passenger removed from aircraft, arrested, jailed and charged with breach of the peace)];
- Violation of Air Carrier's Access Act [Newman v. American Airlines, Inc. (blind passenger with a heart condition claims violation of Air Carrier Access Act (ACAA) after airline refused transportation in the absence of a medical certificate indicating she could safely fly); Brandt v. American Airlines (passenger's

ACAA claim for airline's failure to offer food service dismissed); Rivera v. Delta Air Lines, Inc. (failure to offer wheelchair assistance)];

- Wrongful refusal to board [Chukwu v. British Airways (airline refuses to board passenger's brother); Glavey v. Aer Lingus (passenger not allowed to board unless she wrote a written apology to airline for filing a lost baggage claim 10 days earlier)];
- Failure to confirm or reconfirm reservations [Lathigra v. British Airways (negligent failure to reconfirm flight strands passenger in Nairobi); El-Menshawy v. Egypt Air (failure to confirm flight from Cairo); Burnap v. Tribeca Travel (travel agent fails to confirm reservations and note changes)];
- Discrimination [Mohideen v. American Airlines, Inc. (passenger and children removed from aircraft because of noxious body odour claim religious discrimination); Owolabi v. Air France (blind passenger in wheelchair denied assistance and left unattended in airport for seven hours during which time she urinated on herself; claims discrimination based upon race, age and disabilities); Quinn v. National Railroad Passenger Corp (African-American passengers ejected from train; discrimination based on race and violating ejectment rules); Pearson v. Lake Forest Country Day School (emotional distress and defamation action arising from failure to seat 13 year old boy)];
- Airline overbooking [Minhas v. Biman Bangladesh Airlines (passenger delayed 45 days after being overbooked in New Delhi, India); Lopez v. Eastern Airlines, Inc. (compensatory damages awarded to passenger overbooked on domestic flight); Guerrero v. American Airlines, Inc. (airline not liable for breach of contract for overbooked flight)],
- Wrongful ejection [Hermano v. United Airlines (passenger suspected of having a gun is removed

from aircraft); Huggar v. Northwest Airlines, Inc. (dispute over storage of carry-on baggage in overhead bin leads to removal of passenger from aircraft); Schaeffer v. Cavallero (passenger removed from flight after vociferously demanding a receipt for a piece of carry-on baggage); Rombom v. United Air Lines, Inc. (disruptive passenger removed from aircraft)];

- Failure to assist disabled passenger [Owolabi v. Air France (blind passenger in wheelchair denied assistance and left unattended in airport for seven hours during which time she urinated on herself); Shupe v. American Airlines (failure to meet and assist passenger making connecting flight)];
- Misinformation [Lewis v. Continental Airlines, Inc. (passenger missed connection after being misinformed about flight departure time); Siben v. American Airlines, Inc. (airline misrepresented location and arrival time of lost baggage); Carro v. Parente World Travel Centre (travel agent failed to include tickets as part of package tour)];
- Civil disorder [Jamil v. Kuwait Corp. (four day flight delay because of coup in Pakistan)];
- Shortage of fuel [Daniel v. Virgin Atlantic Airways Limited (25 hour flight delay caused by mechanical malfunctions and shortage of fuel)];
- Misplaced tickets [Ragonese v. Rosenfeld (airline ticket agent fails to locate ticket at airport; passenger forced to buy a second ticket at a higher price)];
- Collapsing ticket counters [Romero v. American Airlines, Inc. (passenger delayed and injured when airport check-in counter sign collapsed on her)]; and
- Altered tickets [Peralta v. Continental Airlines, Inc. (passenger removed from aircraft because of altered ticket lost business deal in Costa Rica and claims lost profits of $30,000)].

RIGHTS AND REMEDIES

The passenger's rights and remedies for a cancellation or

a flight delay will depend upon several factors. Was the flight international or domestic? If it was international then the Warsaw Convention or its progeny may apply. If not then the law of the country having the greatest contacts to the incident may apply [Barkanic v. General Administration of Civil Aviation (air disaster; China not a signatory to Warsaw Convention; Chinese law applied on issue of recoverable damages; $20,000 maximum allowable); Glavey v. Aer Lingus (passenger refused boarding; statute of limitations for asserting claim for intentional infliction of emotional distress determined by law of New York and not that of Ireland); Macintosh v. Interface Group (unruly passenger removed from aircraft; Connecticut law applies to claims)]. If the flight was domestic then the passenger's rights and remedies will depend upon the application of the common law as modified or preempted by the regulations of the DOT. Such regulations give domestic airline passengers greater or lesser rights than would otherwise be available at common law.

These regulations raise the following additional issues:

- If the flight was regularly scheduled domestic air transportation then the passenger ticket may contain disclaimers which limit the airline's liability for flight delays. Under what circumstances are these disclaimers enforceable?
- Was the flight part of a Public Charter Tour?
- Was the delay caused by airline overbooking or discrimination?
- Was the passenger detained because he was unruly or otherwise a threat to the safety and well being of the other passengers on the aircraft?

INTERNATIONAL FLIGHT DELAYS

If the delayed flight was international, *i.e.*, between signatories to the Warsaw Convention, then the obligations of the air carrier are set forth in Article 19 of the Warsaw Convention [" The carrier shall be liable for damage occasioned by delay in the transportation by air of passengers, baggage, or goods "]. To establish liability the passenger must show that

- The air carrier accepted the passenger on the flight [Malik v. Gulf Air (international bumping causes delay; Article 19 of the Warsaw Convention applies)],
- The delay was material [Tasar v. Pakistan International Airlines]
- The delay caused the injury being alleged [Jamil v. Kuwait Airways Corp. (four day delay; damages from loss of business opportunity not foreseeable)].

INTERNATIONAL FLIGHT DELAY DAMAGES

The Warsaw Convention permits the recovery of:

- Compensatory damages which are reasonable and foreseeable,
- Damages for inconvenience but
- Bars the recovery of punitive damages [Daniel v. Virgin Atlantic Airways (25 hour flight delay; damages for inconvenience are recoverable); Harplani v. Air-India (6 day delay in India; compensatory but not punitive damages are recoverable); Pakistan Arts v. Pakistan International Airlines (2 day delay in Pakistan causes cancellation of concert in New York City; all contemplated and foreseeable damages recoverable); Saiyed v. Transmediterranean Airways (delayed shipment of goods; all consequential damages recoverable up to limits provided in the Warsaw Convention); Kupferman v. Pakistan International Airlines (baggage delayed 15 days during tour of South America; passengers were entitled to " fair and just compensation for physical discomfort, inconvenience, humiliation, embarrassment and loss of a refreshing memorable vacation ")].

ALL NECESSARY MEASURES

However, the air carrier may be able to escape liability if it can show that it took " all necessary measures to avoid the damage or...it was impossible...to take such measures "[Duff v. Trans World Airlines, Inc.(flight delay; all necessary measures taken); Peralta v Continental Airlines, Inc (passenger removed from aircraft because ticket appeared altered; airline took all necessary measures to get passenger to Costa Rica after establishing that ticket was valid); Obuzor v. Sabena Belgian World Airlines)(5 day flight delay; airline took all necessary measures to avoid delay)].

WILFUL MISCONDUCT

The Warsaw Convention provides in Article 25 that the air carrier may not "exclude or limit "its liability if the delay is caused by its wilful misconduct. Proving wilful misconduct is difficult but it has been done in cases involving flight delays [Tasar v. Pakistan International Airlines (delay in the delivery of a casket for a funeral; wilful misconduct proven)], baggage loss or delay in delivery [Bank of Nova Scotia v. Pan American World Airways, Inc. (failure to follow internal procedures regarding loss of gold is wilful misconduct); Cohen v. Varig Airlines, Inc.(failure to deliver baggage during extended tour of South America is wilful misconduct); Kupferman v. Pakistan International Airlines (wilful misconduct in the handling of baggage)] and physical injuries and death [Shah v. Pan American World Services, Inc (hijacking in Karachi, Pakistan; fraudulent misrepresentation of adequacy of security system is wilful misconduct); In re Air Disaster at Lockerbie (bomb explodes on aircraft; failure to comply with FAA regulations in screening baggage is wilful misconduct)].

DOMESTIC FLIGHT DELAYS

Air transportation is sold to the general public with the promise that it will depart and arrive at specific times on specific dates. Applying the common law some courts have held that a failure to deliver air transportation "on time" is a breach of contract [Farmilant v. Singapore Airlines, Ltd. (flight delay was a " tortious breach of contract ")]. The breach must be material and may be 2 hours and 16 minutes [Liechtung v. Tower Air, Inc. (flight misrepresented as " non-stop " stops over in Paris causing a delay in arriving in Tel Aviv); 3 hours [Sporn v. Metro International (3 hour delay when airline loans aircraft to film company for background to a movie)], 8 ½ hours [Koczara v. Wayne County (snowstorm at airport results in the stranding of hundreds of passengers on aircraft queued on taxiways for up to 8 ½ hours without food service and toilets overflowing)]; 10 hours[Freedman v. Northwest Airlines Inc. (exculpatory clause in tariff not enforced in breach of contract claim arising from a 10 hour flight delay)]; 2 days [Prechtl v. Travel House of Garden City (flight from Seattle to Hawaii canceled by airline which never informed travel agent who relied upon information in computer reservations system; passengers waited sleepless in Seattle for two days for flight to Hawaii)] and 2 ½ days [(Klakis v. Nationwide Leisure Corp. (charter tour participants stranded for 2 ½ days at airport during snowstorm)]. Such a breach may also constitute negligence [Reservation Desk v. A.L.I.A. (air carrier liable in negligence for failure to advise travel agency that reservations could not be confirmed); Sporn v. Metro International Airways (3 hour flight delay may be the result of negligence] and fraud [Jawal v. British Airways (passenger detained because of stolen tickets)].

Some Courts, however, have refused to find a breach of the contract of carriage stating that timetables do not constitute a " warranty of punctuality " [Chendrimada v. Air-India (passengers forced to stay on aircraft for 11 ½ hours; flight schedules are not guarantees); Padua v. Eastern Air Lines, Inc. (ticket clause stating that timetables not guaranteed enforced; no liability for flight delay and missed connection); Robinson v. American Airlines]. The contract of carriage applies to point-to-point air transportation. There is no continuing common law contractual duty to the passenger once he or she disembarks the aircraft [Martinez v. American Airlines (passenger suffered medical difficulties after arrival at initial destination; airline has no obligation to assist him or transport him to his final destination after becoming ill)].

DISCLAIMERS IN PASSENGER TICKETS

Domestic air carriers are permitted by the DOT to file tariffs limiting their liability and damages for flight delays and other travel problems and to incorporate those terms by reference in the passenger ticket [Wolst v. American Airlines, Inc., (discussion of the incorporation by reference system)]. Although the passenger may never be aware of such disclaimers some Courts have enforced them [Padua v. Eastern Air Lines, Inc. (ticket clause stating that timetables not guaranteed enforced; no liability for flight delay and missed connection); Macintosh v. Interface Group (unruly passenger removed from aircraft; air carrier tariff " Carrier will refuse to carry, cancel the reserved space of, or remove en route any passenger (a) When such action is necessary for reasons of safety " enforced); Robinson v. American Airlines (passenger missed flight because airline advanced departure time by ten minutes; ticket disclaimer " Carrier shall not be liable for failing to operate any flight according to schedule " enforced); Sethi v. KLM Royal Dutch Airlines (passenger denied boarding because of improper visas; tariff disclaiming liability for misinformation enforced); Madia v. Austin Travel Agency (passengers denied entry because of improper visas; tariffs absolving airline of liability enforced)] while others have not [Coughlin v. Trans World Airlines, Inc. (violation of tariff voids liability limit); Freedman v. Northwest Airlines, Inc. (exculpatory clause in ticket not enforced in breach of contract claim arising from 10 hour flight delay); Klakis v. Nationwide Leisure Corp. (2 ½ day flight delay; disclaimer which strikes at heart of the bargain unenforceable); Larken v. Tourlite International, Inc. (tour operator liable for failing to deliver return air transportation; disclaimers unenforceable)].

PRIVITY OF CONTRACT DEFENCE

An air carrier hired by a tour operator may claim that the passenger has no standing to assert a flight delay claim [Carro v. Parente World Travel Centre (travel agent failed to deliver air tickets; summary judgment for air carrier and tour operator; lack of privity of contract)]. It has been held, however, that passengers are third party beneficiaries of the contracts between air carriers and tour operators and have standing to assert a cause of action against the air carrier [Neal v. Republic Airlines; Harris v. Waikane Corp.; Agosto v. Leisure World

Travel, Inc. (tour operator of Rose Bowl package tours fails to deliver rental cars; participants third party beneficiaries of contract between tour operator and rental car company)].

ACT OF GOD DEFENCE

The airline may claim that it was prevented from delivering timely air transportation because of an Act of God [The Majestic (" the act of God is limited...to causes in which no man has any agency whatever; because it was never intended to arise ")] such as a snowstorm [Klakis v. Nationwide Leisure Corp. (charter tour passengers stuck at airport for 2 ½ days during snowstorm)], a typhoon or volcanic eruption [De Vera v. Japan Airlines (Manila Airport closed because of volcano and typhoon)] or a revolution or civil disorder [Jamil v. Kuwait Corp. (flight delayed 4 days due to coup in Pakistan)]. To prevail, however, the air carrier must establish a causal connection between the Act Of God and its failure to deliver timely air transportation. In addition, the air carrier must prove that it acted reasonably to reinstitute the flight once the snowstorm or unexpected event ceased and the airport completed clean-up operations [Bernstein v. Cunard Line, Ltd.].

MECHANICAL MALFUNCTION DEFENCE

The air carrier may assert that the delay was caused by a mechanical malfunction. Such a defence is unlikely to be accepted by the Courts unless the air carrier can prove that the malfunction was truly unforeseeable [Feuer v. Value Vacations, Inc. (48 hour delay due to engine malfunction; disclaimer void)].

PUBLIC CHARTER TOURS

If the air transportation is part of a Public Charter Tour then the duties of both the air carrier and tour operator are governed by DOT regulations. The air carrier is, for example, obligated to return passengers stranded abroad after a tour operator becomes insolvent. Some Courts have held the Public Charter Tour Operator liable for the flight delays caused by a cooperating charter air carrier and other travel suppliers [Irving Trust Company v. Nationwide Leisure Corp. (tour operator strictly liable as principal for defaults of hotels and air carriers in failing to deliver travel services)]. Some Courts, however, have enforced disclaimers in the tour participant contract absolving tour operators for flight delays [Accomando v. Trans National Travel (tour operator not liable for 36 hour flight delay; disclaimer enforced)]. Both Public Charter Tour Operators and cooperating air carriers are required to place consumer deposits into escrow accounts [Neilan v. Value Vacations, Inc. (8,000 passengers stranded; escrow bank liable for failing to properly handle escrowed monies)] and/or to have surety bonds to protect consumer deposits [Irving Trust Company v. Nationwide Leisure Corp. (surety bonds cover all types of claims against tour operator)].

AIRLINE OVERBOOKING

On occasion passengers with confirmed reservations may be "bumped" because the airline has oversold the flight. Domestic air carriers are permitted to deliberately breach the contract of carriage on the theory that it is more efficient to oversell a flight than to fly an aircraft half-empty. If they overbook a specific flight the air carrier must comply with DOT " Part 250- Oversales " regulations which require an " auction " procedure whereby " bumped " passengers may obtain a seat if seated passengers can be induced to give up their position. Otherwise the air carrier must compensate the bumped passenger " at the rate of 200 per cent of the sum of the values of the passenger's remaining flight coupons up to the passenger's next stopover, or if none, to the passenger's final destination, with a maximum of $400 ". If the bumped passenger does not wish to accept the denied boarding compensation then he or she may sue at common law for breach of contract or negligence.

While bumped passengers may not sue for fraud and punitive damages [West v. Northwest Airlines, Inc. (" Federal regulations contemplate overbooking as an acceptable practice so long as passengers received compensation ")] they may sue for compensatory damages alleging a breach of the contract of carriage [Semrod v. Compania Mexicana De Aviacion (overbooking; beach of contract damages include $3000 for loss of one vacation day; food allowance of $300 and a room allowance of $250 per day); Lopez v. Eastern Airlines, Inc. (actual compensatory damages awarded to passenger bumped from flight due to overbooking)].

UNRULY PASSENGERS

Passengers may be removed from airplanes because their actions may endanger the safety of the other passengers. Such grounds may serve as a defence in a passenger's action seeking damages for flight delays [Schaeffer v. Cavallero (passenger removed from aircraft after dispute over carry-on luggage); Macintosh v. Interface Group (unruly passenger removed from aircraft; air carrier tariff allowing removal for safety of passengers enforced); Huggar v. Northwest Airlines, Inc. (passenger removed from aircraft after threatening another passenger over the use of overhead bin)].

DAMAGES FOR FLIGHT DELAYS

Damages arising from a canceled flight may consist of the cost of alternate air transportation which is more expensive than the original flight[McMurray v. Capital International Airways, Inc.]. Consequential damages for cancellations and fight delays that are reasonably foreseeable are recoverable [Reservation Desk v. ALIA (air carrier liable for all consequential damages for failure to deliver air transportation); Smith v. Piedmont Aviation, Inc. (delay due to bad weather; air carrier liable for consequential damages)] including $3,000 for the loss of one vacation day [Semrod v. Compania Mexicana De Aviacion], $2,500 for the loss of " a refreshing memorable vacation " [Vick v. National Airlines, Inc.,] and $240 for " waiting time " [Das v. Royal Jordanian Airlines].

TRAVEL CLASS ACTIONS

Class actions allow many similar claims to be aggregated

into one lawsuit for discovery, trial and/or settlement. Passengers victimized by the same canceled flight [Neilan v. Value Vacations (2,000 stranded passengers)] or delayed flight have been certified as a class and allowed to assert class wide claims for breach of contract, negligence and fraud [Irving Trust Company v. Nationwide Leisure Corp.(charter passengers delayed 2 ½ days because of snowstorm)]. Class actions arising from a failure to deliver a " non-stop " flight have also been certified [Liechtung v. Tower Air, Inc. (unexpected stop over caused a delay of 2 hours and 16 minutes) and the standing passengers for 8 ½ hours in aircraft on runaways during a snowstorm in Michigan [Koczara v. Wayne County].

5

Eco-tourism and Tourism

AN OVERVIEW

Fundamentally, eco-tourism means making as little environmental impact as possible and helping to sustain the indigenous populace, thereby encouraging the preservation of wildlife and habitats when visiting a place. This is responsible form of tourism and tourism development, which encourages going back to natural products in every aspect of life. It is also the key to sustainable ecological development.

The International Eco-tourism Society defines eco-tourism as "responsible travel to natural areas that conserves the environment and improves the well-being of local people."

This means that those who implement and participate in Eco-tourism activities should follow the following principles:

- Minimize impact,
- Build environmental and cultural awareness and respect,
- Provide positive experiences for both visitors and hosts,
- Provide direct financial benefits for conservation,
- Provide financial benefits and empowerment for local people,
- Raise sensitivity to host countries' political, environmental, and social climate,
- Support international human rights and labour agreements.

Aware of the Environment—Today the "Green Laws" of conservation are making people aware of how man and the environment can live symbiotically for more time to come and eco-tourism is the only way to maximize the economic, environmental and social benefits of tourism. Everyone is a stakeholder in the process and we clearly need to avoid our past shortcomings and negative impact that they have had.

Of all the participants in the Eco-tourism activity, the tourism industry is perhaps the most important and the least appreciated by conservationists. Many conservationists dislike having to deal with the corporate, profit- motivated entrepreneurs that they characterize as comprising the tourism industry. Nevertheless, these entrepreneurs are essential to achieving conservation goals via Eco-tourism. They can, and indeed some of them must, become allies and partners with NGOs, protected area managers and communities if Eco-tourism is to become more than an abstract concept. Increasingly, the tourism industry becomes the most powerful advocate for supporting protected areas, and this dynamic should be encouraged by establishing adequate mechanisms for communication and collaboration between protected area managers and tour operators.

The mechanics of international and even national, level tourism require that a complex set of arrangements (transportation, lodging, guides, etc.) exists to facilitate the movement of tourists from their home to the tourism destination. Each arrangement necessitates a specific set of activities and corresponding set of employees, infrastructure and costs. Few tour operators specialize in Eco-tourism. There are, however, many adventure and nature tour operators, most of whom do not fully comply with Eco-tourism standards. Conventional tourism practices still predominate in the tourism industry, just as conventional practices still dominate in every other aspect of our lives, in spite of initiatives for them to become more sustainable.

Nevertheless, the tourism industry is "greening" at an ever-accelerating pace as tourists demand more environmentally-sound services. For example, many hotels now recycle cans and bottles and encourage guests to reuse towels in order to save on water use.

The number of Eco-tourism businesses is also growing as new companies are established. Many of these have developed from the outset with an understanding of and commitment to the principles of sustainability, whereas many of the older, more established nature tourism companies have been slow to integrate all the principles of Eco-tourism into their activities.

- Conservation NGOs working in partnership with private tour operators are ideally placed to provide the Ecotourist technical guidelines which upgrade a nature tourism operation into an Eco-tourism operation. They will be located in the eco travellers country of origin. They produce brochures annually with a series of fixed departures for each tour Programmes, and they often have a loyal clientele who return to purchase trips on a regular basis. They will put together a complete package for the tourist including air tickets, and may provide a tour leader to accompany their client groups but will typically contract with an inbound operator to provide services in the destination country.
- *The Inbound Operator*—Located in the destination country, they provide complete packages of services from arrival in the country to departure. They may have their own facilities (vehicles, lodges) or they may subcontract others in the cities and regions the tourists will visit. Outbound operators contract with them to provide all "on-the-ground" services. With the advent of the internet, they are increasingly competing directly with the outbound operators for clients.
- *Local Service Providers*—outside the big cities, near the natural attractions; these may be local lodge and hotel owners, local transport providers, community-based Eco-tourism enterprises and local guides. These are where local communities typically join the tourism chain.

Implementing Eco-tourism can be a very challenging and

costly venture. If the tourism industry is part of this process from the beginning, costs can be greatly reduced and success made more likely. Including the experience of a private tour operator in the Eco-tourism planning and design process would be invaluable and could not be duplicated by conservation NGO.

Essential inputs by various segments of the tourism industry could include:

- Providing information about the potential market for Eco-tourism activities.
- Providing advice concerning visitor preferences in terms of attractions, accommodations, food and transportation services.
- Marketing an Eco-tourism activity or Programmes.
- Providing one or more of the services needed to facilitate visitor access to and appreciation of the Eco-tourism site.
- Providing training of local guides and entrepreneurs.
- Investing in an Eco-tourism operation. The investment will likely be contingent upon an expectation of a certain level of financial return.
- Operating an Eco-tourism operation. Within a protected area situation, these operators would be considered concessionaires. As such, they would be subject to strict guidelines covering everything from the energy sources used to operators who identified this as one of their primary destinations to the utilization of local supplies and labour. They would also be required to pay a concession fee to the protected area administration.

Eco-tourism is more than a catch phrase for nature loving travel and recreation. Eco-tourism is consecrated for preserving and sustaining the diversity of the world's natural and cultural environments.

It accommodates and entertains visitors in a way that is minimally intrusive or destructive to the environment and sustains and supports the native cultures in the locations it is operating in. Responsibility of both travellers and service providers is the genuine meaning for eco-tourism. Eco-tourism also endeavours to encourage and support the diversity of local economies for which the tourism-related income is important. With support from tourists, local services and producers can compete with larger, foreign companies and local families can support themselves. Besides all these, the revenue produced from tourism helps and encourages governments to fund conservation projects and training Programmes.

Saving the environment around you and preserving the natural luxuries and forest life, that's what eco-tourism is all about. Whether it's about a nature camp or organizing trekking trips towards the unspoilt and inaccessible regions, one should always keep in mind not to create any mishap or disturbance in the life cycle of nature. Eco-tourism focuses on local cultures, wilderness adventures, volunteering, personal growth and learning new ways to live on our vulnerable planet.

It is typically defined as travel to destinations where the flora, fauna, and cultural heritage are the primary attractions. Responsible Eco-tourism includes Programmes that minimize the adverse effects of traditional tourism on the natural environment, and enhance the cultural integrity of local people.

Therefore, in addition to evaluating environmental and cultural factors, initiatives by hospitality providers to promote recycling, energy efficiency, water reuse, and the creation of economic opportunities for local communities are an integral part of Eco-tourism.

Historical, biological and cultural conservation, preservation, sustainable development etc. are some of the fields closely related to Eco-Tourism. Many professionals have been involved in formulating and developing eco-tourism policies. They come from the fields of Geographic Information Systems, Wildlife Management, Wildlife Photography, Marine Biology and Oceanography, National and State Park Management, Environmental Sciences, Women in Development, Historians and Archaeologists, etc.

In India too the movement is gathering momentum with more and more travel and travel related organisation's are addressing the needs of the eco-tourists and promoting eco-tourism in the country. Some basic do's and don'ts of eco-tourism are listed below:

Do's:

- Carry back all non-degradable litter such as empty bottles, tins, plastic bags etc. These must not litter the environment or be buried. They must be disposed in municipal dustbins only.
- Observe the sanctity of holy sites, temples and local cultures.
- Cut noise pollution. Do not blare aloud radios, tape recorders or other electronic entertainment equipment in nature resorts, sanctuaries and wildlife parks.
- In case temporary toilets are set-up near campsites, after defecation, cover with mud or sand. Make sure that the spot is at least 30 meters away from the water source.
- Respect people's privacy while taking photographs. Ask for prior permission before taking a photograph.

Don'ts:

- Do not take away flora and fauna in the forms of cuttings, seeds or roots. It is illegal, especially in the Himalayas. The environment is really delicate in this region and the bio-diversity of the region has to be protected at all costs.
- Do not use pollutants such as detergent, in streams or springs while washing and bathing.
- Do not use wood as fuel to cook food at the campsite.
- Do not leave cigarettes butts or make open fires in the forests.
- Do not consume aerated drinks, alcohol, drugs or any other intoxicant and throw bottles in the wild.
- Do not tempt the locals, especially children by offering them foodstuff or sweets. Respect local traditions.
- Polythene and plastics are non biodegradable and unhealthy for the environment and must not be used

and littered. As a traveller, you will have an impact on the environment and culture of the place you are visiting. Here are some rules of thumb to make this impact positive.

GOLDEN RULES FOR TRAVEL

- Learn about your destination before you get there. Read guidebooks, travel rticles, istories, and/or novels by local authors and pay particular attention to customs such as greetings, appropriate dress, eating behaviours, etc. Being sensitive to these customs will increase local acceptance of you as a tourist and enrich your trip.
- Follow established guidelines. Ask your eco-tour operator, guide and/or the local authorities what their guidelines are for limiting tourism's impact on the environment and local culture. Staying on trails, packing up your trash, and remaining set distances away from wildlife are a few ways to minimize your impact in sensitive areas.
- Seek out and support locally owned businesses. Support local businesses during your eco-travels to ensure maximum community and conservation benefit from your spending. Eco-Tourism in India is still at a very nascent stage, but there are for sure conscious efforts to save the fragile Himalayan Eco System and culture and heritage of the indigenous people, which is probably the largest concentration in the world.

ECO-TOURISM IN INDIA

KERALA

The naturally beautiful and exquisite Kerala landscape is one of the greenest destinations in India and is the perfect place to go on eco-tourism vacations. The clean and tranquil Kerala backwaters, the soothing velvety Kerala hills and a riotous explosion of greens in the intoxicating Kerala wilds offers countless opportunities for eco-tourism and nature vacations. The entire Kerala landscape is generously covered with coconut palms, pineapple groves, banana trees, Pandanus plants, thick leafy plants, dense forests and neatly clipped tea bushes. Acres of submerged paddy fields located in perfect harmony with the winding Kerala backwaters and the gentle rolling Kerala hills are heavenly paradisiacal eco-tourism vacation destinations.

Regale the verdant Kerala beauty on your eco-tourism vacations to Kerala, South India with Kerala India Vacations. Visit the fascinating Kerala wildlife destinations and spot rare wild animals lazing in their natural habitat and enjoy the magic of nature. Eco-tourism in Kerala, South India is a fast developing sector and the state government is making extra efforts to promote eco-tourism. Among the manifold advantages of promoting eco-tourism in Kerala, South India one very important aspect is revenue generation and environment conservation at the same time. The concept of eco-tourism basically means that you get to visit the exotic nature rich tour destinations but at the same time you must take care not to soil the beauty of the region by not using polythene bags and other materials or things such as tin cans, wrappers etc that adversely affect the environment.

Kerala India Vacations guides you through the lush green paths within acres of rubber plantations so that you can experience first hand the incomparable natural beauty of green Kerala, South India on your eco-tourism vacations. Kerala, South India happens to be one of the leading producers of rubber in India though rubber is not a native Indian plant and was introduced by the Dutch colonialists, in fact Kerala accounts for 92 per cent of the rubber produced in India. Stay at a luxury resort or a farmhouse near a Kerala rubber plantation and enjoy the warm hospitality of the Kerala rubber plantations during your eco-tourism vacations to Kerala, South India and be fascinated by the rural Kerala lifestyle while you observe busy twittering birds, brightly coloured butterflies and squirrels scurrying here and there. Admire the thick shapely leaves on straight trunks that glisten in the bright sun.

Botanically known as Havea brasiliensis, a single rubber plant takes about 7 years to mature and can be harvested for latex (processed for natural rubber) for almost 20 years. The local rubber tappers who stay close to these lush rubber plantations harvest latex from these trees. Pineapple is planted as an intercrop in most of the Kerala rubber plantations so you get to taste the juicy Mauritius pineapple variety while on your eco-tourism vacations to the scenic Kerala rubber plantations. Kottayam in Kerala, South India is an important Centre of commercial rubber plantations set on the picturesque banks of the serene palm fringed Kerala backwaters. Extensive rubber plantations cover the hillocks wrapped by silver ribbons of the fascinating Kerala backwaters, not a sight you would like to miss while on your eco-tourism tours to Kerala, South India.

Acres of tea plantations interspersed with shade fruit trees wrap the gentle Kerala hill slopes in a warm embrace and create soothing and striking vistas for you to visit on your Kerala eco-tourism vacations. Rows of neatly clipped tea bushes carpet the Kerala hills on the Western Ghats in Kerala, south India and offer you ample opportunity to gaze at the naturally enthralling Kerala beauty at its beatific best while on your Kerala India eco-tourism vacations.

The Britishers introduced the tradition of tea plantations in India. Tea bushes have the potential to grow to tree heights though they are kept neatly trimmed to waist height to make it feasible for the plantation workers to pluck tealeaves without much difficulty. Gaze at the lovely Kerala tea plantations while on your eco-tourism vacations and mark the fact that each tea bush is planted at a distance of 1 to 1.5 metre from each other along the contours of the landscape. Stay at the resorts and clean home-like accommodations on the Kerala tea plantations and spend your eco-tourism vacations in Kerala, South India in the midst of pure undulating greens. Watch the plantation workers plucking tealeaves and filling the baskets slung on their backs while you enjoy nature treks. Usually it's the women who are employed for plucking tealeaves on these tea plantations in Kerala, South India. These women work in unison and sing peppy songs while plucking tealeaves and move along the rows of tea bushes in perfect rhythm. Kerala, South India has some of the highest tea estates located in India. Munnar is one of the most popular Kerala hill stations, which is known for its sweeping tea plantations. Some of the popular tea plantations in Kerala, South India are located at Peerumadu that is situated at a height of 914-meters above the sea level, Anayirankal that has acres of tea plantations located in the midst of dense evergreen forests and a few other Kerala hill stations that are definitely worth visiting on your Kerala eco-tourism tours to Kerala, South India.

Wander at leisure on the aromatic Kerala spice plantations during your Kerala India eco-tourism Vacations. Stay at the spice plantation farmhouses with the plantation owners and experience the magical charm of staying in the midst of luxuriant plantations laden heavily with a combination of scents of the various spices that are grown on these extensive plantations. Though you can visit spice plantations almost all over beautiful Kerala, Periyar is one of the most popular spice districts in Kerala, South India. This absolutely beautiful hill district is covered with a variety of spice plantations that lie close to the famous Periyar wildlife sanctuary.

Shop for rare spices at the local Kerala spice markets and inhale the intoxicating aroma of cinnamon, cardamom, pepper, ginger, turmeric, curry leaves and other spices. Besides the cultivation of these traditional Kerala spices the Kerala plantation owners have also taken to growing spices such as rosemary, oregano, mint, vanilla, bay leaves, basil, thyme and others. Discover the secret of the mouthwatering Kerala cuisine as you visit the acres of Kerala spice plantations on your eco-tourism vacations with Kerala India Vacations. Spices are basically fragrant substances of vegetable origin with distinct flavours used in selective combinations to give a special flavour to the exotic Indian cuisine. Enjoy bird watching tours and nature treks to the lovely Kerala spice plantations with Kerala India Vacations and experience the Kerala natural beauty at its aromatic best. Watch the locals work on the extensive spice plantations and observe closely the way of life in these Kerala spice plantations and enjoy your eco-tourism vacations thoroughly.

ORISSA

Organized by Tourism of Orissa offers you the best seats in the house to attend what is essentially a spectacular show of competing colours, cacophony of voices, a jumble of animal instincts and raw emotions. No, we aren't talking about a Broadway show or a Hollywood musical production. Eco-tourism in Orissa is what concerns us at Tourism of Orissa. With Eco-tourism in Orissa tour package, offered by Tourism of Orissa, you get to see all the shades of the diverse ecological system that reside within the state of Orissa. Eco-tourism in Orissa may revolve around water bodies or beaches or national parks and wildlife sanctuaries alone or, it can be a combination of all these features that make Orissa such as enticing choice as a destination for eco travel and tours.

While hot springs (Atri and Tarabalo), lakes (Chilika), waterfalls (Badaghagra, Khandadhar) and reservoirs (Hirakud, Indravati) in Orissa have tourists lining up, the beaches of Orissa (Puri, Chandrabhaga, Gopalpur, Chandipur) have dazzled international and national tourist for centuries with their pristine beauty and positive vibes. Orissa's varying topography—from the wooded Eastern Ghats to the fertile river basin—has proven ideal for evolution of compact and unique ecosystems. Thereby creating such treasure troves of flora and fauna that even seem inviting to many migratory species of birds and reptiles.

Bhitar Kanika National Park is famous for its second largest mangrove ecosystem. The bird sanctuary in Chilika (Asia's biggest brackish water lake) and the tiger reserve and waterfalls in Simlipal National Park are integral part of any eco tours in Orissa, arranged by Tourism of Orissa. The Gharial Sanctuary at Tikarpada and the Olive Ridley Sea Turtles in Gahirmatha turtle sanctuary also feature on the list of avid nature watchers.

The city wildlife sanctuaries of Chandaka and Nandan Kanan are a must visit for the lessons they teach is conservation and revitalization of species from the brink of extinction. Since Orissa is so rich in culture—history, traditions and people, Tourism of Orissa can even have your eco tour clubbed with other tours in Orissa so that you get the best of the worlds at a single destination called Orissa.

CHHATTISGARH

Chhattisgarh, the 26th state of the Indian Union, is located in the central part of India. The newly formed Indian state of Chhattisgarh is famous for its enchantingly beautiful natural landscapes, rich cultural heritage and unique tribal populations. With over 44 per cent of its total area under forests, Chhattisgarh is also amongst the greenest states of India. The Chhattisgarh region is known as a great repository of biological diversity. The unique combination of rich cultural heritage and biological diversity makes Chhattisgarh an ideal eco-tourism destination with immense potentials for the growth eco-tourism the region. The Indian Govt. is actively collaborating with the local officials of the state to realise the full potential of Eco-tourism growth of the region in order to make Chhattisgarh as one of the most important eco-tourism destinations in India.

Chhattisgarh is one of the greenest states of India with over 44 per cent of its total area under lush forests. The forests of Chhattisgarh are not only known for their diverse flora and fauna but also contain about 88 species of medicinal plants. In addition, Chhattisgarh has also formulated several ecological plans and working in the direction to become the country's first bio-fuel self-reliant state by 2015. And to achieve this goal the green state has devised a plan to plant over 100 million saplings of Jatropa Carcus. Chhattisgarh is also unique in its wildlife population and has 3 National Parks and 11 Wildlife Sanctuaries, housing some of the rare wildlife and bird species. With so much of variety for Eco-tourism, Chhattisgarh promises to be an ideal holiday destination for nature lovers, wildlife enthusiasts and also for those who want to discover the unique tribal life of the region.

Chhattisgarh has identified some regions with a very high potentiality for eco-tourism. The green state has launched an eco-tourism project covering three potential tourist tracks—Raipur-Turtiria-Sirpur, Bilaspur-Achanakmar and Jagdalpur-

Kanger Valley National Park. In addition, a number of herbal gardens and natural health resorts have been created with increased local participation. The use of ethno-medicine, which has been practiced by aboriginal tribes since centuries, predating even Ayurveda, is also being promoted in Chhattisgarh. The major eco-tourism attractions, which are getting prime attention in Chhattisgarh, include the protection and development of the wildlife areas, camping grounds and trekking facilities. With so many initiatives, Chhattisgarh is destined to become the most Favourite eco-tourism destination in India and few among best in the world.

RAJASTHAN

The Cultures of the Rajasthan Desert are some of the most well preserved in India. We, at Marwar Eco-Cultural Tours and Travels, are passionate about this land, its cultures and its people and we want to share this passion with you. The Desert and its people will captivate you.

Because we are able to provide you with in-depth cultural information that you would not receive on other Tours. If you have an adventurous spirit or a cultural thirst to quench, we have a Tour that should surpass all of your expectations. We also offer opportunities to get involved with the people and assist in ongoing, non-profit projects. As an NGO, we have assistance projects in most villages we will visit. All of our guides are from Rajasthan, and most are village natives or indigenous people.

They have a great knowledge of local and regional history and are great storytellers. They will keep your attention for hours next to a fire, counting tales of kings and warlords; castles, forts and Havelis (mansions); rituals and traditions. You will see the camel herds, observe villagers' craftsmanship, and gain insight into indigenous nomadic lifestyles. We will show you the best of Rajasthan, and we are very flexible and can modify our tours according to the group's needs. You can also design your own tour. You dream it up; we'll do the rest. We will organize the tour and guide you according to your wishes. Among other things, we can arrange a visit to a marriage ceremony, a farming or agricultural tour, Handicraft and Jewelry making, a stay in an Ayurvedic (traditional Indian Medicine) clinic, and more.

MADHYA PRADESH

Eco-tourism signifies to save the environment around us and preserving the natural luxuries and forest life. Whether it's about a nature camp or organizing trekking trips towards the unspoilt and inaccessible regions, one should always keep in mind not to create any mishap or disturbance in the life cycle of nature. A destination enveloped in magic, Madhya Pradesh is one of the most popular tourist destination in India. It's many tourist destinations are, by far, some of the most magical locales in the world.

With the highest mountains, beautiful wildlife, a cosmopolitan heritage from different civilizations, it is so rightly called tourist paradise. It has lot to offer from breathtaking natural vistas, amazing architecture, rich culture, and a warm hearted society of people living in virtual harmony.

HIMACHAL PRADESH

The majestic coniferous trees from an enchanting backdrop to the mountains with broad-leafed species like the Oaks, Maples, Birdcherry, Hazelnut, Walnut, Horsechestnut and Rhododendrons adding grandeur to the landscape. Whereas the ivies clinging to the trunks of stately Cedars appear to veil secrets of Nature, the vines flowing from atop the trees seem to invite the visitors with open arms. The violas popping up from under the forest floor and the riot of colours provided by the anemones, primulas, buttercups and many other herbs in the alpine meadows lay a colourful feast before eyes of the beholder.

Besides plants the State also provides a very congenial habitat to a wide variety of Himalayan fauna. The Himalyan Tahar and the Ibex can be spotted as silhouettes on the high ridges in the trans-Himalayas. The Brown Bear and Musk Deer roam happily in the temperate forests, in the company of colourful pheasants including the Monal, the Western Hornes Tragopan, the Koklas and the Kalij. The lucky ones can even be traeted to rare sight of critically endangered species like the Snow Leopard and Snow Cock.

Also known as the 'Abode of Gods', the State conjures up visions of ancient temples, with exquisitely carved wooden panels, occupying almost every hilltop and the festivities associated with these religious places. Even a casual glimpse at the traditionally attired local deities being carried in meticulously decorated palanquins, devotees dancing to the rhythmic play of traditional drums and clarions, leaves a lasting imptint on one's mind.

This natural and cultural richness of the State coupled with its simple peace loving people and traditional hospitality makes the State a most favoured tourist destination. Anybody with a zest for life, a spirit of adventure and a love for nature will find all that his heart desires amongest the pristine environs of Himachal Pradesh.

UTTARANCHAL

Uttaranchal blessed with magnificent glaciers, majestic snow-clad mountains, gigantic and ecstatic peaks, valley of flowers, skiing slopes and dense forests, this Abode of Gods includes many shrines and places of pilgrimage. Char-dhams, the four most sacred and revered Hindu temples: Badrinath, Kedarnath, Gangotri and Yamunotri are nestled in the Mighty Mountains. A picturesque state, with a breathtaking panoramic view of Himalayas, Uttaranchal promises its tourists a visit full of fun and unforgettable moments.

Uttaranchal blessed with magnificent glaciers, majestic snow-clad mountains, gigantic and ecstatic peaks, valley of flowers, skiing slopes and dense forests, this Abode of Gods includes many shrines and places of pilgrimage. India's first National Park is cradled in the foothills of the Himalayas and spreads over an area of 520 sq. kms., along the banks of the Ramganga river. The dense Sal forests of the Himalayan foothils and the tall grassy neadows make it one of the richest areas of northern India for the habitation of the big mammals.

ECOSYSTEM IN INDIA

The Himalayan region is a particularly fragile ecosystem. The interconnections between the different types of vegetation, between plant life and the soil, between the soil, vegetation and water are so close and so precariously balanced that the slightest change in one plunges the entire system into jeopardy. Ecosystems on seismic belts, for example, are literally 'at the mercy of the land'. Nature plays havoc in other ways too: the monsoon pattern often spells drought in the dry season, and terrible floods during rainfall.

DEFORESTATION

Growing Population

- Way back in 326 B.C., when Alexander the Great came to India, his advance was checked by almost impenetrable forests along the Indus. By the time Emperor Ashoka ascended the throne, stretches of forests had already been cleared to make roads. Ashoka realised the importance of conserving forests, and even appointed an officer for the purpose.

Sher Shah Suri was also farsighted, and planted trees all along the route from Delhi to his capital Patna. However, the Mughals' interest in forests was sadly limited to a rather hedonistic passion for big game. Under the British rule, deforestation became rampant in order to procure timber to build furniture, railway sleepers and ships for the British navy. However, the British soon realised that forests had to be spared the ordeal. After Independence, forests were cleared whenever wood was needed either for timber or agriculture, or for setting up townships. Forests were razed to the ground mindlessly till the eastern hill people decided to say a collective 'Stop'.

Forest Distructions Through Fire

Forest fires have largely contributed to deforestation. Forests in India are very susceptible to fires, especially in summer. All it takes is one little spark and a forest fire could reduce considerable green stretches to ashes in a matter of a few hours. Earlier the Bishnois of Jodhpur (Rajasthan) even laid down their lives to save trees. The Bishnois are a religious community, famous for their loyalty towards animals and trees. In fact, they are known to worship the blackbuck as a sacred animal. Various measures are being taken to curb the felling of trees. Clearing forests is now an offence under Indian law, unless approved by the concerned authorities. However, deforestation has acquired alarming proportions in India. The country's total forest cover today has fallen to a little more than approximately 10 per cent –a dismal situation for a country with a population of over a billion.

Land Degradation

Every year, valuable topsoil is swept away by floods in the rainy season and deforestation contributes to the problem of soil erosion. Man may well have compounded the problem.

Chemical Farming

To sustain the country's enormous population, intensive chemical farming was introduced in the 1960s, ushering in the 'Green Revolution'. Chemical fertilisers and high yield grains were used on an unprecedented scale. Although production tripled, the quality of the land took a battering. Chemicals and toxic substances too have taken their own toll on the land. Desertification (cultivable land turning barren) is a serious problem in some parts of the country, especially in Rajasthan.

Water Conditions

Despite high rainfall, water levels have dropped alarmingly in many places in the country. Obviously this is due to the demands of a burgeoning population. In any case, the monsoon cannot always be relied upon; it is not uncommon for a region like Rajasthan to be stricken by drought once every two to three years. While hydroelectric projects are a partial solution to the problem, their overall 'efficiency' is not beyond interrogation.

The Narmada Valley Project – a vast project of several dams aimed at providing water and power for Gujarat, Rajasthan, Madhya Pradesh and Maharashtra – when completed, is projected to submerge an estimated 350,000 hectares of forest and 200,000 hectares of cultivated fields, and displace nearly 400,000 people. Spearheaded by the environmentalist Baba Amte, Medha Patkar, and more recently Arundhati Roy, a vigorous campaign is in progress against the building of the dams. Another controversial project is the Tehri Dam in Uttar Pradesh. Besides the displacement and loss it is projected to cause, another dread is that the dam may burst as it is being constructed on an earthquake-prone zone. The distinguished man in white, Sunderlal Bahuguna has once again spared no effort at raising public consciousness about the issue at hand.

Pollution

Despite having some of the strictest laws in the world against pollution, India is one of the most environmentally polluted countries in the world. Air pollution is so grave in cities like Delhi, Calcutta, Kanpur and some others, that simply breathing the air is equivalent to smoking 10-20 cigarettes a day! Recently, Delhi acquired the dubious distinction of being one of the five most polluted cities in the world. The rivers in the country have not been spared either.

Industrial waste and a combination of other factors have contributed to the plight of these 'dying' rivers. In some places, safe drinking water, is a rare commodity. Lakes and river habitats too have been polluted. The Yamuna Action Plan was a project undertaken at a tentative cost of Rs 20,000 crore to cleanse the river of pollutants. A similar project was undertaken for the mighty Ganga River.

Conservation

Ancient texts including the epics, the Buddhist Jatakas, the Panchatantra or the more recent Jain scriptures, all preach non-violence towards even the lowest forms of animal and plant life, a philosophy that the Indian Maharajas and their British guests chose to overlooked for a while. The Indian Government has an uphill task to perform. It has been able to protect only about 4 per cent of the total forest cover in the form of National Parks and similar reserves. Underhand activities like poaching are not entirely unheard of even in these restricted areas. Currently there are about 80 National Parks and 441 sanctuaries in the country. Massive tree plantation Programmes are also being undertaken. The Vana Mahotsava, first started in 1950, is an annual tree-planting festival celebrated across the nation.

Individual Efforts

Vishweshwar Dutt Saklani of Garhwal, in Uttar Pradesh, is a small time farmer who started planting trees to seek solace after the death of his brother (who had initiated the practice) in 1948. In the last 50 years, Vishweshwar has overlaid 100 hectares of land with oak, cedar, walnut and rhododendron. Pecple were dismissive of him until they saw the sea change that his work had brought about in the village.

Denuded hills became green, land became more fertile and dry streambeds filled up. Fodder and fuel were in plenty and everyone was happy. Vishweshwar received the Indira Priyadarshini Vrikshamitra Award in 1986. Bikkalu Chikkaiah and Thimmakka were a childless couple who worked in a quarry close to Bangalore. They decided to raise banyan trees in lieu of the children they were unable to have. So they chose a barren piece of land en route to their quarry.

The couple planted saplings and put protective barriers around them. In the evenings, they lugged water from a well a kilometre away. 40 years later, 284 banyan trees provided shade to a 3km stretch. Thimmakka received the National Citizen's Award in 1996. Abdul Karim of Kasargod, Kerala too did something similar. He turned a dry piece of land into a veritable forest after 19 years of hard labour. His deciduous trees brought water back into the soil. Karim went a step ahead and got some animals in this forest, to successfully replicate a healthy ecosystem.

ECO-TOURISM POLICY

The Draft Tourism Policy 1997 states that "in the context of economic liberalisation and globalisation being pursued by the country, the development policies of no sector can remain static. "The policy further states that" the emergence of tourism as an important instrument for sustainable human development including poverty alleviation, employment generation, environmental regeneration and advancement of women and other disadvantaged groups in the country" requires support to realise these goals. India's tourism resources have always been considered immense, in a tourism audit. The geographical features are diverse, colourful and varied.

The coastline offers opportunities for developing the best beaches in the world. There are a wealth of eco-systems including bio-sphere reserves, mangroves, coral reefs, deserts, mountains and forests as well as an equally wide range of flora and fauna. The Policy further states that "international tourists visiting interiors of the country for reasons of purity of the environment and nature contributes to the development of these areas particularly backward regions". Thus Tourism "should also become a reason for better preservation and protection of our natural resources, environment and ecology". The policy recognises that sustained growth of tourism can give rise to conflicts.

To ensure that the growth of tourism takes place along desired lines, certain guidelines have been framed:

- To remove the constraint of the information gap.
- To create a tourist product that is desirable and supported by an integrated infrastructure.
- To involve all agencies, public, private and government, in tourism development.
- To create synergy between departments and agencies that have to deliver the composite tourist product.
- To use both the circuit and scheme approach so that peoples participation through panchayats, local bodies, NGO's, and youth organisations will create a greater awareness of tourism. The Central Government can thus concentrate on larger investment oriented projects.
- To create direct access for destinations off the beaten track.

- To diversify the product with new options like beach tourism, forests, wild life, landscapes and adventure tourism, farm and health tourism.
- To ensure that the development does not exceed sustainable levels.
- To develop the seven north-eastern states, the Himalayan region and Islands for tourism.
- To maintain a balance between the negative and positive impacts of tourism through planning restrictions and through education of the people for conservation and development.

DEVELOPMENT PLAN

The strategy for development should take into consideration the carrying capacity, local aspirations and benefits likely to accrue to the community. In particular specific policies and guidelines for eco-tourism development and adventure tourism are to be formulated, primarily through a regulatory framework. The Draft Guidelines have been approved at a State Ministers Conference and have been circulated to various trade and industry bodies. The guidelines draw a distinction between mass or resort tourism and nature or Eco-tourism, as the kind of tourism that has a lower impact on the environment and requires less infrastructural development. The Ministry hopes that the environment conscious international tourist will be made aware that India is taking steps to protect its ecology and environment.

Apart from the do's and don'ts, the guidelines are governed by a tourism management plan, the key elements of which are the protection of natural resources and a positive involvement of local communities, along with an optimum number of environmentally conscious visitors. The principles of management are scientific planning, effective control and continuous monitoring, development of physical infrastructure, zoning and a Management plan for public use of natural sites. The management plan should establish standards for resort development, style and location of structures, waste disposal, treatment of sewage, control of litter, use of public spaces and fragile areas. The operational guidelines rely on sensitisation of all the role players and this Programmes is based on a self-regulated environmental code.

Area specific rather than universal development plans keeping in mind the unique character of the location and its economic and social environment are important. This would help the State Government to coordinate with the industry in managing visitors and their activities. NGO's working on socio-economic Programmes in forest and remote areas could have a closer coordination with tourism service operators to transfer economic benefits, particularly the handicraft production and marketing sector. The guidelines are only a beginning, and it is hoped that with increasing awareness of the visitor the industry will regulate its practices.

TOURISM ADVISORY COMMITTEE

There is an emphasis on the needs and perceptions of the international tourist running through the discussion on the guide lines although the data from the National Parks makes it evident that the domestic tourists outnumber international visitors, although they do not pay the same amount as the foreign visitor either in entry fees or for board and lodging and transport facilities. They do however demand a much higher per capita use of resources like water, fuel for heating and cooking and transport. They also make the same intensive use of time and try to maximize their stay by the number of animals and birds they can view in the 24-hour period.

It is interesting to note that no democratic participation has been called for in the policy formulation process, and all the amendments to the policy have come from trade associations and government think tanks. The tourism Advisory Committee also consists of eminent persons and community representation has been ignored.

The policy clearly recognises the debate on the tourism issue which has surfaced wherever tourism development, particularly in the case of tourism projects relating to the "gifts of nature" like beaches, rivers, mountains and forests, have already been developed. However, mere recognition of the hostility of people to tourism development is not enough to change the nature of tourism development or the resistance to tourism or what many have termed a poor tourism culture.

Perhaps to understand this in a better perspective, we should look at the issue of sustainable development in a critical way. Perhaps we can question the impact of sustainable development on the environment and sift through the jargon of development planners, international agencies, and environmental activists to see how sustainable development can be achieved without all the contradictions that are apparent as in the case of the tourism sector.

DEVELOPMENT IN TOURISM

The concept of sustainability originated in the context of renewable resources like forests and fisheries and was subsequently adopted by the environmental movement. In most cases it is understood to mean "the existence of the ecological conditions necessary to support human life at a specific level of well being through future generations." However, in addition to ecological conditions there are social conditions that influence ecological sustainability in a nature-people interaction.

The social connotations have been described by Barbier (1987) who has defined social sustainability as "the ability to maintain desired social values, traditions, institutions, cultures or other social characteristics." The term sustainability came into usage in 1980 when the IUCN presented the World Conservation Strategy where sustainable development was linked to conservation of living resources. However, the fundamental goals have often been lost sight of because of operational goals (*e.g.* food, water, shelter, health are fundamental goals to be realised through self reliance, cost effectiveness, appropriate technology, people centred-ness etc.)

Consequently, the WCED made its definition brief: Social Development is development that meets the needs of the present without compromising the ability of future generations to meet their own needs. They did not make any assumptions on the direction in which changes in demand would take place.

(*e.g.* equity, social justice, self-determination, or cultural diversity). India's tourism policy follows the mainstream SD (Sustainable Development) thinking by adopting all the critical objectives: revive growth change the quality of growth meet essential needs for jobs, food, energy, water and sanitation ensure sustainable levels of population conserve and enhance the resource base reorient technology and management risk merge environment and economics in decision making reorient international economic relations make development more participatory.

These objectives are responsible for building a very broad consensus on the issue of sustainable development, yet the debate at the operational level continues. Most participants in the debate now accept that many human activities are reducing the long-term ability of the natural environment to provide goods and services, which will eventually affect human health and well being.

ENVIROMENTAL DEGRADATION

Many also accept that poverty is devastating the lives of millions in the Third World since there is no consensus between what is environmentally necessary and what is economically and developmentally feasible. The level of inter-dependence between the two insights is yet to be incorporated in the concept of Social Development. Some problem areas are: Environmental degradation, already affecting millions in the Third World, is likely to reduce human well being across the globe.

Who is responsible for this rapid degeneration? Is it the poor or the rich? The poor have no option but to exploit resources for short-term survival. If we take the example of forests and their resources, which have been traditionally outside the market system and in the sphere of tribal or indigenous peoples rights, they are today seen as exploiters of the forests as against tourists, with all their demand for infrastructure and superstructure, who are seen to be conservationists.

The inter-linked nature of the problem of sustainability is such that the impact of degradation will be quicker on the poor than on the rich. Can Sustainable Development be the metafix it claims to be in reconciling increasing industrial, agricultural and resource use productivity with environmental needs. The weakness of the Social Development argument lies in the techno-economic approach to solutions with regard to common property resource management, through know how transfers, resource pricing, subsidy policies and building management capabilities. (World Bank, 1987) Deeper processes such as land reforms, industrial demands on raw materials, over consumption, changing legal and political structures are either ignored or looked at in a cursory manner.

For instance how can we claim a consensus between those who are concerned for the survival of future generations with those who are concerned with the survival of wild life, or human health and subsistence? Unless we can identify the trade-offs necessary for each specific objective of sustainability, we will not have clarity in the discussion. We will also fail to understand why, even when there is a broad consensus, projects on the ground result in conflicts.

Suggested refinements could be:

- A distinction between ecological and social sustainability and in the process an identification of the inter-linkages a distinction between renewable and non-renewable resources, between environ-mental processes crucial to human life and crucial to other forms of life dependent on the resources a distinction between the techno-economic aspects of social sustainability (infrastructure, services, government) with political and cultural sustainability.
- A distinction between equitable development and local participation, and decentralisation, what many have called NGO organization of sustainable development. This is because no rigorous testing of local participation leading to social equity or to sustainable resource use have been reported.

ENVIRONMENTAL IMPACT

Case studies reflect personal, organisational or political

preferences. Tourism is one of the activities which have caused concern because of the effects of increasing human traffic on fragile environments. Countries which are looking towards Tourism as a means of economic growth, like India, have limited resources and cultural restraints and they have the greatest need to pay heed to the possible negative impacts of tourism. The environmental impact of tourism is a basic issue, whether we are looking at a developed or an underdeveloped area, region or country.

The costs of tourism for a country like India include extensive investment in fixed assets with a low rate of return for infrastructure, transportation, accommodation, cultural institutions, exhibition centres, and park facilities. To this maybe added the social and cultural costs like additional demands on infrastructure like land, water, health services; the creation of new jobs for displaced people; the cost of positive community relationships; the disparity between the lifestyle of visitors and those who serve them; the possible friction between local residents and new users of valued local resources; the perception of local residents of the spending of scarce capital resources on what they consider low priority areas like tourism; cultural cost of alterations in local ceremonial or traditional values; loss of privacy for local communities as tourists come to gape at their living conditions and rituals.

Tourism also causes increasing congestion and pollution as thousands of visitors flock to parks and sanctuaries in motorised vehicles; there are changes in accessibility, landscape and the ecological balance between man and nature; there is the cost, both monetary and human, of creating conservation zones (core/buffer) with unforeseen or undesirable side effects; which have been observed in the Eco-tourism movement. The benefit of revenue from tourism does not always redress these problems but goes towards the cost of administering the project. The tourism industry is generally self-centred and not given to educational, cultural or exchange Programmes on a philanthropic basis. The natural environment, with the best will in the world, cannot escape damage with the volume of visitors. As more and more tourists, both domestic and international seek the exotic and remote destinations around the world, the likelihood of the environment suffering as a result become greater.

Forests can suffer from trampling, fires, tree felling for facilities and waste. Wildlife, despite the protection in national parks, has suffered a loss of habitat, hunting and poaching, viewing and photographing, leading to an interruption of feeding and breeding patterns or hunting for food undisturbed. These are the prized moments for the viewer. The trade in wild life trophies or tourist souvenirs is the more deliberately destructive aspect of such tourism.

SANCTUARIES

The building of tourist lodges in materials that are not integrated with the environment and the pressure they put on the land and water bodies is also wilfully destructive. Management techniques that include being less user friendly or control of numbers by closing access or by multiplying the number of attractions and areas or charging higher admission fees are generally not popular with the tourist or the tour operator and are also difficult to implement because of high administrative costs.

Equations, through its involvement in the field have had a variety of experiences relating to the debate on Eco-tourism and sustainable development. The major issues that have emerged after the policy of notification of wild life sanctuaries and their management by the Forest Departments are quite disturbing.

Wherever notification has led to displacement of people the experience of rehabilitation has not been successful and the conservation aims have not been met. Several sanctuaries have witnessed militant action by displaced communities against the developers of tourism.

In many cases the tourism aims have also not been met in making the sanctuary accessible to viewers, naturalists, wild life photographers. Tourism has not been able to counteract poaching and the most extensive and the oldest conservation project, Project Tiger has not been able to save the tiger population. The commercialisation of the experience, like the privileging of one species, for example the tiger, has led to congestion and noise pollution and this has put a pressure on the management of the sanctuary to organise tiger shows which are putting a pressure on the feeding and mating habits of the tiger. These are very invasive techniques of experiencing the wild. On the plus side, the concept of beneficiary led development has helped indigenous people to organise against their displacement and exploitation as well as to fight for the retention of their traditional rights and life styles.

Environmentalists have not only been involved in such organisations and movements but have done valuable documentation. This has influenced many urban visitors to be more sensitive to the wild and to follow the rules when participating in eco-tourism. This has also led to the development of a code of conduct for the tourist, the industry and the administrator. These attempts are in a very nascent stage. The kind of co-ordination that is required between the environmentalist and economist is just beginning to emerge and have still to counter the myths of neo-classical economists in the field of tourism. But a beginning has been made.

COASTAL ISSUES

The Coastal Regulation Zone (CRZ) came into existence on February 19, 1991, with the gazetting of the notification by the Union Ministry of Environment and Forests (MoEF) under Sec. 3(1) and Sec. 3(2)(v) of the Environment Protection Act, 1986, and Rule 5(3)(d) of the Environment Protection Rules, 1986. Through the Notification the Central Government declared the coastal stretches of seas, bays, estuaries, creeks, rivers and backwaters, which are influenced by tidal action (in the land ward side), up to 500m. from the high tide line (HTL) and the land between the low tide line (LTL) and HTL as CRZ. In the case of rivers, creeks and backwaters, the Notification stated that the CRZ could be modified on a case by case basis, on the basis of reasons to be recorded during the preparation of the coastal zone management plan (CZMP).

However, the width of the CRZ from each bank could not be less than 100 m., or the width of the water body, whichever was less.

Activities Prohibited in the CRZ:

- Setting up of new industries and expansion of existing ones, except those directly related to waterfront or requiring foreshore facilities.
- Manufacture, handling, storage or disposal of hazardous substances.
- Setting up and expansion of fish processing units including warehousing (excluding hatchery and natural fish drying in permitted areas).
- Discharge of untreated wastes and effluents from industries, cities, towns or other human settlements. The existing practices would have to be phased out by the concerned authorities within three years.
- Dumping of ash or any waste from thermal power plants.
- Land reclamation, bunding or disturbing the natural course of sea water with similar obstructions. Exceptions are made for activities required for the control of coastal erosion, the maintenance of water ways to ports; clearing sand bars; and for the construction of regulators, storm water drains and structures for the prevention of salinity ingress.
- Mining of sand, rocks and other substrata materials, except those raw minerals not available outside the CRZ areas.
- Drawing or harvesting of groundwater and construction of mechanism within 200 m. of the HTL. Between 200 and 500 m. it will be permissible only if done manually through ordinary wells for drinking, horticulture, agriculture and fisheries.
- Construction activity in ecologically sensitive areas.
- Any construction activity between LTL and HTL except facilities for carrying treated effluents and waste water discharge into the sea, facilities for carrying sea water for cooling purposes, oil, gas and

similar pipelines and facilities essential for facilities permitted under the notification.

- Dressing or altering of sand dunes, hill, natural features including landscape changes for beautification, recreation and other such purposes, except as permitted under the notification.

Regulated activities (requiring environmental clearance from MoEF):

- Construction activities related to Defence requirements for which foreshore facilities are essential. Residential office, hospital, workshops will not normally be permitted in the CRZ, except in very special cases.
- Operational construction for ports and harbors and light house.
- Foreshore facilities of thermal power plants for transport of raw materials, in-take of cooling water and out fall for discharge of treated wastewater or cooling water.
- All other activities with investment exceeding. 5 crores.

COASTAL ZONE MANAGEMENT PLAN (CZMP)

All the coastal states have to prepare, within one year, CZMPs identifying and classifying CRZ areas as per the Notification guidelines. These plans have to be approved by MoEF All further development activities should be within the framework of these plans. In the interim period, before the approval of the plans, development activities should not violate the provisions of the Notification. Violations are punishable under the provisions of the Environment Protection Act of 1986. For regulating developmental activities, the coastal stretches within 500m of the HTL are classified into CRZ-1, CRZ-11 and CRZ-III.

CRZ-I—Areas that are ecologically sensitive and important (national parks, coral reefs, mangroves, areas close to the breeding and spawning grounds of fishes, areas of high natural beauty, historical heritage, high genetic diversity, and those likely to be inundated by global warming, 'etc.); and areas within the LTL and HTL.

Regulations in CRZ-I

- No new construction shall be permitted within 500 m of the HTL.
- No construction activity except for facility for carrying treated effluents and waste water into the sea or carrying sea water for cooling, oil, gas or similar pipelines will be permitted between the LTL and the HTL.

CRZ-II—Areas that have already been developed up to or close to the shore-line. 'Developed areas' that come within municipal limits or other legally designated urban areas which have been substantially built up and which have been provided with infrastructural facilities like drainage, approach road, water supply and sewage mains.

Regulations in CRZ-III

- Buildings will not be permitted in the seaward side of existing roads (or those proposed in the CZMP) nor on the seaward side of the existing authorised structures.
- Reconstruction of authorised buildings to be permitted subject to the existing floor space and without change in existing use CRZ III Areas that are relatively undisturbed and do not belong to either CRZ-I or CRZ-II. This will include coastal zones in the rural areas and also areas within municipal limits or urban areas that are not substantially built up.
- Areas up to 200 m. from the HTL earmarked as no development zone (NDZ). No construction will be permitted within this zone except for repairs of existing authorised structures not exceeding the existing plinth area and covered apace. Raising of horticultural crops, gardens, pastures, parks, play fields, forestry and salt manufacture from sea water permitted in this zone.

- Development of vacant plots between 200 m. 500 m. from the HTL, in designated areas with prior approval of MoEF, permitted for hotels and beach resorts.
- Construction or reconstruction of dwellind units between the 200m and 500m of the HTL permitted so long as it is within the ambit of traditional rights and customary uses such as existing fishing villages and gouthans. Building conditions would be based on the conditions that the total number of dwelling units does not increase more than double of the existing units; the total covered area is not more than 33 per cent of the plot area; the overall height is not more than two floors and 9 m. Guidelines for development of beach resorts in the designated areas of CRZ-III · No construction within 200 m. from the HTL and in the area between LTL and HTL.
- The total plot size should not be less than 0.4 hectare and the covered area should not be more than 33 per cent. · The total height of the construction should not be more than 9 m. and the building should not be more than two floors. Groundwater cannot be tapped within 200m of the HTL. Between 200 and 500 m. it can be tapped with the concurrence of the State or Central Groundwater Board.
- Extraction of sand, leveling or digging of sandy stretches, except for the structural foundation will not be permitted within 500 M. of the HTL.
- The quality of treated effluents, solid wastes, emissions and noise levels etc. must be within the standards laid down by the central or state pollution control boards. Untreated effluents and solid wastes should not be discharged into the water or beach.
- To allow public access there should be a gap of 20m. width between two hotels. Two consecutive gaps should not be more than 500 m. apart.

THE WORLD SCENARIO OF TOURISM

In recent years tourism has emerged as a major economic

activity that is employment oriented and earns foreign exchange. Its share in the worlds GDP in 1994-95 was 10 per cent which is more than the world military budgets put together. In global terms, the investment in tourism industry and travel trade accounts for 7 per cent of the total capital investment. Today 21.2 crore people around the globe are employed in travel trade and tourism. In future, this industry is likely to see unprecedented growth.

According to the World Tourism Council at Brussels, the revenues from travel and tourism in Asia Pacific region will grow at the rate of 7.8 per cent annually over the next decade. Amongst the economic sectors, the tourism sector is highly labour intensive. A survey by the Government of India notes that the rate of employment generation (direct and indirect) in tourism is 52 persons employed per Rs.10 lakh investment (based on 1992-93 Consumer Price Index). This is much higher than the rates of employment generation in most other economic sectors.

Indian tourism industry has also recorded phenomenal growth. The rate of international arrivals in India in recent years has been to the tune of about 19 lakh arrivals per year. The unprecedented growth in tourism in India has made it the third largest foreign exchange earner after gem and jewellery and ready-made garments.

This is not surprising since India possesses a whole range of attractive normally sought by tourists and which includes natural attractions like Iandscapes, scenic beauty, mountains, wildlife, beaches, major rivers and manmade attractions such as monuments, forts, palaces and havelis.

However, in global terms, in spite of such attractions, tourist arrivals in India are a mere 0.30 per cent of the world arrivals. Receipts are similarly low, just a 0.50 per cent of the world receipts. We are still quite far from the target of 50 lakh tourist arrivals per year.

Travel and Tourism is the world's largest industry and creator of jobs across national and regional economies. WTTC/ WEFA research show that in 2000, Travel and Tourism will generate, directly and indirectly, 11.7 per cent of GDP and nearly 200 million jobs in the world-wide economy. Jobs generated by Travel and Tourism are spread across the economy—in retail, construction, manufacturing and telecommunications, as well as directly in Travel and Tourism companies. These jobs employ a large proportion of women, minorities and young people; are predominantly in small and medium sized companies; and offer good training and transferability. Tourism can also be one of the most effective drivers for the development of regional economies. These patterns apply to both developed and emerging economies.

CONTRIBUTING TO SUSTAINABLE DEVELOPMENT

The 1992 United Nations Conference on Environment and Development (UNCED), the Rio Earth Summit, identified Travel and Tourism as one of the key sectors of the economy which could make a positive contribution to achieving sustainable development. The Earth Summit lead to the adoption of Agenda 21, a comprehensive Programmes of action adopted by 182 governments to provide a global blueprint for achieving sustainable development. Travel and Tourism is the first industry sector to have launched an industry-specific action plan based on Agenda 21.

Travel and Tourism is able to contribute to development which is economically, ecologically and socially sustainable, because it:

- Has less impact on natural resources and the environment than most other industries;
- Is based on enjoyment and appreciation of local culture, built heritage, and natural environment, as such that the industry has a direct and powerful motivation to protect these assets;
- Can play a positive part in increasing consumer commitment to sustainable development principles through its unparalleled consumer distribution channels; and
- Provides an economic incentive to conserve natural environments and habitats which might otherwise be allocated to more environmentally damaging land uses, thereby, helping to maintain bio-diversity.

There are numerous good examples of where Travel and Tourism is acting as a catalyst for conservation and improvement of the environment and maintenance of local diversity and culture. (Some of these are set out in Section B of this paper and a fuller illustration of the range of industry action can be found on the World Travel and Tourism Council's Of course, there are also examples where development has not been sustainable. (Some of the lessons learnt from these poor practices are illustrated in Section C of this paper.)

PROVIDING INFRASTRUCTURE

To a greater degree than most activities, Travel and Tourism depends on a wide range of infrastructure services—airports, air navigation, roads, railheads and ports, as well as basic infrastructure services required by hotels, restaurants, shops, and recreation facilities (*e.g.* telecommunications and utilities).

It is the combination of tourism and good infrastructure that underpins the economic, environmental and social benefits. It is important to balance any decision to develop an area for tourism against the need to preserve fragile or threatened environments and cultures. However, once a decision has been taken where an area is appropriate for new tourism development, or that an existing tourist site should be developed further, then good infrastructure will be essential to sustain the quality, economic viability and growth of Travel and Tourism. Good infrastructure will also be a key factor in the industry's ability to manage visitor flows in ways that do not affect the natural or built heritage, nor counteract against local interests.

CHALLENGE FOR THE FUTURE

Travel and Tourism creates jobs and wealth and has tremendous potential to contribute to economically, environmentally and socially sustainable development in both developed countries and emerging nations. It has a comparative advantage in that its start up and running costs can be low compared to many other forms of industry development. It is also often one of the few realistic options for development in many areas. Therefore, there is a strong likelihood that the Travel and Tourism industry will continue to grow globally over the short to medium term.

Of course, if Travel and Tourism is managed badly, it can have a detrimental effect—it can damage fragile environments and destroy local cultures. The challenge is to manage the future growth of the industry so as to minimise its negative impacts on the environment and host communities whilst maximising the benefits it brings in terms of jobs, wealth and support for local culture and industry, and protection of the built and natural environment.

OBJECTIVES

The main objective of the States Tourism Policy will be to undertake intensive development of tourism in the State and thereby increase employment opportunities.

The following related objectives are dovetailed with main objectives:

- Identify and develop tourist destinations and related activities.
- Diversifications of tourism products in order to attract more tourists through a varied consumer choice.
- Comprehensive development of pilgrimage centres as tourist destinations.
- Create adequate facilities for budget tourists.
- Strengthen the existing infrastructure and develop new ones where necessary.
- Creation of tourism infrastructure so as to preserve handicrafts, folk arts and culture of the state and thereby attract more tourists.

APPROACH AND STRATEGY

In addition to the facilitation role assigned to itself by the Government in the development of tourism, the Government will adopt the following strategy towards the private sector with the objective of securing its active involvement in leading the development of tourism in the State.

- The tourism will be given the status of industry in order that the facilities and benefits available to the industry are also made available to tourism projects.
- A special incentives package will be made available for encouraging new tourism projects as well as expansion of existing tourism units.
- Infrastructural facilities will be strengthened and developed within the State, particularly in Special Tourism Areas which will be notified latter and which will be developed by adopting an integrated-area.
- Effective mechanisms will be set up to build meaningful co-ordination with the Central Government and the State Governments agencies, the local self-government bodies and the NGOs.
- Government will encourage building effective linkages with the relevant economic agents and agencies such as the national and international tour operators and travel agents of repute, hotel chains and global institutions connected with tourism such as WTO.

So far, the lending from the State Financial Institutions has been largely confined to hotels only. In reality, the range of activities for tourism projects is far larger than just hotels as can be seen from the following illustrative list

TEN COMMANDMENTS

- Respect the frailty of the earth. Realise that unless all are willing to help in its preservation, unique and beautiful destinations may not be here for future generations to enjoy.
- Leave only footprints. Take only photographs. No graffiti! No litter! Do not take away souvenirs from historical sites and natural areas.
- To make your travels more meaningful, educate yourself about the geography, customs, manners and

cultures of the region you visit. Take time to listen to the people. Encourage local conservation efforts.

- Respect the privacy and dignity of others. Inquire before photographing people.
- Do not buy products made from endangered plants or animals, such as ivory, tortoise shell, animal skins, and feathers. Read Know Before You Go, the U. S. Customs list of products which cannot be imported.
- Always follow designated trails. Do not disturb animals, plants or their natural habitats.
- Learn about and support conservation-oriented Programmes and organizations working to preserve the environment.
- Whenever possible, walk or use environmentally-sound methods of transportation. Encourage drivers of public vehicles to stop engines when parked.
- Patronize those (hotels, airlines, resorts, cruise lines, tour operators and suppliers) who advance energy and environmental conservation; water and air quality; recycling; safe management of waste and toxic materials; noise abatement, community involvement; and which provide experienced, well-trained staff dedicated to strong principles of conservation.
- Encourage organizations to subscribe to environmental guidelines. ASTA urges organizations to adopt their own environmental codes to cover special sties and ecosystems.

Travel is a natural right of all people and is a crucial ingredient of world.

6

Intellectual Tourism

RESEARCH

Although tourism as an activity has a long tradition, as an academic subject it is a development of the 1960s. Initial concentration of the subject development was in Europe but it is now seen as a worldwide phenomenon. In the 1960s there were few academic institutions which offered tourism courses (as differentiated from travel trade and hospitality specific programmes). Consequently, there were only a few academics who could term themselves as 'tourism lecturers'. However, as tourism expanded as both a domestic and international activity, it inevitably attracted the interests of academics from many disciplines with a consequent development of courses and degree programmes.

Tourism has developed at undergraduate level during a period of continual structural change within higher education institutions (HEI) and during changes in the purpose of the wider Higher Education (HE) system. There has been, without doubt, extraordinary growth of provision for Tourism in both further and higher education in the last ten years in the United Kingdom.

Together with the arrival of other new subjects such as Media, Communication and Theatre Studies, Tourism represents an alternative to the traditional, yet popular, disciplines such as Geography, English and History. Over a four year period, the number of students accepting a place on an undergraduate Tourism programme in a UK HEI increased from 1666 to 2363, a rise of 42 per cent.

The study of Tourism as a subject has focused previously on the existence of, and need for, a minimum core curriculum. Research has also concentrated on the growth of provision and concerns of over provision of tourism graduates due to the proliferation of tourism programmes in the last ten years or so, since the first two programmes at undergraduate level were introduced at Dorset Institute and Newcastle Polytechnic in 1986. However, no study to date has attempted to understand why Tourism has developed in the manner it has, and what factors have contributed towards that development.

This significant gap in research to date in the field of Tourism in HE offers the opportunity for this paper to evaluate Tourism lecturer perceptions of the key factors influencing the development of Tourism undergraduate programmes.

In the last few years, Leiper and Tribe have re-opened the debate surrounding Tourism's disciplinary status, following its initial airing in the early 1980s well before provision at an undergraduate level featured in HEIs in the UK. Tribe maintained that Tourism is not a discipline but two distinct fields, the business of tourism and the non-business aspect of Tourism. He defended the non-disciplinary nature of Tourism and proposed that 'tourism studies should recognise and celebrate its diversity' rather than 'hankering after an overly idealised concept'.

Leiper responded directly to Tribe's assertions of Tourism's non-disciplinary nature and favoured a recognition that a discipline can be seen to be emerging, and that 'the debate about whether or not a discipline of tourism studies exists is similar to debates about whether or not the industry exists'. These debates have played an important role in allowing the nature of Tourism as a subject and the extent of its academic maturity to be aired in the increasing number of academic Tourism journals.

In the 1990s there still appears to have been greater support for the view that tourism is still a subject rather than a discipline due to its relative youth as a subject area and because it lacks what Cooper and Westlake described as 'antecedents of a mature field'.

Tourism as a subject for study could strive to build a reputation not as a discipline, but based on its ability not only to draw on a wide range of established disciplines as above, but on its diversity and multi-disciplinarity.

Tourism is still a relatively new phenomenon which has featured at postgraduate level for nearly 30 years and at undergraduate level for less than 20 years. While the existence or emergence of Tourism as a discipline and the need for a common curriculum has been disputed during this period these issues will not form the focus of this paper. Rather the aim of this paper is to analyse two key factors which have, according to Tourism lecturers, influenced the development of Tourism in HE against a backdrop of constraints at a national, institutional and departmental level.

METHODOLOGY

The research developed in two stages, firstly content analysis (of discussion documents, a new research tool, and programme validation documentation) and secondly, in-depth interviews with a variety of lecturers. The methodology is, in part, experimental in terms of the use of a previously untested research instrument, the 'discussion document', but also includes a more traditional method, *i.e.* in-depth interviews.

The process of content analysis involved the identification of 'bits of data which can be relied upon for the purpose of comparison'. Comparison in this case was between one lecturer's views and another's (in the same or different institution). As the research progressed, drawing on information from the two stages, certain influences on the development of Tourism programmes emerged as being more or less critical in terms of the actual nature of programmes.

The detailed 'discussion document' was designed to allow one representative from each of ten institutions delivering undergraduate Tourism to respond to a number of statements regarding programme structure and content. To date this type of research instrument has not been used to examine lecturers' views about aspects of programme development in HE and as such, the discussion document was an innovative test case which could be useful for future similar studies. A major problem which was recognised regarding the introduction of a new, untested research tool, is the fact that there could be no guarantee that it would result in collection of the necessary, or sufficient usable, comparable information.

For this reason piloting of the document was crucial in terms of highlighting potential problems which needed to be eradicated before completion by the actual selection of institutions. Piloting the discussion document with two institutions not involved in this stage of the research allowed the testing of wording (avoiding ambiguity), sequencing and layout of questions as proposed by Fink, Folz (1996) and Veal (1992) and very importantly in this case, finding out if the 12 page document was manageable in terms of the length of time it would take to complete.

A number of changes were made to the structure and design of the original piloted discussion document following telephone or personal interviews with the two respondents involved and analysis of the completed documents. The key change made involved a reduction in the number of open-ended questions and an increase in closed questions to make the instrument less demanding for the respondent and as a result, less time-consuming.

Criteria for selection of institutions to be analysed at the second stage were considered carefully and nine institutions, collectively covering the 'descriptors' of institutions delivering Tourism at undergraduate level, were approached and subsequently agreed to take part.

The description included:

- Tourism programmes delivered in England, Scotland and Wales
- New Tourism programmes delivered at the former polytechnics
- Established Tourism programmes delivered at 'old' universities
- Tourism programmes delivered by colleges of higher education and university sector colleges, franchised and validated by a named university

- Tourism programmes of a 'general' or specialist nature (by programme title)

Respondents at this stage of the research held various positions within Tourism sections, schools and departments, *i.e.* lecturers, programme leaders, heads of departments and deans of faculties. The second stage of the research concerned the opinions of 27 lecturers responsible for teaching and researching Tourism in HE in the 1990s, as research to date in the field of Tourism education appears to have focused primarily on the quantitative aspect of programme delivery, rather than widespread interviewing of Tourism lecturers. According to McCracken 'the long interview is one of the most powerful methods in the qualitative armory...no instrument of inquiry is more revealing'.

Unlike the research carried out by Johnson where in-depth interviews were carried out with key Tourism educators who were known to be knowledgeable and to hold strong views regarding common core curriculum, this research aimed to interview not only the knowledgeable in terms of the subject, but also those lecturers who were relatively new to Tourism, and heads of department/school whose influence over programme structure and content was limited.

The aim was to gather views and opinions from individuals who had a wide range and level of interest and involvement in the development of Tourism programmes, from the highly informed, involved and influential individuals to those whose role in course delivery and programme structure was more limited.

This indicates the paper's emphasis on lecturers' views regarding Tourism's development, which needs to be viewed in the light of the recognition of three further possible levels of potential influence, at the national, institutional and departmental level. As it was not possible to undertake detailed interviews with staff across all the institutions which had completed the discussion document, it was decided to select a small sample of institutions which would represent these. Each of the five institutions selected met one or more of the criteria listed above.

The interviews were designed to focus on those substantial issues that emerged from the analysis of the discussion and validation documents and were semi-structured with specific objectives or outcomes. An informal approach was adopted with participating respondents being offered a list of topics or themes to be discussed prior to the interviews. Kahn and Cannell describe the in-depth interview as 'a conversation with a purpose' which is believed to be more fruitful than highly structured interviews. The aim of these interviews was to 'unfold' the respondents' perspectives on the 'phenomenon', in this case the nature of Tourism as an undergraduate degree subject.

Although there did need to be some form of systemisation in terms of the questioning (to aid the analysis and comparison of findings), it was vital to ensure that a flexible approach was maintained throughout in order to encourage openness and honesty on the part of the respondent.

Interview transcriptions and discussion documents were coded manually by the author according to four potential levels of influence on Tourism; national, institutional, departmental and individual. This allowed the critical issues to jump out due to their re-occurrence at two or more of these levels. Analysis of the documents could have been carried out using one of the many software packages available, for example, QSR Nudist, which enables the analysis of qualitative data, possibly after the researcher's initial step of open coding of data. Nudist was, in fact, used to analyse and code the two pilot discussion documents.

However, it was not deemed successful due to the length of time it took to get the documents in a format which was acceptable to the Nudist package. It was felt that this time was better spent analysing and coding the discussion documents manually and subsequently the package was not used at the content analysis and coding stage of interview transcripts. As a research tool, Nudist was not designed to 'displace you as the researcher or your process as the central area of activity. Rather it supports the processes or activities that you engage in as you go about the business of doing qualitative research'.

As Nudist was not seen to support the research process—if anything it appeared to hinder progress—it was rejected accordingly. A limitation of the study with regard to methodology concerns the number of respondents interviewed. Although the interviews were comprehensive, allowing individuals to offer detailed explanations of their opinions and beliefs regarding Tourism in HE, the fact that they were relatively few in number means that it would be inappropriate to regard them as statistically representative of all Tourism lecturers.

From the outset the study was planned primarily as a qualitative, not quantitative study. The views of these lecturers should, therefore, be regarded as individual cases which illustrate the range of views and opinions at the five institutions. Additionally, the tendency for respondents on occasions to moan about certain issues regarded as important to their job satisfaction, rather than focusing on the concerns of the interview, resulted in a number of protracted interviews (nearly two hours) and a need to approach these grievances with a degree of caution. As only five institutions (and 27 respondents) were included it would be inappropriate to regard these grievances as being reflective of all institutions and individuals involved in the design and delivery of undergraduate Tourism programmes.

Tourism as a subject is now found in many academic institutions throughout the world and many academics now designate themselves as 'tourism lecturers'. It is now possible for an academic to foresee a career in the academic study of tourism with a range of institutions in many countries offering a varied career path. The growth of tourism as a subject is reflected in the continuously expanding number of publications related to the subject in books, specialist journals, conferences and increasingly through postings on the Internet.

As a group, academics have three main characteristics based on their traditional role of being thinkers, researchers, analysts and teachers:

1. To advance both the knowledge and understanding of the subject;

2. To disseminate information via teaching, publications and conferences;
3. And, through teaching and publications, to educate and influence students, other academics and the industry.

Although there may be some debate about these characteristics they do seem to represent what most academics do. In the area of teaching the purpose is not only to inform students but also to influence their thinking by equipping them with concepts and techniques which are relevant to their future careers, an objective supported by the growing literature on tourism.

The need to publish in academic journals and through subject-specific books seeks to influence (if not always impress!) the peer group-fellow academics. The dissemination of information is essentially career-motivated and scholarly. Some of the central and continuing debates, for example defining the subject area, the nature and definition of 'sustainable' tourism, the role of tourism in society are all topics which advance our theoretical understanding of the subject but are unlikely to be of much interest to practitioners.

A further difficulty is that given the need for academic rigour in publications and the review system, many publications become dated and lose their usefulness before they are published. There may be a further problem where tourism practitioners do not read the academic press. It is suggested, from the basis of experience, that this is often the case. It follows therefore that academics write for and seek to inform fellow academics. Much of the innovative work being done by academics will tend to have a very limited influence on tourism development practice unless the academic is also a practitioner.

For example, the extensive and growing literature on ecotourism, on community participation in tourism development planning, and host-guest relationships are three areas of current interest to academics. Although these issues are also of concern to practitioners their concerns are essentially pragmatic, resource-constrained and implementation-oriented. Of necessity, practitioners must be focused within the parameters of the project and do not seek more general prescriptions.

PRACTITIONERS

In relation to development planning, tourism practitioners are either individual consultants or consulting companies. Consultants, unlike academics, operate in a business environment and may be identified as having three broad operational characteristics.

- Their work is contractual, project specific and profit driven.
- Knowledge dissemination is through project-specific reports, plans and studies which are commissioned by the client and have a limited circulation.
- They aim, by the development of expertise and reputation, to secure future contract work.

Consultants by the very competitive nature of their work do not readily make available to enquirers their past reports unless these are likely to be influential in securing future work. As most projects are in two stages, that is project preparation and subsequent implementation, consultants tend to protect their client base and are always, like any business, seeking to ensure their company sustainability through further contracts.

Much tourism development planning is funded by international agencies, for example World Bank, European Union, United Nations Development Programme, and, for regional development, by banks such as the Asian Development Bank. Many projects are large, long-term and require a variety of technical skills inputs. Few academic institutions would have either the resources or flexibility to compete for large contracts with the major consultancy companies in the area of tourism development.

For these reasons, where large contracts are available many consulting companies subcontract specialist requirements to individuals, often academics and sometimes academic institutions. In this way, there is a 'cross-over' between the academic and the practitioner.

CROSS-OVER

Although it is postulated that academic institutions cannot realistically or effectively compete in the international tourism contract market, academics are employed as project specialists offering skills and experience usually on a short-term basis, for example tourism economists, forecasters and marketing specialists. However, these posts are filled after the contract has been signed and the project strategy and methodology agreed. A brief description of the project preparation stage will support this point.

PROJECT PREPARATION

Although projects vary in scale and complexity there are basically five steps in the project cycle which are briefly discussed here:

1. *Project identification:* Depending on the nature and scale of the project there are usually three sub-components involved in this stage:
   - *Technical specification:* At this stage of project identification the concept, for example to develop a tourism resort, or to specify a tourism planning exercise, is formalized into a project proposal. The project's objectives, activities and expected outputs (results) are identified. The aim is to establish wherever possible measurable indicators to eventually evaluate the project if it should go ahead.
   - *Feasibility studies:* For some projects a feasibility study will be done to assess the viability of the proposal. For international lending agencies a particular area of interest will be to determine how the proposed project fits into any indicative programme of general guidelines for cooperation between the beneficiary country and the lending institution. For example, what priority is given to the tourism sector in a particular country (perhaps indicated in a national development plan) and to what extent will the proposed

project contribute to national and sectoral development aims? In some African countries, such as Zambia, tourism is not only recognized as a priority sector by the Government, but as Zambian tourism is almost exclusively based on wildlife viewing, which obviously takes place in rural areas, tourism development contributes to increasing rural development, incomes and employment-all national economic objectives.

– *Financial proposal:* If the feasibility study confirms the viability of the proposed project and the overall objectives meet national development objectives, then a financial proposal will be drawn up for the project. At its simplest, the financial proposal sets out the budget for the project. At the project identification stage it is usual to employ a consultant(s) to prepare the various working documents. The technical specification and the financial proposal are used to prepare the Terms of Reference.

2. *Terms of Reference:* The Terms of Reference is the project 'bible'. It sets out in detail what the project aims to achieve, what activities are necessary, what outputs (results) are expected within a given budget. Usually incorporated into a comprehensive Project Document, the Terms of Reference not only guides the consultants undertaking the project but is also the main evaluating instrument to check performance against specification.
3. *The tender process:* Consultants may be invited to bid for a contract either on an open or restricted basis. The open system means that, with perhaps some qualification, any company can bid for the contract. A restricted tender operates where only selected companies are invited to bid. In the latter case this may be as a consequence of time pressures or more likely due to the specialist nature of the contract. The bids received will usually have three dimensions: a

profile of the tendering company (including a record of previous experience); a technical proposal to indicate how the contract specifications are to be met (*i.e.* project methodology and the proposed team of consultants); and a financial proposal. It is not always the case that the lowest bid price wins the contract. Evaluations of tenders should involve careful scrutiny of past experience, an evaluation of the proposed methodology and of the team of consultants assembled to carry out the project, and of the financial proposal. The evaluation of tenders is a fairly mysterious process. The quality of the evaluation will depend very much on those doing it-their knowledge, experience and their understanding of the proposed project. Some project evaluations are guided by attempts to systematize the process often by using a points-scale reference to assess different project components. In some cases the process may proceed along more subjective lines. The outcome of the tender process is to award and sign a contract with a consultant(s).

4. Project implementation: The consultant implements the project by using the financial resources provided in the contract. Implementation will require the consultant to prepare a plan of operation and to present reports on the progress of the project as specified in the contract. It is also usual to appoint a project Steering Committee to oversee the operation of the contract and to monitor and discuss any issues arising. The Steering Committee is the main operational channel between the consultant/ contractor and the client.
5. Project evaluation: This involves the review and analysis of results and the impact of the project. Project evaluations can take place during or after a project has ended. In the case of a multi-stage project, the start of the next phase will usually depend on the conclusions of the previous stage.

Although the outlined project schematic may vary between agencies depending on a variety of circumstances and practices, the main stages are common to development planning exercises. What is important to note is that the methodology for the project is devised by the bidding company/ consultant.

PROCEDURE

Despite the increasing funds which are being channelled to tourism planning and development, very little is known about how project methodology is chosen, and on what basis. For example in the WTO report a brief synopsis of various country development plans is given for country projects, but there is no discussion of how a particular methodology was chosen, what alternatives might have been considered, and how this selection was made. Although much has been written on micro-methodologies, such as cost-benefit analysis, economic impact studies, social impact analysis, environmental assessment techniques, little has been written on macro-project methodology for tourism.

Methodological issues are usually conceptual, for example the debates on sustainability, on community participation and empowerment through decentralization. It is these conceptual but essentially pragmatic issues which are often project-relevant and are the main focus for academic writing and research. For many academics the issue is to ask 'why?' rather than 'how'; the latter question could be interpreted to be the main concern of the consultant.

It is suggested that in most projects, methodology is derived from past experience and it is the tried and tested methodology which prevails over anything innovative. In projects where profit margins are often tight, innovation might be costly. For example if, as is now generally agreed, community participation in tourism development is desirable, this might be written into the Terms of Reference.

How it is to be implemented is a challenge despite the extensive academic writing on this topic. In practice, participation may only involve consultation, and perhaps the consultant employed to undertake this task (academic or otherwise) may be methodologically constrained by the project manager, or the budget, or both.

In most large projects there are a series of methodological issues. At the project (or macro) level the main concern is to devise a methodological approach to cover the activities and to produce the outputs required within both the time-scale and budget. At the component (or micro) level, for example economic impact study, marketing survey, analysis of demand and forecasting, the same constraints apply but methodology and techniques are more firmly established. At all times, methodology is driven by pragmatism and is informed by experience rather than theory.

Although methodology is an area where one would expect academics to be most comfortable, it appears that few academics actually are involved in this at the project level. Some of the important contributions to tourism in the developing countries remain enshrined in the literature often unread by consultants. This statement is of course impressionistic and is based on the author's experience. It is a contention which might be tested via a survey of tourism practitioners or from responses to this chapter. A more important source of information could be derived from the financiers of tourism development and in particular, the institutional lenders.

Although organizations such as the European Union, the United Nations Development Programme, development banks and country-based donor organizations have and continue to fund tourism projects, very little information has been released about the relative success or failure of these projects. These lenders have the ability, and probably need, to create institutional memory, that is, to compare through project appraisal and evaluation a major databank of tourism-related information.

Such information is not only relevant to the prospects of future projects but, if disseminated, would become a stimulant to debate. Such an innovation would have to come from a project's lender; client confidentiality would preclude the consultant from revealing such information. Methodology has a particular significance in tourism because of its multidisciplinary nature. Various aspects of a single project can include economic, social, environmental and political inputs, each of which might require a specific methodological approach which will have to be harmonized within the operational framework of the project to meet the Terms of Reference.

Some of the major current debates in tourism development include: sustainability; the environment; social impacts; community participation; local empowerment; type, scale and location of development; globalization; indigenization; women in development and host-guest relationships. These are issues which have attracted major academic interest and publications-how can tourism practitioners and funding agencies be made more aware of this output? How can it be fed into project methodologies?

From the brief discussion of the project cycle it can be deduced that there are two points where the methodological approach can be influenced. First is at the stage of preparing the Terms of Reference for the project and second, at the implementation stage where the project's activities are undertaken. As noted previously, the Terms of Reference set out the activities, inputs and expected outputs from the project.

To a considerable extent the writer of the Terms of Reference can exert a direct influence on methodology by specifying certain activities which are integral to the project, for example that the planning process must incorporate some degree of community involvement; that the scale of the project take into account possible impact on the social and natural environment; that measures be devised to increase participation of women in the development process.

In each case the Terms of Reference will not normally specify how these activities will be done-but that they have to be incorporated into the implementation or operational phase. Well-written Terms of Reference can incorporate within a project most of the concerns that are of current academic debate-for example, how is the sustainability of the project to be achieved? The Terms of Reference are also informed by the client's perspective and any legal and planning framework perspective which might exist in the project's locale.

Where clients are international development agencies they will insist on certain development parameters which directly affect project methodology. For example, many development agencies, such as the World Bank, require that more development initiatives have to be channelled to and through the private sector. Long experience of state-dominated capitalism, for example in both Eastern European and African countries, has not generated the expected levels of development benefits.

In African countries, for instance Zambia, a 'privatization unit' is selling off the state's commercial assets such as copper mines to international and local private investors. Where part of a project's remit is to support more private sector involvement in the development effort specific measures have to be devised to do this. In both Zambia and Zimbabwe, although private sector companies were and are involved in the tourist sector, there was no representative body which had the recognized stature to provide an 'industry view'.

In both countries, aided by development assistance, industry representative associations were initiated in the Tourism Council of Zimbabwe and the Zambia Tourism Council which in the latter case is being formally incorporated within the proposed Tourism and Hospitality Bill. In terms of community participation in tourism development the Zimbabwean 'Campfire' project provided benefits for village communities in return for anti-poaching and wildlife conservation activities.

This type of initiative meets the requirements for more local participation in tourism development and also helps to increase rural development particularly related to employment and income. From these examples it can be seen how the Terms of Reference of a project can ensure that general development objectives are included within the parameters of a specific project. The Terms of Reference guide the formulation of project methodology-how the project is to be implemented. It is useful here to make a distinction between project methodology and project management. The methodology determines 'how to' and project management monitors, changes and ensures that time-scales are adhered to. As noted above, very little is known about how project methodology in tourism is formulated. It is determined at the contract tender stage where the methodological proposal itself becomes an important aspect of the tender.

In fairly large projects, such as national development plans, experience suggests that methodology is derived from the 'tried and tested' approaches. These types of plans tend to break down into well-recognized components: marketing, transport, human resources development, environmental impact etc. To conform to the activities of the project and to meet the expected outcomes as specified in the Terms of Reference, little innovation is required.

The main opportunities for methodological innovation are related to the component activities. It is in these areas of activities where academics can become practitioners themselves through subcontracted inputs to the project or through academic writing which informs practitioners of developments in the field. This is the 'great divide' and where little is known about 'cross-over' activities.

To what extent are academics involved in tourism development projects as advisers or as temporary practitioners? How can they influence project methodology and/or implementation? Are tourism practitioners aware of the latest issues/developments/concepts in the field? It is these questions, largely unanswered, which should be incorporated into a new agenda. If it is accepted that there is a gap between tourism academics and tourism practitioners then how might it be bridged to the mutual benefit of both parties? The following suggestions are not exhaustive but hopefully focus on some of the fundamental concerns raised by this chapter.

RESEARCH

At a country level it should not be difficult to identify

those consulting companies with interests in and experience of tourism development projects. By means of a survey and probably personal interviews the issue of the formulation of methodology could be explored, as could the relevance and knowledge of academic publications on tourism. Information might also be gathered on the links with and use of academics in projects. A carefully structured research effort could yield information to lighten what is at present a black hole.

PUBLICATIONS

As noted above, the review system often has the effect of considerably delaying publications. In an era where the electronic media predominate, it should become increasingly possible to 'post' at least preliminary data and draft articles on specific networks accessible both to consultants and academics. There are the problems of copyright and plagiarism. However, it is one means of getting work more widely and quickly disseminated.

Another problem is that many academics would say this approach is essentially one-sided; what would the consulting companies offer in return? It may be that this type of information distribution would provide the consultancy companies with more information of what academic interests are, and who is working in what field-which may also lead to consulting opportunities for more academics.

This would facilitate 'cross-over' but some academics might argue that this would tend to compromise their objectivity as commentators on and analysts of the tourism sector. The required outputs of the project might limit if not preclude debate and experimentation on the more theoretical and conceptual issues which academics are mostly interested in.

MEETINGS

It is noticeable that in most academic conferences on tourism issues-of which there is a growing number-very few consultants or consulting companies attend. This may be due to pressure of work or perhaps because the practitioners do not have much interest in what academics are discussing?

More effort should be given to inviting and involving practitioners in these fora, probably by asking for a written or/oral presentation. Creation of more common interest will again facilitate 'cross-over'. For many younger academics it may be an occasion to understand what the consultancy imperatives are.

EDUCATION

In an increasingly professional era, most consultants will have received a university-level education. The proliferation of tourism programmes and the growth of the industry worldwide, is creating more awareness of the career potential in tourism. Academics have an opportunity to influence students with a balanced view of tourism, how it has developed and what issues might have importance to its future. A well-rounded education in the subject area should become the basis for life-long learning.

The knowledge base must be continually refreshed. Academics can help to do this. The task would be facilitated if more of the practitioners' output could 'cross-over'. Unfortunately, as most of the practitioners' work is client-confidential, it will require dispositions from the clients to release non-sensitive project materials. For example, the large number of national tourism development plans which have been completed rarely find their way into the public domain. These project outputs could become very useful teaching aids and perhaps shed light on some of the methodological issues raised in this article.

ACADEMIC PARTICIPATION

There are four areas where academics can influence tourism projects. First, is where they are invited to write the Terms of Reference for a project. Second is where they are employed by a consulting company to help devise the methodology for a project tender. Third is at the implementation stage usually involved as a specialist (*e.g.* economist, environmentalist). Fourth, where the academic is appointed to the project's Steering Committee which monitors the progress of the project. It is often possible through this involvement to input to the project methodology or to suggest changes as necessary and appropriate.

Participation will require that the academic has a reputation in the specialist field. Herein lies a problem. Although the academic may be perceived by his or her peers as a leader in the field, the practitioner may yet regard him as a citizen of an 'ivory tower'. Grossly unfair though this designation may be, tourism academics who do not engage in practical project work may find their influence marginalized or not even heeded at all. In part of course, this situation does derive from the nature of the academic's work which often involves theoretical and conceptual thinking which may not have an immediate application.

There does seem to be empirical evidence that there is a divide between tourism academics and tourism practitioners. There is a postulated need to facilitate more 'cross-over' and some measures have been suggested in this article. However what is important is to recognize that there is a synergy between the tourism academic and the tourism practitioner. There is a possibility of increasing mutual benefit, an objective which both groups should strive to achieve.

Essentially, tourism development is all about implementation. Sound or even innovative projects have no impact on development unless they are implemented. Perhaps too much of the concern of academics is about impact rather than the process of implementation. The two aspects are inextricably linked because the process of implementation is itself a methodological issue which can directly affect the impact of what is done.

To have a more central role in formulating methodology would allow the academic a real-world participatory function which should benefit the project, and the experience gained would also benefit teaching and future research. There are considerable 'cross-over' benefits to be gained by both parties if the great divide can be effectively bridged.

Integration has become a common and frequently used term in the tourism literature, particularly in the context of planning and development. Apart from Innskeep's volume relating specifically to the topic, the term finds considerable reference in writing by authors such as Gunn, Haywood, Murphy, Pearce, and Wall (1997) on general issues relating to tourism planning and development. In the more specific area of sustainable tourism, for example, we can find the term being supported in a considerable number of publications such as those by Bramwell et al. (1996), Priestley, Edwards and Coccossis (1996), Nelson, Butler and Wall (1993), Stabler (1997) and Wahab and Pigram (1997).

This is not surprising, as the concept of sustainable development implies the linking or integration of elements of the environment in an appropriate manner, Wahab and Pigram (1997:4) commenting that 'sustainability is an integrative concept'. Although the term is widely used, like sustainable development, it is rarely adequately defined. A dictionary definition describes the verb to integrate as meaning 'to make or be made into a whole; incorporate or be incorporated', and goes on 'to amalgamate or mix... with an existing community'.

In the context of tourism, therefore, we can regard integrated planning and development as meaning the process of introducing tourism into an area in a manner in which it mixes with existing elements. It is implicit in such an understanding that this introduction and mixing is done in an appropriate and harmonious way, such that the end result is an acceptable and functionally successful community, in both ecological and human terms.

Successful integration in many cases is similar to the basic principles so eloquently presented by Ian McHarg (1967) in his book Design with Nature over three decades ago. As pressure from supporters of Agenda 21 to incorporate tourism development with the principles of sustainable development increase, the successful integration of tourism with other processes and activities in destination areas becomes more significant and important. It is possible to note at least three principles which should make the concept of integration in the context of tourism appropriate and appealing to those involved in tourism development:

- Acceptability
- Efficiency and
- Harmony

The successful integration of tourism development into a community or destination should make the development more acceptable to local residents and existing resource users than when a tourism development is imposed in a segregated and unrelated manner. Successful integration can also be a much more efficient process. To most planners, developers and managers efficiency is a goal to be achieved, and steps and processes which speed the process of completion and acceptability of development are to be welcomed.

As important, perhaps, is the fact that successful integration can avoid problems that could otherwise materialize later in the operational phase of development through achieving synergy and even symbiosis with other existing activities and resource processes rather than competition or conflict. Finally, at a time when conflict resolution is an increasingly common process in development, the achievement of harmony and the avoidance of conflict through appropriate and acceptable development is another situation that is desired by planners and developers alike.

Despite this general support for the concept of integration in tourism development and planning, particularly in the last decade, in reality it is hard to find true examples on the ground. In many cases there are significant gaps between the concept as described in many plans and what actually appears and is operationalized in specific tourist destinations.

There are a number of reasons which can be put forward for this pattern of events which are discussed below. It can be argued that it is often not a lack of intent nor a lack of desire to achieve integration, but rather like the implementation of sustainable development, more a case of a lack of understanding and information about the nature of tourism which prevents the goal being achieved.

As with any process relating to development, the successful achievement of goals depends on a variety of factors. In the context of integration and its inclusion in planning there are a number of what may be termed policy issues which have to be taken into account. The integration of tourism development implies inevitably that tourism is being added to a set of one or more existing activities and processes in the particular destination. Of key importance are the intra-relationships within this set of activities and processes and potential inter-relationships between them and tourism.

- *Priorities:* In the real world very few economic or social-cultural activities are equal in priority. There is normally a constant state of competition or at best uneasy alliance between activities in most communities, some being in the ascendance and others stagnating or being in decline. In many parts of the world in which tourism has been introduced, traditional primary activities have had a long established priority, both in terms of economic importance and because of their often intricate links with cultural patterns and behaviour. Tourism is often seen as being in direct competition with these traditional activities and in such situations integration rather than imposition is essential if development is to be successful.
- *Control:* In many areas in which tourism is being introduced or expanded control of resources and governance is often vested in those community members involved in other activities. In such situations tourism may be seen as a threat to the established power structure, as a force which seeks to obtain control of resources and space. Thus acceptance may be difficult if tourism is not carefully and appropriately fitted into the existing systems. This situation is often compounded by the fact that in the case of large-scale tourism developments, ownership and control of these developments commonly lies outside the local community, and the element of external control can make acceptance of such development much more problematic. Lack of appreciation of local preferences, patterns of activities and priorities can exacerbate such a situation.

- *Scale:* Clearly, small-scale developments can generally be integrated into communities and systems more easily than large complex developments which make major demands on local resources. Tourism development occurs in a wide range of scales from generally small local operations such as the provision of accommodation in private homes or itinerant selling of souvenirs to large, often foreign-owned inclusive resorts with major space and labour requirements.
- *Stage or timing of development:* Unless tourism is being introduced into an area devoid of settlement, the destination will contain a variety of activities at various stages of development and can itself be categorized as being developed, developing or undeveloped. Even where tourism development is taking place in an unsettled area, consideration has to be taken of natural processes. In a community the stage of development can be of crucial importance with respect to the probability of the successful integration of tourism. Mature, complex or sophisticated (in the economic sense) communities have a greater chance of successfully integrating tourism development into their pattern of activity and absorbing the economic impacts of tourism than more basic economies, where the effects may be much more severe and unanticipated.
- *Community harmony or conflict:* Communities rarely have uniform views, particularly on factors such as tourism that are seen as capable of causing considerable change to and within the community. Tourism, as other forms of development, is capable of generating the full range of emotions from enthusiastic support to outright antagonism, not only over time as in Doxey's over-simplistic unidirectional model, but also from the initial suggestion of tourism before development ever occurs. The issue may be not so much how feelings towards tourism develop

over time, but whether there are opposing views at any time. There need to be policies and practices in communities to determine views towards development and to enable the community to decide what type and scale of development can be accommodated in the community before development occurs, If such processes are in place and operational, then integration of the appropriate type of development should be much more easily achieved.

Other issues are also involved in determining whether tourism development will be successfully implemented in a particular community or not, and many are place and time specific, as well as relating to the nature of the specific development.

While the issues discussed above are perhaps more abstract and general in nature, there is also a range of practical issues which significantly affect the likely success or failure of the integration of tourism in specific locations.

- *Multiplicity of form*: As Simpson and Wall note, tourism comes in many forms and its effects are extremely varied. What may be appropriate procedures for the integration of tourism development of one form may not be suitable or successful for another form. Further-more, it is rare for a destination to experience only one form of tourism or one form of tourism development during its life cycle. Thus the successful integration of one type of tourism does not guarantee that all development will be accepted and integrated in the same way, or that new forms of tourism will be able to be incorporated into the community as successfully. Different sectors, even within the same form of tourism, can place very different demands upon the destination resource base with varying levels of acceptability.
- *Dynamics:* In many respects the dynamic nature of

tourism is the most difficult and greatest problem to be overcome in achieving the successful integration of tourism. Rates of development and change are themselves inconsistent, and the faster the rate of development the more difficult the task of integration because the time available for consultation with the community and the study of ecological processes in the destination is reduced. As has been discussed elsewhere the agents of change themselves are subject to change, causing an infinite variety of inconsistency. Thus the integration process has to be dynamic and flexible itself, and capable of adapting to changing circumstances. The dynamism in the system extends to views about tourism, as well as change in economic activities and processes, in cultural behaviour, and in political viewpoints.

- *Benefits and costs*: It is not unreasonable to assume that if the attributes noted above accrue from the successful integration of tourism, then they can be regarded as benefits and will have a tangible economic form. An absence of conflict, increased speed and efficiency of planning and development and then of operation, coupled with an absence of post-development adjustment because of inappropriate scale of development, all have potential social and environmental benefits as well. However, the fact that benefits can accrue from integration does not necessarily by itself ensure the success or viability of the development. In many cases the benefits may be derived mostly or even exclusively by the developers and external agencies, allowing for dissatisfaction and opposition to continue or to develop at the local level. Benefits generally have a mirror effect, in that benefits in one area or at one level may be matched by costs in other areas and sectors. Successful integration needs to ensure that costs at the local level are at least matched by the benefits at the same level, and hopefully that they accrue to the same sectors which face costs because of the development. In many cases the benefits of tourism may accrue to new actors on the economic scene, while to other established operators there are only costs incurred by accommodating tourism development or expansion. If the principles of sustainable development are to be implemented in tourism development, then equity will become a major consideration, applying to the allocation of benefits and costs in the present as well as in the future.

In addition to the above factors, other elements such as politics and the origins of the actors involved can become significant influences on the success or failure of attempts to integrate tourism into a community. In reality the political structure and relationships within a community and with external agencies and levels of government can create strange associations and groupings of views. This can be complicated further by the origins of proponents and opponents of development and the ways in which tourism could be integrated into a community. The varying backgrounds, familiarity with the destination, and different levels of knowledge about tourism and the context for development can all affect the success or failure of attempts at integration.

The gap between the successful integration of tourism and partial or symbolic integration can be wide. A great deal depends on the attitudes of those with responsibility for tourism planning and development and the approaches which they take to co-ordinate and include the full range of viewpoints on proposed developments including those of local residents. It has been argued that if local participation is to be effective in overcoming the often inherent problems of entrenched decision-making and inequality in the allocation of benefits from development, then it must originate within the local communities themselves.

The level of involvement and the ability to bring about changes in development proposals so that the final results are truly integrated into the local systems vary widely. One of the first researchers to describe the various stages of participation was Arnstein (1969), who proposed six 'steps' in her 'Ladder of Public Participation'. More recently, Pretty (1995) has described seven stages in a typology of participation. The five categories noted below reflect the same basic elements of level of participation and decision-making power vested in the communities involved, as do Arnstein's and Pretty's typologies. They range from 'imposition' through to 'equality', reflecting to a large degree the nature of decision making in the host country and community.

- *Imposition:* Clearly the least desirable, and probably the least effective, form of integration is where it is forced upon a community without input from that community. In such cases the development is normally controlled and financed from outside the community and has the support of external and higher levels of government. The Nusa Dua development on Bali serves as an example of such a type of development. A complex of international franchise hotels and associated facilities developed by external financing with strong support from the central Indonesian government was constructed over a period of years in southern Bali in the 1980s. The resort can be said to be integrated on the basis that it has strong economic links through transportation developments and employment with other parts of Bali, is promoted as a part of Bali, not as a separate destination, and to some extent has integrated water and other elements of environmental planning and operations. It is spatially segregated from the rest of Bali by virtue of its location and design, and by the market at which it aims, which is considerably higher than that attracted by most of the rest of Bali.

- *Petition:* Whereas the previous category implied a total absence of local involvement in the decisions on location, scale, design and other elements of integration of development, this category suggests an opportunity for input. However, that input is made without obligation on the part of the decision-making agencies to accept such input or to modify their intentions. In these cases the proposal is presented to local communities for comment only after demands and petitioning for such an opportunity has been made and often at a point at which major decisions have been made. The opportunity for integration is mostly one-sided, that is, local operators and resource users may have an opportunity to adjust their patterns of operation to allow integration with the development before it is begun, or at least completed, thus allowing for an easier and possibly more successful insertion of the development. To some extent this situation reflects the process at Anuha Island discussed by Sofield, where the situation deteriorated rapidly following changes in ownership and operation and the perceptions of the level of involvement of local decision makers were abruptly changed with disastrous results.
- *Advice:* This category represents a situation in which local advice is sought as to the ways in which the development could be designed, located and operated in order to make it more integrated into the community, although the final decision-making authority still remains outside the community. There is the opportunity for local expertise and priorities to be reflected in the development, not only in its scale and operation, but also in its design and location. Integration that is effective is more likely to be achieved at this level and beyond in that there is for the first time the opportunity for adjustment to achieve integration on both the part of the

developers and of the local communities. This process was followed by National Park authorities in Canada in the 1970s when public participation was introduced to park planning for the first time.

- *Representation:* At this stage the communities have formal rights to be involved in the process of integration through planning and operation of the development. This may take the form of representation on local boards or agencies to oversee the design, construction and even operation of the development. With involvement from an early stage local expertise can be incorporated more fully into design and operational procedures and the effects of development and use on the environment be minimized. The greater the sharing of knowledge about the local environment and the operation of the development the greater the opportunity for avoiding conflict and incompatibility as tourism develops. In Canada, tourism developments in those national parks which have permanent settlements are now designed and operated in such a way, and the residents are actively involved from the early stages (Parks Canada 1994). Final decisions are still taken outside the local area, and the process can still cause concern and generate opposition, because compromises still have to be made.
- *Equality*: True equality in the integration of tourism developments is rare. It can be taken to represent the situation in which the proponents and recipients of development are treated as equals and all elements of the integration process are agreed to by all parties. Adjustments in the design and operation of developments are as likely, or perhaps even more likely than adjustments in the operation of existing activities and lifestyles. Decision making rests in both locations, the communities and the source of the development. Clearly, where development is coming from within the community and the community

operates on a democratic or equally acceptable format for its residents, then this situation should be automatic. Where development is proposed from outside, then procedures need to be in place to ensure that proponents are required to treat the communities as equals. A workable veto is obviously one way of achieving this situation. It is likely that such a situation or something equivalent may materialize in Nunavut, the soon to be established Inuit controlled section of the Canadian North West Territories, where the local governing body will not only have control of development but also the funds to carry it out.

The categories which have been discussed above represent generalized levels of local involvement in decision making, and have been discussed in a variety of forms with respect to planning, but have not been applied specifically to the integration of tourism developments. As will be discussed below, one of the major problems is that it has taken a long time for the idea of local involvement in the tourism planning process to become a reality in many areas. In many parts of the world, unfortunately, a large proportion of which are the scenes of major tourism development and expansion, it still does not exist. However, the involvement of local actors in planning does not necessarily carry over into involvement in development and even less so in operations. Integration is much more than planning, however, and involves all elements from design, planning, construction and operation if it is to be truly successful. The presence of local involvement does not guarantee successful integration, but one may argue strongly that its absence is very likely to result in unsuccessful integration.

If it is accepted that current thinking and attitudes with respect to tourism development are strongly in favour of an integrative approach, and that such an approach is very much in line with the principles of sustainable development, which also appears to have widespread political and popular support, it is perhaps surprising that examples of the successful integration of tourism are hard to find. Pearce's example of such an approach in Sarawak is one case where external advisers have gone much further than most in clearly expressing the need for and utility of integration. The Integrated Rural Tourism Development Programmes for Andalusia, discussed by Cavaco represent another. In reality, while the intent may be present in other areas, although one may question whether there is little more than symbolic intent in some situations, there are a number of factors which make implementation difficult to achieve.

- *Lack of equality:* Despite long-standing calls for local and community involvement in tourism, echoed strongly in Our Common Future, local communities do not have the same power as higher levels of government or large-scale external development agencies. Local activities, especially where these are small-scale and highly fragmented, for example small family farms or individually owned fishing boats, can rarely be effectively and strongly represented when large-scale developments are being promoted and discussed. Different priorities are involved at different levels of government and local concerns may be subordinated to national or regional level policies. Such a situation can often mean that while tourism may be integrated in planning at national and regional levels, in reality it becomes imposed at the local level. Efforts may be made to integrate it at the community level, but in such situations existing activities are more likely to have to be adjusted to accommodate tourism than tourism significantly modified to fit in with established local activities. Such situations are common to development of all types. It is rare for local interests, generally represented by a small and limited power base, to be able to successfully achieve and retain equality with higher levels of government and large external private sector corporations. When they are able to do so, it is often because specific local conditions such as geographical attributes and timing, along with the contributions of key individuals, provide the means to achieve such equality of power.

- *Lack of desire*: To achieve successful integration can require considerable resources of time and money, as well as consistent commitment. In most countries elected representatives have relatively short-term viewpoints, often only as far as the next election. To ensure proper integration requires involvement from the first stage of the initial proposal for development through to monitoring the operational phase of developments. Even if the same decision-makers and officials were in power throughout that period, their priorities and commitments are likely to change and their concerns for specific developments in specific areas likely to wane after development has occurred. There are marked similarities with the issue-attention cycle of impact analysis. The environmental impact analysis process often attracts considerable attention in the early stages of a project, but decreasing attention is generally paid as the project continues, and in very few cases does monitoring continue and rarely are the original projections of impact reviewed and verified once the development is in place and operating. Resources are rarely allocated to ensure that integration of development continues into the operational phase, even if integration was achieved during the planning and development of a project. Development rarely stops when initial construction is completed and the dynamic element of tourism noted above almost always results in modifications to the physical and operational characteristics of most projects over time. Such modifications should also be reviewed and assessed as to their likelihood of being successfully integrated into the local environment.

- *Lack of appreciation*: Despite all of the research and attention given to tourism over the past two or three decades, there is still considerable ignorance of its effects and the way in which it operates at all levels. The blindly optimistic view of tourism as an economic panacea promoted in the 1960s, when it was seen as the salvation of declining areas and thus pushed forward at almost any cost, has fortunately changed as the costs as well as the benefits of tourism are being more accurately assessed. However, to some extent the pendulum has swung too far the other way, and tourism is now often envisioned as a supplementary form of economic activity which can be easily accommodated in many peripheral or marginal areas with little adjustment. It is often assumed that tourism will automatically be compatible with existing activities, for example, that local farmers will supply hotels with food and local fisherman have ready markets for their catches, ignoring the fact that many hotel chains prefer to buy in bulk from offshore suppliers to ensure reliability and consistency in supply and quality, and that many tourists demand foodstuffs that cannot be produced locally. Tourism is a complex, resource-specific industry operating at a global scale, often with scant regard for local priorities. Failure to appreciate that it is an industry with global links, dependencies and relationships can result not only in an inability to achieve integration, but ultimately the replacement of a weak monoculture by one that is strong and dominant, at least in the short term.
- *Lack of mechanisms:* There is a general lack of appropriate mechanisms for ensuring the integration of tourism. There is widespread acknowledgment of the fragmentation and complexity of tourism, and the

difficulty of exerting consistent control over the industry, along with its general failure to successfully regulate itself. For many other economic activities there are established agencies which are designed and empowered to control such elements as production, quality, price, marketing and participation, for example, agricultural marketing boards such as the Wheat Board in Canada, the White Fish Authority in Great Britain or Atomic Energy Authorities in many countries. No such bodies exist for tourism, and control and regulation is left with agencies not normally specifically equipped for the task. Planning authorities in most countries at the national level are either concerned with broad strategies or with promotion of development or both, and control and regulation including integration are found at regional and local levels if they exist at all. Whether tourism is sufficiently unique to require a specific mechanism to ensure its regulation and integration is uncertain. What is certain is that without appropriate mechanisms (along with the desire to enforce them, as noted above) tourism is not likely to be effectively integrated on principles of equity at even the planning stage, let alone the operational stages of development.

- *Lack of data and knowledge*: The lack of detailed knowledge of the way that tourism relates to and impacts on other activities has been noted above. One of the main reasons for this lack of knowledge relates to the lack of data on tourism and on the environment in which it operates. Traditionally data have been collected and analysed sectorally, which has mitigated against a holistic and integrated approach. In addition, data were often from one limited time period only, making it extremely difficult to identify and attribute changes over time to any particular causal agent. Monitoring change was not only expensive and time consuming, but often impossible on the scale necessary. Such change as was identified was often limited to small areas and was rarely placed in a regional, let alone a national context. Much data were collected for administrative units rather than for natural ecosystems, which made identification of causation and scale of effect much more difficult also. Only in recent years has it become possible, through the use of remotely collected data, for example from satellite imaging systems, to collect data at a scale suitable to be able to understand and monitor change in natural systems. Even then, analysis of such data was difficult until suitable techniques such as Geographic Information Systems became available and were applied to tourism. The advent of a wide range of relatively user-friendly systems for the spatial analysis of data combined with increasing ease of access to large scale data means that one of the major blocks to effective integration planning may be removed.

The concept of integration is a popular one in the tourism literature and calls for its adoption have increased significantly with the popularization and support for the concept of sustainable development. Successful sustainable development inevitably neither requires the application of an integrative approach, since by definition it demands that the development process not eliminate future options nor prevents the continued operations, especially of indigenous peoples. In discussing planning the management of tourism for the future, Maitland comments:

There is increasing interaction between tourism and other industries and between visitors and host populations unconnected with tourism. The consequence is that we need tourism planning which integrates tourism development into broader strategies for the development of places, and of non-tourism businesses.

As tourism becomes tied ever more firmly to global processes and agents, so it will increasingly be involved with many activities and processes unrelated directly to leisure, and it will only be successful if its development is integrated with these other processes. While failure of a tourism enterprise at the global level through a lack of integration may be unfortunate, tourism development at a local level which is not suitably integrated with local activities and processes can be disastrous. The complete integration of tourism development is unlikely in many communities, just as the attainment of sustainability is more of a goal than a reality in most situations. However, sincere attempts at integration which include the involvement of local communities are more likely to be well received than development for which no effort is made to reach compatibility, if not symbiosis, with local ecological, economic and social systems. Even where sustainability is not an issue, development which is a part of a community is generally more successful than development which is apart from a community.

FACTORS INFLUENCING TOURISM

Before presenting the case findings, a number of broader comments need to be made regarding lecturers' perceptions of uncontrollable or system-wide factors which have been emerging as influential in the development of Tourism. Additionally influences are revealed which influence the way in which Tourism has developed at more than one 'level', for example, the issue of modularisation which, according to most lecturers, features at both the institutional and the department/school level, and the perceived importance of the subject's status or respectability which features at all four levels of influence. Despite the fact that there are system-wide factors or issues beyond Tourism lecturers' control which have had implications for the nature of the subject, Tourism is seen to have remained within the subject specialists' control during its developmental years.Some of the general trends in HE, for example, the perception of a decline in students' academic ability and the increasing importance of quality assurance policies such as the Research Assessment Exercise (RAE) and Subject Review, have featured in the way in which Tourism has evolved, but are not perceived to have hindered its development.

At an institutional level lecturers felt that Tourism has represented for most, an opportunity for solid recruitment at minimal cost, rather than an opportunity to expand into previously uncharted academic waters. Competition between institutions is perceived to have heightened in the mid 1990s, resulting in the possible emergence of a virtual 'league table' of providers of Tourism at the turn of the century, and changing priorities with regard to research agenda at the institutional level compound similar frustration felt at department level.

Modularisation in HE receives mixed reactions from lecturers who perceive a reduced level of curriculum space and problems of contextualisation for Tourism as being unfortunate by-products of a system which is applauded within the wider HE system because of associated increased flexibility of provision and widening choice for students. Policies and activities at department or school level which influence Tourism subject development are numerous and in many cases filter down from the institution as a whole.

The issue of subject status is again prevalent at the department level and the extent of lecturers' concern about the appropriateness of individuals to teach Tourism is a reflection of their insistence that the subject still has to prove itself in academic terms.

There is a clear message which emerges, that inappropriate individuals teaching Tourism have hindered the quality and integrity of the subject's development. In an environment where goal-posts regarding teaching and research are seen to change constantly, the importance of maintaining personal aims and agendas is regarded as critical in ensuring healthy development of the subject. The remainder of the paper focuses on the two critical factors which have influenced Tourism's development, that of the individual lecturer's influence and the subject's perceived status in HE. The first of the two critical influences on Tourism's development focuses on individual Tourism lecturers. Members of the Tourism academic community interviewed have been seen to cope in the face of institutional change and constraints, resolute in their need, on occasion, to swim against the tide as a relatively content community.

At the same time they have accepted the continual, and what they regard as frustrating changes, whilst ensuring the community maintains a voice at department and institution level when human resources are being allocated and programme additions and deletions considered.

In spite of the fact that lecturers interviewed regarded the Tourism academic community as playing a critical role in the way the subject has developed, this is not a community which can be characterised by togetherness, or involving a team approach to subject development. Becher has argued that 'being a member of a disciplinary community involves a sense of identity and personal commitment'.

Whilst the sense of identity for the Tourism academic community has not become as apparent (linked to a perceived lack of respectability) or consistent as one might have expected after 15 years of the subject's existence at an undergraduate level, the commitment of individuals to the teaching of courses cannot be doubted in the light of this study's findings.

The academic community which has emerged is one characterised by individuals' expectations, personal goals and values which have been critical in shaping Tourism and its developing curriculum. Trowler (1997) has emphasised the importance of individuals in HE and the potential impact that their aspirations and values can have on HE, and this study would lend support to this view.

The fact that Tourism lecturers appear to cope in the face of considerable teaching pressures could also reflect, on the part of institutions' management, a soft approach to managing people where a committed group of individuals is developed by allowing Tourism lecturers a considerable amount of academic freedom regarding what they teach and how they teach it.

However, this soft approach, whilst encouraging committed individuals to pursue their own course development, does not appear to have been as successful in encouraging a truly committed Tourism academic community at institutional level when programme teams have been required to work together on programme validations or revalidations. Trowler noted that those lecturers who appear to be coping with their teaching workloads are likely to place activities like programme planning meetings very much at the bottom of their list of priorities.

The fact that a number of lecturers all but 'stick their heads in the sand' when such meetings are called, is reflective of a community which will busy themselves with what they perceive to be the more important issue of ensuring the delivery of their own courses. This is not to say that Tourism lecturers lack professionalism, which is evident in their commitment to research and teaching and interaction between these two key activities in HE.

This relatively young, still developing specialism remains at the evolutionary stage and realistically, is delivered by a diverging community, owing to the enthusiasm and determination of its members in delivering courses which meet their own personal aspirations and goals, rather than those of a collective, cohesive community.

This does not, however, undervalue the achievement of those individuals in contributing towards a new subject which remains, for the time being, economically viable and diverse in its nature, reflecting the changing interests of the Tourism lecturing community.

What has emerged is a process of self-alienation from opportunities to contribute to subject development by the specialists who have, at the same time, made clear their discomfort with the lack of control they have over recruitment and promotion of the subject. This might be a reflection of the fact that some Tourism lecturers do not perceive the programme planning process to contribute towards the development of Tourism as a subject, perhaps favouring individual course development and research as the key factor in this process.

However, the trend which has emerged for lecturers to concentrate their efforts on course rather than programme development, could have implications for the subject's wider development as a cohesive curriculum, particularly if tensions emerge between those lecturers who do get involved in programme development and those who effectively choose to ignore it.

A concern has been emerging for the appropriate matching of lecturer to course, extended in some cases to a concern that lecturers from other departments or schools have been drafted in to cover courses which require the knowledge and experience of other disciplinary areas.

Full-time Tourism lecturers interviewed expressed considerable concern over the fact that non-Tourism specialists were delivering generic Business courses to Tourism undergraduates, who were left to take responsibility themselves for providing the necessary contextualisation.

The existence and quality of Tourism- specific knowledge amongst non-Tourism specialists appeared then to be of more concern to Tourism lecturers who have been defending 'their own patches of intellectual ground' in their attempts to ensure some level of influence over who is recruited from outside the specialism to deliver courses which contribute towards Tourism degree programmes.

Although there has been no evidence of a need to see Tourism recognised as a discipline per se, Tourism lecturers have been inclined to exert some level of ownership over their subject and to ensure the appropriate content of the curriculum, which has been after all, delivered by members of a wide variety of academic communities beyond the boundaries of the 'Tourism community'. This might account for the need amongst many lecturers to see Tourism's profile and respectability as an academic subject enhanced. Little evidence has emerged to support a view that Tourism lecturers should take a step back from their teaching and consider the wider implications for the programme as a whole of removing entirely or amending the contents of a course.

In the light of this evidence, not only has the Tourism curriculum been changing all the time, but it has been changing without any real attention paid to the implications of minor course amendments, exclusion and new additions to the overall thrust of programmes.

Individual desires and enthusiasms to alter the nature of a course or even to eradicate a course altogether could have been threatening the ability of students to meet programme aims and objectives. With regard to the subject's future in HE, the ad hoc addition and removal of courses from programmes could threaten the achievement of programme aims and learning outcomes. The nature of this divergent academic community is by no means unique to Tourism.

Previous studies have been able to clarify 'tribes' within disciplinary communities. For example, economists, sociologists and marketers are just some of the individual tribes within the Business Studies disciplinary community which has been described by Macfarlane (1998) as diverging in nature, made up of a number of 'refugees, nomads and tourists' due to its reliance on so many disciplines.

Tourism lecturers appear to belong to a community which is characterised by individuals from a wide variety of academic disciplines, although there does appear to be an increasing number who are gaining named Tourism academic qualifications at higher degree level.

It might, however be inappropriate to talk about the Tourism community in terms of a tribe, as this might imply that there is, in fact, a sense of togetherness and working towards a common goal which has not yet, according to this study, come to light.

In short, this paper has revealed the critical role played by the individual Tourism lecturer which is indicative of a still developing subject, reflected in the rapid movement of Tourism staff into and out of institutions, coupled with the frequency of inappropriate matching of staff to specialist courses and the incidence of curriculum change to suit particular circumstances rather than careful planning. In essence, a situation has emerged where control of the logistics of offering Tourism as a subject in HE rests at the institutional level, as it is here that decisions are made about who studies Tourism at undergraduate level and what information is communicated to potential students regarding the structure and content of their Tourism programmes.

However, individual lecturers in their teaching have been given the freedom to deliver the subject according to their own personal desires and aspirations, but have not necessarily taken up opportunities to make changes to the curriculum through the programme planning and validation process. Having analysed the significant role played by individuals within the Tourism academic community on the subject's development, the discussion now turns to an evaluation of the continuing importance of the academic-vocational debate in the context of the developing curriculum, with particular reference to its contribution to the subject's status in HE.

TOURISM IN HIGHER EDUCATION

The academic-vocational debate and the perceived status of Tourism in HE clearly involves the individual lecturers described earlier playing a vital role in the subject's development. Interviews with Tourism lecturers reveal the continuing importance of the academic-vocational debate which surrounds the purpose and development of HE programmes and the perceived importance of academic respectability.

Whilst the two issues have not necessarily been explicitly linked in the context of Tourism's development in the first two decades in HE, this paper offers evidence which might support a view that the subject's status is inextricably linked to the Tourism academic community's relationships with the tourism industry.

The extent to which Tourism programmes are delivered in accordance with the more vocational aims detailed in promotional literature and validation documents can certainly be challenged. Undergraduate Tourism programmes have been promoted in recent years as preparation for work in the tourism, or other service industry, as evidenced in Airey and Johnson's study of 1997. However, this study found that the majority of Tourism lecturers appear to have been taking on a form of liberal vocationalism in their approach to delivering their courses, which saw them combining academic and vocational aspects in what Raffe described as an aggregative approach to education, despite a tendency for stated aims to favour the employment preparation focus.

This flexible approach to focusing vocational programmes in HE on preparation for work in general rather than stating explicit Tourism careers has also been reflected in the emergence of undergraduate Tourism programmes which could be described as simultaneously offering both an education for, and an education about, Tourism, as in the case of Business Studies.

Tourism's development, according to Tourism lecturers, has been influenced by both a focus upon subject specific knowledge and skills development, and upon the development of transferable, academic skills. The critical factor here was the recognition that developing knowledge for Tourism was seen as just as important an aspect of preparation for work as the industry specific practical or skills-based aspects of Tourism education.

Some lecturers were even beginning to argue that an education about Tourism could actually be a better preparation for employment in the tourism industry than an education for Tourism. This supports an argument proposed by Ainley who felt that 'the independent ability of students to pursue knowledge, up to degree level and beyond' was even more useful to them in preparation for a given vocation than perhaps vocational information during their studies.

It is now clear that lecturers are placing greater emphasis on traditional academic abilities than vocationally oriented skills at course delivery level, even when a Tourism programme's aim was essentially to provide graduates for the tourism or other service industry. There is, however, a further possible explanation for lecturers' tendency to avoid the overtly vocational courses, and to focus instead on the more academic aspects of the subject. However clearly an institution promotes the vocational aims of its Tourism provision, the individual lecturers' need to focus on the academic, more respected aspects of the subject, might have overshadowed the vocational intent of that provision.

Whereas respectability for Tourism as an academic subject has been viewed by lecturers interviewed as an issue over which they feel they have little influence or control, their decision to focus on the academic aspects of Tourism, and to distance themselves from courses which have clear vocational links, is to an extent, evidence of the considerable impact they have exerted over the subject's perceived respectability. There are in fact a number of further reasons why lecturers focus upon the provision of academic courses, other than reasons of respectability.

Firstly, lecturers might be intrinsically interested in the academic aspects and, as long as they have the apparent freedom to teach what they are interested in, they will continue to do so. Secondly, as mentioned earlier, institutions might not be capable of delivering vocational courses due to the nature of the lecturing staff they recruit; this might be the reason why institutions do not lean heavily on staff who are not delivering what the documentation states should be happening.

Thirdly, there might be a total misunderstanding on the part of programme planners about the needs of the industry. Given that lecturers probably know more about these needs (which may involve general as opposed to specific skills) than senior programme planners, they may believe they are, in fact, delivering what the industry wants. With this evidence in mind, therefore, a contradiction has been unearthed regarding the provision of Tourism as an undergraduate subject in HE.

Whilst the stated focus remains that of preparing graduates for the world of work in the Tourism and other industries, lecturers admit to being reticent in involving tourism industry professionals in the planning, design and delivery of Tourism courses.

This is despite the fact that much of the validation documentation and institutions' mission statements highlight the importance of industry involvement. Whilst institutions say they are offering an education for Tourism in programme validation material which reflects the mission of the institution as a whole, the industry which could benefit the most from graduates with that education is rarely offered more than a token role in its delivery.

The vast majority of Tourism industry involvement in an education for itself, and other service industries, involves a seat on the validation or revalidation board and the occasional guest lecture arranged by individual Tourism lecturers on an ad hoc basis, which are regarded as one-off insights into industry practice rather than a valuable contribution to the overall Tourism education package.

This might not, however, be indicative of approaches to industry involvement at all institutions which offer Tourism undergraduate programmes but is, nevertheless, an emerging trend which featured in this study.

This apparent trend for some individuals to distance themselves from opportunities to work with the tourism industry in preparing programmes and coursescould be further evidence of an attempt, on the part of Tourism lecturers, to rid the subject of vocational links which they perceive to be detrimental to its respectability in the wider academic community.

Another reason for avoiding links with the tourism industry could be that many Tourism lecturers come from other disciplines or subjects and do not necessarily want to sever these links. Reluctance amongst Tourism academics to foster links with the industry might also account for the difficulties experienced by the National Liaison Group for Higher Education in Tourism (NLG), now the Association of Tourism in Higher Education (ATHE), to gain widespread support over the last seven years.

Despite its aim to 'promote the development and recognition of tourism as a subject for study in the UK' and 'to identify and communicate good practice, statistics and other information about first degrees and postgraduate qualifications in tourism', it has been perceived by Tourism lecturers interviewed to be a body made up of committed individuals but was regarded as having been 'an outside body looking in' to Tourism in HE.

In this sense, lecturers interviewed did not feel that they had any control over the activities taken on by the Group. In view of the efforts of the NLG to bring as many representatives from HE and the industry together in the last seven years or so to discuss the nature and direction of the subject, it is difficult to understand why this perception has emerged.

What is more, of the 50 institutions which offered Tourism at undergraduate level in the academic year 1998/99, only 30 were paid up members of the NLG therefore it could easily be argued that membership of the Group would itself lead to opportunities to influence its key activities.

The NLG has reported continual problems in encouraging a greater proportion of institutions to become active members of the Group, and this could be put down to its professed industry links which have been regarded as countering Tourism academics' desire to see vocational links severed in order to enhance the subject's academic respectability.

If you do not agree with the fundamental aims of the organisation, you are simply not going to join. It is important to note that four of the five institutions which took part in the interview stage of this study were members of the NLG during the academic year 1998/99.

Therefore, it would appear that comments reflecting a lack of awareness of the Group's activities and its key purpose might reflect gaps in communication between NLG representatives and Tourism lecturers within institutions/ schools or an unwillingness or inability for tourism lecturers to take on board the potential importance of a group whose remit has focused on facilitating and advising on the nature and delivery of Tourism in HE.

Whilst the activities of the NLG have been perceived by some lecturers as being beyond their control, the Group has in fact been committed to increasing its membership, widening participation in its conferences and encouraging those involved in the design and delivery of Tourism, (in education and industry) to produce practical written guides which reflect the developing Tourism curriculum and areas of good practice in its design and delivery in higher education.

The debate surrounding the role and effectiveness of the NLG continues into 2001. In adopting its new name, ATHE has in fact opted to drop its industry-link role and to take on the role of subject association for Tourism in HE. If this is an indication of a more direct approach to gaining academic respectability for the subject, then ATHE might well see its membership increase and a true community approach to curriculum development emerge.

In spite of this apparent trend for Tourism academics to distance themselves from the tourism industry, one of the key concerns of lecturers regarding the RAE was the fact that the exercise was not supportive of practical or industry based research.

A key characteristic of Tourism research carried out by Tourism lecturers in the last few years has been the fact that it was in most cases 'RAE-led'. In short, lecturers felt that departments and institutions as a whole were seen to be very supportive of individuals who would and could write for the RAE and were seen, in fact, to create research appointments and sabbaticals for that very purpose, irrespective of the increased teaching workloads for non-research active lecturers.

This has led to criticism from some who felt that industry relevant research output which would not be suitable for contribution to the RAE was not supported or encouraged. Completion of academic or pure research which was sure to get published in one of the handful of highly acclaimed, refereed Tourism journals was the only way in which Tourism lecturers could be sure of gaining valuable remission from teaching to carry out research.

This approach to research, whilst recognised as a fact of life in HE in the late 1990s, was regarded as unfortunate in the context of Tourism as an emerging subject, as it has important vocational content which, it could be argued, had just as much right to contribute to research evaluations. These complaints from a few lecturers, however, need to be considered in the context of an academic community which, for the most part, is not all that supportive of links with the tourism industry and are contradictory to the more general view that academic aspects of the subject need to be pursued if respectability is to be gained.

6

Indigenous Tourism and Service

INTRODUCTION

Aboriginal tourism gives Indigenous people the chance to tell their story in their way, to share cultural insights, traditional practices and contemporary concerns with non-Indigenous Australians and international visitors. Indigenous communities view tourism as a means of both educating others about Indigenous culture, and creating employment and training opportunities at a local level. Aboriginal tourism experiences are varied, but a common thread is the inclusion of insights about the cultural knowledge, lifestyle and beliefs of Australia's Indigenous people.

Aboriginal tourism goes beyond the lifestyles and traditions of Indigenous people who live on homelands, out-stations and remote communities to include the urban experience of Australia's Indigenous persons. Rock art tours, politically themed art exhibitions, live theatre and stories from the Dreamtime told around a campfire are all expressions of Indigenous culture. The National Aboriginal and Torres Strait Islander Tourism Industry Strategy defines Indigenous tourism as including all forms of participation by Indigenous persons in tourism:

- As employers
- As employees
- As investors
- As joint venture partners
- Providing Indigenous cultural tourism products
- Providing mainstream tourism products.

In Aboriginal culture the significance of land is intimately bound in the spirituality surrounding the origins of landscapes, animals, plants and people. Traditional owners, or custodians, have a responsibility to look after the environmental, cultural and spiritual wellbeing of the land. This unique relationship and respect for the land is increasingly attracting visitors seeking to 'touch the earth'.

Another key element of Aboriginal tourism is cultural control, considered crucial to maintaining authenticity and preventing cultural exploitation and cultural appropriation. Intellectual and cultural property rights, along with copyright issues, are of particular concern to Indigenous. Authenticity is important to international visitors.

The Wet Tropics World Heritage Area (WHA) was declared in 1988. It covers an area of 894 420 hectares and mainly includes tropical rainforest extending from Townsville to Cooktown in northeastern Queensland. It is managed by the Wet Tropics Management Authority (WTMA) based in Cairns, and the Queensland Parks and Wildlife Service (QPWS) is responsible for field management and permits for activities in the WHA.

There are twenty Indigenous language groups in or near the Wet Tropics WHA, which also includes Indigenous communities such as Yarrabah, south of Cairns, Mona Mona, near Kuranda, and Wujal Wujal, in the Daintree region. The involvement of Rainforest Indigenous communities is set out in Wet Tropics WHA legislation, the Wet Tropics Management Plan 1998, and in the key policy document Protection through Partnerships.

WTMA negotiates with Rainforest Indigenous groups on cultural protocols, planning, site management, infrastructure, walking-tracks, and joint management agreements. Three Indigenous community liaison officers are employed on contract by WTMA, to consult Indigenous groups on management issues.

Rainforest-based nature tourism and ecotourism is a major activity in the Wet Tropics WHA. In 1998, more than 210 commercial tour operators had permits to operate in the Wet

Tropics region. Half of all Queensland nature-based tour operators are located in Far North Queensland, with the majority visiting sites in the Wet Tropics. The region has an estimated 2.8 million visitors per year. High-use areas include Mossman Gorge with 500 000 visitors and the Daintree with over 300 000 visitors per year.

Indigenous tourism ventures include Kuku Yalanji Dreamtime Walks in Mossman Gorge; Native Guide Safari Tours conducted by Hazel Douglas in the Daintree; Tjapukai Aboriginal Cultural Park in Cairns; Menmuny Museum in Yarrabah; Nganyaji Cultural Centre in Ravenshoe; and guided rainforest walks at Malanda Falls with Ngadjonjii elder, Ernie Raymont. Kuku Yalanji art and craft workshops, storytelling and Indigenous-guided rainforest walks are included at the Daintree Ecolodge.

New Indigenous tourism ventures in 2002 include Kuku Yalanji Coastal Habitat Tours marketed by Daintree Ecolodge; Bunda Dibandji Art Site Tour near Kuranda, a joint venture between Djabugay Tribal Aboriginal Corporation and Cedar Park Resort; and Gugubarabi Echo Creek Walk in the Tully Valley, a partnership between El Rancho del Rey and local Jirrbal guides, Robert and Ernie Grant. Other Rainforest Indigenous participation in Wet Tropics tourism includes employment as QPWS rangers, the construction of boardwalks, and cultural heritage signs in national parks.

Tourism in the Wet Tropics WHA directly generates $179 million, while flow-on tourism expenditure in the local region is around $753 million. At present, Rainforest Indigenous groups do not receive any licensing income from tourism operations in the Wet Tropics and visitors do not pay park entry fees at popular rainforest sites such as waterfalls, lakes and rainforest boardwalks in National Parks.

Tourism use should contribute to the conservation and understanding of Aboriginal cultural heritage and help Aboriginal people as tourism industry participants to achieve economic and social benefits.

Apart from consulting with traditional owners about site management, there is limited Indigenous participation in the development and management of tourism in the Wet Tropics WHA. Indigenous cultural and land issues are addressed by the North Queensland Land Council representing Wet Tropics native title claimants, Indigenous land management agencies and by Indigenous community liaison officers. New cultural protocols will guide consultations with Indigenous peoples about permit applications in the Wet Tropics. Wet Tropics nature-based tourism strategy Indigenous involvement in rainforest-based tourism is a central part of the Wet Tropics Nature Based Tourism Strategy.

This tourism strategy for the Wet Tropics World Heritage Area of North Queensland aims to 'facilitate Aboriginal involvement in (nature) tourism and tourism management'. It also acknowledges that 'Rainforest Aboriginal people have native title rights and are partners in management of and participation in nature-based tourism in the Wet Tropics'.

The Strategy has policy statements on 'Rainforest Aboriginal People's Rights and Interests', including the cultural responsibilities of native title landholders, visitor site management involving traditional owners, and Indigenous involvement in nature-based tourism. This included participation, employment and training in tourism, interpretation of natural and cultural values and partnerships in tourism, such as cultural tours at Mossman Gorge.

The Bama Wabu Rainforest Aboriginal Association was listed as a key partner in Wet Tropics marketing guidelines, monitoring visitor sites, and setting accreditation levels for tour operators. Indigenous groups, though, were not involved in permit approvals for commercial tour operators in the Wet Tropics. This Strategy endorsed nature-based tourism in the Wet Tropics WHA that promotes Indigenous cultural heritage values and empowers Indigenous peoples as participants in the tourism industry. ATSIC, Bama Wabu and local Indigenous groups contributed to the policies and principles for the Wet Tropics Nature Based Tourism Strategy.

Consultation with traditional owners about site planning and management was required for most of the popular visitor areas in the Wet Tropics WHA. Rainforest Indigenous interests in tourism or cultural interpretation were also mentioned for eighteen visitor sites, including Mossman Gorge, Cathedral Fig Tree, Lake Barrine, Lake Eacham, Tully Gorge, and five scenic waterfalls: Murray, Josephine, Millstream, Blencoe and Wallaman Falls.

Other sites are under review with traditional owners about tourism concerns. The Strategy also states the need for assessment of the impacts of tourism on Indigenous cultural landscapes in the Wet Tropics. It does not address the specific programmes or training required for developing Indigenous tourism ventures at key visitor sites.

Wet Tropics Walking Strategy

The Wet Tropics Walking Strategy identified 145 managed walks in the Wet Tropics WHA region. Rainforest peoples were identified as key stakeholders with opportunities for walk management and cultural tourism. This Strategy acknowledged the cultural significance of walking tracks with many based on traditional trading routes through rainforest areas. Indigenous participation in this Strategy included employment through tourism operations, guided walks, track construction and maintenance.

Negotiation on walking-track routes, protection of cultural sites, permits for commercial operations, and resources to fund Rainforest groups in track construction were highlighted. The Indigenous cultural setting was one of four key criteria used to assess walk experiences, focusing on Indigenous history, use, perceptions, names, cultural associations and stories about walkways.

Walkingtrack management by community rangers and Indigenous cultural walks were also identified for key rainforest areas such as Malanda Falls, Bare Hill, Wabunga Wayemba, Echo Creek Falls, Barron Gorge, and Murray Falls/ Kirrama Range. Some eighty per cent of the Wet Tropics WHA is claimable under native title legislation and sixteen claims covering 282 966ha have been lodged to date.

Land-use agreements have been negotiated recently by WTMA with the Mona Mona and Wujal Wujal Aboriginal communities. Indigenous Land Use (ILU) agreements have also been reached with major tourism developments in the Cairns region. These agreements cover Skyrail Rainforest Cableway and Tjapukai Aboriginal Cultural Park, located on adjacent sites under a native title claim, with guarantees of employment for the local Djabugay people, protection of cultural heritage, and Indigenous approval of cultural presentations.

In 2002, the Mamu Aboriginal Corporation and Johnstone Shire Council, based in Innisfail, signed an ILU Heads of Agreement for a proposed new rainforest canopy walkway in the Wooroonooran National Park.

This Agreement also provides for Indigenous employment, protection of cultural heritage, and cultural tourism input at the Mamu canopy walk, during and after construction. The Queensland Ecotourism Plan 2003-2008 (Tourism Queensland 2002) also recognises the importance of negotiating native title claims in managing protected areas for ecotourism.

Indigenous Tourism in the Wet Tropics WHA

Kuku Yalanji Dreamtime Walks in Mossman Gorge won the 2002 Tourism Queensland Award for Aboriginal and Torres Strait Islander Tourism, previously won by Tjapukai Aboriginal Cultural Park. However, this tourism venture operated by the Mossman Gorge Aboriginal Community depends on CDEP wages for guides and is not open on weekends. Indigenous tour operators also require QPWS permits in national parks and approval from WTMA to build new infrastructure such as visitor centres and walking tracks in the WHA.

Indigenous tours also compete with other rainforest day tours offered from Cairns, Port Douglas and Mission Beach, and mainly attract self-drive independent travellers rather than regular tour groups. Thus new Indigenous guided tours in 2002 are partnerships with established rainforest lodges in the Wet Tropics. There are other key issues for developing Rainforest Indigenous tourism in the Wet Tropics WHA.

Tasting rainforest fruits (bush tucker) are part of an Indigenous cultural experience that may be constrained by seasonal availability, or environmental laws that prohibit taking or using natural resources in protected areas. One Indigenous tour operator in the Wet Tropics used to let visitors taste rainforest fruits, but a sign in the operator's vehicle now asks guests not to touch or eat anything in the rainforest. Telling tourists how (Rainforest) Indigenous peoples ate bushfoods and utilised the natural environment, as a past practice, seems to contradict the image of Indigenous culture as 'alive and authentic'.

Since 1990, Rainforest Indigenous peoples have sought to have the Wet Tropics officially re-listed by the World Heritage Convention for its Indigenous cultural values, along with current natural heritage values, in order to manage jointly the WHA. With this official cultural recognition, 'they would become equal partners rather than seen as "stakeholders"' in Wet Tropics' management, including tourism. Rainforest Indigenous groups did not consent to WHA listing of the Wet Tropics region, neither have they benefited economically from rainforest tourism in the area.

Funding for new tourism infrastructure such as rainforest walking tracks and cultural centres has been provided through the Queensland Heritage Trails Network. Ongoing funding for Indigenous groups to maintain and preserve Wet Tropics WHA values is required, drawn from an environmental levy on visitors. ILU agreements for major tourism projects such as Tjapukai, Skyrail and the Mamu Canopy Walk have generated Indigenous employment and protection of cultural heritage.

Allocation of commercial tourism permits to Rainforest Indigenous groups for key sites, with leaseback or licensing arrangements for tour operators, would also increase the economic benefits of tourism for Indigenous communities.

Putting the 'ECO' in Tourism

Bicycling on back roads. Trekking a 2,000-year-old trail. Crouching in the sand to measure a giant sea turtle. Sipping chai and savoring chapati prepared at a local Indian restaurant. However diverse the modern vacation, there's a common thread that ties each together: the traveller's thirst for discovery, passion for authenticity and interest in helping preserve and protect the planet.

"We're longing for gung-ho, do-something, learn-something, give-back-something vacations that will exhilarate us and leave us feeling good," write Daniel and Sally Wiener Grotta in The Green Travel Sourcebook, eloquently capturing the sentiment of the globe-trotting environmentalist. "We want vacations that will allow us to experience intimately the people and places we visit, while not inadvertently polluting the environment or contributing to an oppressive political regime, and perhaps make the world a better place."

Defining Green Travel

Ecotourism, or ecotravel, strives to do just that. "Ecotravel helps conserve fragile ecosystems, support endangered species and habitats, preserve indigenous cultures and develop sustainable local economies," sums up Megan Epler Wood, president of The International Ecotourism Society. "By looking at travel alternatives and making informed choices, you can minimize your impact and positively contribute to the conservation of natural environments, local economies and cultures."

That's something the mainstream travel industry has yet to accomplish. In popular resort areas like Cancun and Hawaii, overbuilt waterfront hotels have contributed to beach erosion, flooding and the disappearance of natural wetlands, while generating mountains of garbage without adequate means of disposal. The rapid growth of the trekking industry in Nepal has increased pollution in Kathmandu and caused dangerous crowding and destruction of trails; logging for hotel building materials and cooking fires has led to deforestation, flooding and landslides as far away as Bangladesh.

More than 500 million people travel for leisure each year, making tourism the world's largest industry at $425 billion and climbing, according to the World Tourism Organization.

Tourism provides 10 per cent of the world's income and employs almost one-tenth of its workforce. Ecotourism, although growing by 20 to 30 per cent a year, still represents less than one-tenth of the total tourism industry.

Although "ecotourism" attempts to recognize the incredibly complex interactions among the environment, culture, economy and travel, it often eludes a clear definition. Guidelines are offered by such diverse groups as the United Nations Environmental Programme, Conservation International, the American Society of Travel Agents, Sierra Club and Mountain Travel Sobek. "Certified ecotourism" has recently been introduced in Australia, offering consumers a "Good Housekeeping"-type seal like those used for certified organic produce and sustainably harvested wood.

Touring with a Purpose

Ultimately, however, the responsibility for the impact of your travel rests not with a label, but with you. Be an activist—traveling the world as a dedicated ecotourist is not a spectator sport. "Ecotravellers ask lots of questions," says M.J. Kietzke, team coordinator of Co-op America Travel Links, which matches members requesting ecotravel with the operators or destinations that meet their needs.

"Because ecotourism is consumer driven," she says, "these questions help create a green demand for responsible travel options." If you choose all organized ecotour, ask about the trip fee. Besides responsibly sourced food and lodging, it can also help defray the cost of fieldwork, support local education or health programmes and leave economic dividends with the host community.

(Often, if paid to a nonprofit organization, the fees for service trips are also partially tax-deductible.) Ask whether you'll be visiting a place during the most heavily traversed time of year, contributing to overcrowding, and whether you'll be using mass transportation, to reduce pollution, and eating regional cuisine, to support local markets.

The answer to the most vital question, however, still hangs in the air: Can ecotourism help connect us with the rest of the world, and by doing so, actively make it a better place? There are many who believe it can. The following examples are but a sampling of the vast array of ecotravel options and operators, for all budgets and for all age groups.

Whether you have a few days or a few months, these ideas offer a glimpse into an amazing world, one we must either learn to protect or lose forever. Participants on Oceanic Society Expeditions need no prior scientific training, but their enthusiastic contributions will support the research that leads to environmental protection of marine life in Belize. This small, diverse Central American country nestled along the Caribbean Sea is still captivatingly wild. As of 1992, 90 per cent of Belize's forests were very much intact, and much of the reef system—the second longest in the world—was considered so valuable that it received World Heritage protected status.

Oceanic Society groups in Belize, under the guidance of top specialists in the field, alternate between conducting scientific research on dolphins—including observing their behaviour and recording their vocalizations—and taking naturalist-guided excursions, snorkeling in the pristine waters around Sergeants Caye, or birdwatching in the mangrove lagoons. To avoid tourist-saturated San Pedro on Ambergris Caye, the Expeditions are now based on Spanish Lookout Caye at the Belizean-owned Spanish Bay Resort.

The solar-powered resort offers its guests sun-washed cabanas over the water and native family-style cuisine in the main lodge. Evening slide shows and discussions about the dolphins, reef and mangrove ecology supplement the daily experiences. "These trips help us learn, grow and give back," says Elly Schaefer, a recent volunteer. Beginning in 2001, the dolphin project will move to the Blackbird-Oceanic Society Field Station at Blackbird Caye, and Spanish Bay will host a project on coral reefs.

For over 30 years, Mountain Travel Sobek has helped thousands of cubicled office workers transform themselves into modern-day replicas of Indiana Jones. Although this ecotravel doesn't scrimp on comfort and cuisine, environmentally sensitive practices like solar showers and leave-no-trace camping are part of the painstakingly planned cultural and wilderness experience.

Breathtaking describes both the spectacular landscape and high-altitude effects that come from trekking with Mountain Travel Sobek's ecotrip in the Annapurna Himal region of Nepal. The magical panorama includes some of the highest mountains on the planet, 20,000-plus-footers like Annapurna South, Annapurna I and III and Machapuchare, the so-called "Matterhorn of Nepal." A tattered topographic map will lead you along ancient, stone-stepped passageways and narrowly carved trails, through terraced rice paddies, rhododendron, oak and bamboo forests. The journey brings you, too, in close contact with the Gurung and Tamang clans, who have practiced sustenance agriculture in the region for centuries.

An active supporter of global nonprofits, Mountain Travel Sobek and the grassroots conservation work of white-water rafters led in 1993 to the preservation of the Tatshenshini River in Canada and Alaska as an international park, saving it from development as a giant, open-pit copper mine.

In the rainforests of Guatemala, slash-and-burn agriculture and other deforestation pressures continue to close in on the four-million-acre Maya Biosphere Reserve, which contains the popular Mayan temple complex of Tikal and the El Peru and Tikal National Parks. Conservation International (CI), along with USAID/Guatemala, the Guatemalan government, the National Council for Protected Areas and local conservation organizations, has set out to redirect development there in a more life-preserving direction.

The Mayan Trails, or Caminos Mayas, provides ecotravellers with the opportunity to explore both the cultural and natural heritage found beneath the forest canopy of Guatemala's Peten region. Three distinct trail systems await the ecotraveller: The Scarlet Macaw, El Mirador, and Zotz-Tikal. Hosted by communities along the path and guided by local experts, each offers a spectacular glimpse of flora and fauna—tropical birds such as Mot Mots, Macaws, Toucans and Trogons, and spider and howler monkeys—and the ancient Mayan ruins. Accommodations are at rustic campsites where guests rest in hammocks with protective mosquito nets, falling asleep to the late-night symphony of nocturnal rainforest life.

"The services, including meals, lodging, guides and horses or boats, are offered by the communities themselves," says Juan Carlos Bonilla, former coordinator for CI's Ecotourism Enterprise Development and Marketing Programme. "Conservation International is trying to build community-based, conservation-savvy entrepreneurship, not that big of a stretch."

Scotland is a hill walker's paradise. A journey there features rugged mountains, heather-covered moors, sparkling lochs, swift-flowing streams and cragged coastlines. The country's wilderness—from alpine flowers to colonies of Max shearwaters, guillemots, razor bills and Arctic terns—complements its ages-old castles and ancient Standing Stones.

Ecotravellers on the Wilderness Travel trip make their way through the highlands to the poignant Isle of Sky, rich in tradition and a spectacular landscape created by ancient volcanic activity. At a local pub, the Gaelic language still hangs heavy during discussion of the latest rugby match. After a spirited day of hiking, you'll find yourself warmly invited into this proud culture—perhaps for a "wee dram." A quaint country inn will welcome you to stop and rest for the night.

"Many of [our clients] see tourism as contributing to a more sustainable economy," says Barbara Banks, director of marketing and new trip development for Wilderness Travel. Rather than engage in destructive activities that may "benefit a region in the short term," she says, "the host communities can safeguard their land and bring money into the economy for years to come."

The sun-bleached and wind-swept slope on which Concordia Eco-Tents rests contrasts with the lush green landscape of the surrounding Virgin Islands National Park on the island of St. John. It's difficult to imagine that Maho Bay Eco-Tents, Concordia's sister resort, nestles among the forested terrain just a short drive away.

Concordia Eco-Tents is an ongoing experiment in the practical use of sustainable design. On St. John, where water is a precious commodity, owner and developer Stanley Selengut was inspired to create truly low-impact accommodations—a resort that brings people literally closer to nature. Guests collect their own solar-heated water in a cistern. Solar panels and wind generate much of the electricity that powers energy-efficient lighting and a small refrigerator. Floors and boardwalks are made with a recycled composite wood and each eco-tent includes a composting toilet with low-water flush.

"Living within the Earth's resources is something that we have to do to survive as a race," says Selengut. "There are a growing number of people interested in these problems, and we're probably one of the most popular resorts in the Caribbean because of it." Vistas of undeveloped coastline and sparkling turquoise water, accompanied by a constant breeze, certainly don't hurt either.

Great, fluttering butterflies, dragonflies the size of softballs, and huge spiders resting on shimmering strands of web, melt into the lush forest understory of the Gunung Leuser National Park in Sumatra, Indonesia. This steamy, tropical rainforest is also home to endangered orangutans, known locally as the "humans of the forest," and the subject of the Earthwatch expedition called Orangutan Health.

Joining an Earthwatch expedition is an opportunity to both explore the world and assist the scientific community. Volunteers for the Sumatran project follow orangutans, making behavioural observations from close distances, in the hopes of learning how these lumbering primates use specific plants to heal themselves.

Situated at the edge of the park along the Bohorok River, the base camp is what you might expect from such a jungle adventure: a simple, clean bungalow with a bed and mosquito net, cold-water showers, Asian toilets and freshly made Indonesian dishes of rice, fish, chicken, vegetables and amazing tropical fruit.

The diverse projects and global presence of Earthwatch attracts volunteers from all over the world. The trips, which usually last several weeks, are organized by research focus, and the fee, which covers the meals and accommodations of volunteers, also directly supports the research of leading scientists in the field. On the Sumatra expedition, besides tough hiking terrain, high humidity and manic mosquitoes, the nearly two-million-acre park also harbors 130 mammal species (including gibbons, leopards and Sumatran rhinos) and 325 species of birds. So there's plenty to do when not observing orangutans. When travellers to any of the U.S. national parks venture forth from their cars for more than just a quick bathroom break, their experiences can be transforming.

Numerous wildlife interpretive programmes, which offer travellers valuable insights to area flora and fauna as well as the unique histories of the parks themselves, help put the all-important aspect of education in ecotravel. Grand Teton National Park in the U.S.

Rocky Mountains is one of the most majestic—high enough to support a dozen mountain glaciers, with 12 Teton peaks that reach above 12,000 feet. Grand Teton itself rises 13,770 feet above the bucolic valley of Jackson Hole, the Snake River threading the terrain below. Plant communities thrive there, from ribbons of riparian plants to sagebrush fiats, lodgepole pine forests, subalpine meadows and alpine stone fields. The nonprofit Teton Science School offers Wildlife Expeditions, a programme in which locally trained wildlife biologists teach people not only about the wildlife, but also wildlife viewing ethics and habitat preservation.

These specialized safari-style tours help visitors turn a casual trip to the park into a more intimate, ecologically friendly experience. "Often times, people approach wildlife, endangering themselves and disturbing an animal's natural behaviours," says Christy Bradburn, administrative coordinator for Wildlife Expeditions. "We teach people how to enjoy wildlife and understand their natural history."

Immeasurably rich in geography, ecology, culture and history, Bolivia is home to expansive cloud forests, unique salt flats, savannas and the snow-capped Andes, making it one of the most biodiverse portions of the Amazon region. Tread Lightly trips to Bolivia, completely set up through in-country operating partners, offer backstage views of the prehistoric ruins and indigenous villages of the mystical islands of the Sun and Moon in the expansive Lake Titicaca, at 3,810 feet the highest navigable lake in the world.

Tread Lightly provides intimate cultural and natural experiences for ecotravellers to Latin America. It favours lodges that respect natural surroundings, carefully use water and other valuable resources, and employ alternative energy and waste-disposal techniques. Tread Lightly partners sponsor guide-training courses that provide rich careers for locals, helping preserve community integrity while increasing awareness for the environmental diversity and fragility of their surroundings.

Visits to Potosi and the magnificent capital city of Sucre offer ecotravellers an opportunity to enjoy Bolivia's unique cultural, as well as natural, attractions. Located at an altitude of nearly 13,100 feet, Potosi is one of the highest cities in the world and best known for the extraordinary quantities of silver extracted from Cerro Rico, "Rich Mountain."

Amidst a sea of cruise ships competing for the honour of biggest and most grandiose, the 100-passenger Galapagos Explorer II is putting luxury in a more intimate, and environmentally sustainable, context. "We want to be the most environmentally friendly ship in the Galapagos," says Freddy Espinel, hotel manager of the Explorer II. He proudly points to practices like on-board desalinization of water; its purification with ozone, rather than chlorine; composted biodegradable waste and recyclables flown to the mainland; and the use of only biodegradable soaps and detergents.

While the service is impeccable and on-board atmosphere inviting, the islands themselves are the real showstoppers. On excursions escorted by the ship's naturalists (trained by Galapagos National Park) visitors see firsthand the unique adaptations of island fauna, such as flightless cormorants, marine iguanas, giant tortoises and Darwin's finches. Opportunities for photography are rife, as is snorkeling with schools of brightly-coloured fish or hiking in search of the more perfect vista.

Small group size and tight Park Service control help protect the fragile ecosystem and ensure that even on this limited terrain more wildlife than tourists are encountered. The new interpretation centre on San Cristobal Island is well worth exploring, and after you return to the ship for some native Ecuadorian cuisine and to sail to your next destination, you can watch a slide show about the natural history of the archipelago, discuss with fellow shipmates environmental challenges faced by the islands, or browse through the science library on board.

Winding along the sweeping valleys and rolling hills of unglaciated southwestern and central-western Wisconsin, the Elroy-Sparta State Trail tempts both bicyclists and walkers alike. Interrupted occasionally by cavernous rock tunnels through which bikers pass, the trail showcases local history and wildlife as it crosses trout streams and weaves through farmlands and hardwood forests.

By staying in quaint bed and breakfasts, eating at family-owned restaurants and shopping for unique gifts or handmade Amish furniture along the 32-mile trail, visitors help preserve the area, support struggling agricultural communities and revive interest in natural corridors for wildlife and recreation.

The Elroy-to-Sparta trail is among the first of the U.S. rail-trails, recreational trails created from abandoned railroads, advocated by the nonprofit Rails-to-Trails Conservancy. Such trails provide a link among historic, cultural and natural sites, boost sagging local economies and, in some cases, completely revive economically depressed towns.

Playing hopscotch across the landscape, the number of trails has grown from 75 in 1986 to more than 1,000 today; they cover 11,000 miles.

Ecotourism operators and "free independent travellers" each share a commitment to tread lightly on the land and culture, and support the local economy at their destination. Ecotourism is not defined by the distance traveled, but rather how it's accomplished and what is experienced, so don't overlook natural attractions like rail-trails right in your own backyard.

After all, for most travellers, a fully satisfying journey can be one of less than 100 miles.

Eco-Cultural Tourism in India

There is an urgent and growing need for local/regional/ national/international peace and security. This may be broadly ascribed to the increasing conflicts arising out of social, economic, religious and political factors. Peace and sustainability, considered as the indicators of development are threatened due to a myriad of conflicts and they are more visible than ever before in India. Tourism considered as a Global Peace Industry has greater potentials to reduce these conflicts. This paper analyses the threats to peace and sustainability and indicates that the newly emerging Heritage Eco-cultural Tourism holds the key for the promotion of peace and sustainability.

As we enter into the next millennium and the birth of a new global era, we are confronting the urgent need for local/ regional/national/international peace and security more than in the past. This may be broadly ascribed to the increasing conflicts arising out of social, economic, religious and political factors. The widening gap between the haves and have-nots, have further accelerated these conflicts.

Hence, we are seeking universal human rights and universal human progress and prosperity. One powerful indicator of such a development is the fact that more people are traveling from more countries than ever before, making travel and tourism the worlds largest industry. Its growth is expected to continue with globalization and as people everywhere seem determined to exercise their right to travel and to make their world a more familiar place in the spirit of peace and friendship.

Tourism itself has always been a peace-based industry and may be considered as a Global Peace Industry. In the face of current human population increases and worldwide ecological degradation, intact and healthy ecosystems are becoming the world's most sought-after tourism destinations. Culture and Heritage besides peace and harmony in such areas attract special groups of tourists, who demand quality products. Peace and sustainability, considered as the indicators of development are threatened due to a myriad of conflicts—Social, Economic, political, cultural and Environmental. These conflicts usually confront multiple and diverse stakeholders such as state institutions, religious organizations, communities, indigenous ethnic groups, local institutions, private development and non-government organizations, international organizations, and many other players.

Wide differences in culture, knowledge, power, influence, and resources characterize these groups. Even though most conflicts essentially develop in a local framework, they are also frequently connected at regional, national and even international levels, transcending political and geographical boundaries including non-represented interests (*e.g.* future generations).

Such complexity explains, in part, the lack of sustained attention that conflicts receive. In addition, many conflicts in India are often dealt with unprofessionally and result in frustrations, violence, greater inequities, and negative impacts on quality of life, economic and social processes and in the natural resources themselves.

The most common methods of intervention in conflicts tend to be centralized, hierarchical, and sectorial, with a predominantly technical and adversarial (judicial) and at times political. Seldom do they achieve a reasonable level of satisfaction for all interested parties.

Hence, we are urgently in need of alternative paradigms for development—we are moving from the narrower 'reductionist', 'reactive' and 'bureaucratic' approaches to 'wholistic/Integrated or Systems' view of looking at issues, 'pro-active' policies and 'participatory' strategies. How quick and how effective we are in reorienting ourselves according to these shifting paradigms will determine our sustainable futures.

The word 'conflict' carries negative connotations. It is often thought of as the opposite of cooperation and peace, and is most commonly associated with violence or the threat of violence. This view of conflict is not always helpful. In many settings it should be seen as a potential force for positive social change—its presence a visible demonstration of society adapting to a new political, economic or physical environment. A potential non-violent approach to solve these conflicts at the least social/economic/Environmental costs may be through evolving alternative tourism strategies.

In the midst of growing tensions and worries everywhere "Getting away from it all," is understandably popular. With so many wonderful places in the world, prices of international travel falling, and the stresses and strains of everyday life increasing, more people are traveling. And as the population grows and incomes rise in many societies, the trend is steeply up. In 2000, international tourist arrivals reached an all time high of 698 million, an increase of 7.4% that was double the growth rate of 1999, according to the World Tourism Organization. Tourism sector employs 11 per cent of the global workforce—over 200 million people—either directly or indirectly.

The Tourism Sector in India

India's tourism potentials are immense—with a large variety ranging from rich cultural diversity, world-renowned historical, religious, heritage and architectural monuments, unique fairs, festivals, folklore and folk dances besides the costumes and customs to wildlife sanctuaries with exquisite flora and fauna. Besides, there are cool hill stations and long stretches of sunny beaches all round the peninsula.

The diversity is not only in climate but is all pervasive and as J. Nehru put it, "India is a land of contrasts—with the rural tranquility of simplicity and urban bustle, pomp and show". Added to this, there are plenty of traditional arts and crafts to carry back as souvenirs; Indian hospitality and variety induce tourists to make repeated visits. India's wide choice of adventure sports ranges from the daring to the exotic—trekking, camping, rock climbing, white water rafting, skating, air/water gliding, etc. In spite of such attractions, tourist arrivals in India are less than 1% of the world arrivals.

Tourism in India is different from other sectors by some special characteristics that include: A wider variety of stake-holders but with lack of communication and coordination. Uniformity of artificial structures in Tourism areas does not blend with the natural diversity of undisturbed areas. Inter-sectoral linkages and complexity with several intangible costs and benefits; conflicts leading to problems in analysis, monitoring and coordination; mixed priorities and conflicts, make cooperation and participation difficult. Research on tourism especially on policy and planning has been given low priority—as a result, it is poorly studied and understood as a sector in general and its Environmental and Social/Cultural impacts in particular; hence, we are confronted with fragmented and poorly coordinated policies, riddled with ad-hoc decisions for short term gains at the cost of long term sustainability.

Multiplier effect is prominent—can enhance poverty alleviation and alternative livelihoods; but is rarely understood by the planners and the implementing agencies. Seasonality in Tourist influx has implications for carrying capacity analysis and Tourism policy/planning/implementation, but rarely taken into account by the planners/policy makers Spatial and temporal dimensions—implications for Physical planning:

Positive and negative feed backs—implications for absorbing capacity, carrying capacity, Sustainability, and resilience; a typical tourism cycle would involve—Exploration/developmen/tconsolidation/stagnation/decline/rejuvenation; however, negative impacts, on a cumulative basis destroy the resource base, affecting the natural, cultural, and Heritage attractions, culminating in declining tourism trends. Life supporting systems are impacted, culminating in debates on Ecological integrity Vs Economic security.

'Profit maximization' is the prime motto of Tourism enterprises (irrespective of whether they are private or Govt. sector undertakings) and hence, tourism is largely out of control for planners; some impacts are irreversible and hence tourism itself is affected due to degradation in Environmental health/quality. The Ecological impacts of tourism are more on Common Property Resources—air, soil and ground water, leading to tragedy of the commons as they are treated as 'open access commons'. Lack of know how and trained man power in Govt. agencies on Eco-cultural tourism lead to lack of appreciation and Govt. support for community based initiatives. Tourism industry is fundamentally dependent on the diversity and quality of the natural and cultural resources. Hence, it has grater reasons to conserve/protect the same. But are we giving adequate attention/priorities for natural and cultural resources while planning and implementing tourism projects in India? Though tourism is India's one of the largest foreign exchange earners and one among the fastest growing industries, the natural resource base that supports tourism is "heavily stressed" in and around the main tourist destination areas. In spite of the overwhelming technological and information revolution, we have trapped ourselves in a vicious circle of self-destruction by adopting the typical "boom and bust" tourism paths paved by the ill-conceived and unplanned/uncontrolled mass tourism, promoted for short-term profit maximization at the cost of degradation in Environmental quality. Ironically, this in turn, ultimately detracts the tourists and destroys the Tourism industry itself.

The question is whether we, in the blind pursuit of rapid Economic growth and earning more foreign exchange Q an afford to sacrifice the higher Environmental quality and our rich cultural Heritage upon which tourism so strongly depends. Though we have already learnt many bitter lessons, we tend to overlook them.

Changes in the physical, spatial, and socio-economic structure of a tourist area as well as the existence of several, sometimes burdensome, environmental/social problems testify to the presence of these conflicts and the crying need for evolving appropriate strategies to sustainably manage the Environmental quality, and to improve the local livelihood opportunities.

However, the researchers as well as policy makers in India largely ignore the inseparable links between the Environmental quality (EQ), sustainability, peace and tourism and pay little attention to participation of local communities, by focusing only on setting up infrastructures, promoting marketing strategies and make only *ad hoc*/piece meal efforts to improve the EQ, sustainability and peace in the destination areas. This is self-evident from the "tell-tale symptoms" or "indicators" such as garbage dumps, foul smell, very high rates of pollution, over exploitation of natural resources, alienation of local communities, increasing conflicts and violence in several destination areas.

The industry has learned these bitter lessons only after the irreversible damages have already set in. Examples can be seen every where the mass tourism went out of control—starting from Ooty and Kodai lakes in the South to Dal lake in the North; from Kovalam in the South to Goa in the North; even our nation's pride Taj Mahal is not spared!

As a result, tourism has become a dirty word amongst many communities, environmental groups and human rights campaigners. This is really unfortunate as the tourism sector has greater potential to enhance local livelihoods, if it is properly planned.

The Ills of the Tourism Industry

Though tourism could lead to a variety of potential benefits, uncontrolled mass tourism, the most predominant form of tourism today, inevitably increases the already existing conflicts, besides creating new ones. Tourism's voracious appetite for basic resources—land, water and energy—has meant that the tourism industry and Government Agencies are increasingly finding themselves opposed over land rights and water rights by local people. Lack of access by locals to public beaches, violation by hotels of environmental regulations, and heavy-handed tactics by local authorities to free-up beach areas for hotels' use, have all been cited in legal disputes throughout the world.

For instance, three quarters of the sand dunes on the Mediterranean coast between Spain and Sicily have now disappeared, largely because of the construction of hotels and holiday flats. One of the most famous long-term tourism protests has been in Goa, India. With one five-star hotel consuming as much water as five local villages and one five-star tourist consuming 28 times more electricity per day than a local Goan, local discontent over resource-use is understandable. Thus, the modern world is characterized by mass concentrations of people, mass production, and mass activities. Diversity and beauty of land and life are more and more replaced by uniformity and ugliness. Human settlements in their mad rush for development have turned beautiful tree-clad landscapes into desolate concrete jungles, and fertile lands with diverse native vegetation are increasingly destroyed by monocultures. Tourism is no exception to this general rule.

The Green Signals

Over the last decade, understanding of these complex and interconnected issues by the world tourism industry, tourists, governments and communities has increased as indicated by the evolution of numerous alternative forms of tourism such as 'green' tourism, 'alternative' tourism, 'responsible' tourism, 'sustainable' tourism, 'eco' tourism, 'eco-cultural' tourism (ECT), 'eco-development' tourism, 'Heritage eco-cultural' tourism (HECT), 'community' tourism, "ethical' tourism, 'fair-trade' tourism and even, most recently, the particularly un-catchy, 'pro-poor' tourism (PPT).

Unfortunately, we, in India have not sufficiently re-oriented ourselves, to meet the future international market demand for these specialized forms of tourism. The concept of sustainable tourism should not be confused with ECT. According to WTO, all tourism activities, be they geared to holidays, business, conferences, congresses or fairs, health, adventure or ECT itself, must be sustainable.

This means that the planning and development of tourism infrastructure, its subsequent operation and also its marketing should focus on environmental, social, cultural and economic sustainability criteria, so as to ensure that neither the natural environment nor the socio-cultural fabric of the host communities will be impaired by the arrival/activities of tourists; on the contrary, enterprises, as well as the communities in which they operate, should benefit from tourism, both economically and culturally. Eco-tourism, a growing trend, is the most commonly understood term as tourism that focuses on an appreciation of the environment. In 1993 the World Tourism Organisation (WTO) estimated nature tourism generates 7 per cent of all international travel expenditure. More recent research reveals this is now much higher, accounting for 20 per cent of international travel in the Asia-Pacific region and some areas, such as South Africa, experiencing a massive growth in visitors to game and nature reserves, of over 100 per cent annually. Research by The International Ecotourism Society (TIES) reveals that coo-tourists are likely to be higher spenders on their holidays than 'ordinary' mass tourists. And high spending, nature-loving, responsible tourists are undoubtedly an attractive option for governments looking for ways of earning foreign exchange.

The recent Amman Declaration on Peace Through Tourism reflects many of the strategies discussed above and has recognised that peace is an essential precondition for travel and tourism and all aspects of human growth and development. Hence, it has recommended the development of tourism as a global vehicle for promoting understanding, trust and goodwill among peoples of the world through an appropriate political and economic framework.

The New Threats

The alternative tourism strategies, evolved in response to the concern for the Ecology, culture, Heritage and local livelihoods, have created both new opportunities as well as new threats. One of eco-tourism's first problems is one of definition. Although, there are several definitions, there is no certification system to abide by or international monitoring body. The term can be used by anyone at anytime for anything from a small-scale locally run rainforest lodge where the money goes to support a local community, to a large, luxury, foreign-owned resort which has little community involvement and uses masses of natural resources.

Eco-tourists may even visit areas of national beauty and wildlife significance without realizing that local people have been evicted from the area in order for eco-tourism to be developed, as has happened in East Africa, India, Southern Africa and many other destinations. Ill-conceived and/or ill-planned Eco-tourism, as practiced now by a majority of the business communities has caused serious, irreversible negative impacts in environmentally and culturally sensitive areas, even in countries that are well known as eco-tourism destinations like Belize or Costa Rica.

The Malaysian-based Third World Network working with the Thailand-based Tourism Information Monitoring team (TIM-team) cite examples throughout Asia, including the eco-tourism policy promoted by the tourism working group under the Greater Mekong Sub-region (GMS) development scheme, led by the Asian Development Bank, which covers a vast area across Burma, Cambodia, Laos, Thailand, Vietnam and Yunnan/China. They are riddled with several problems relating to accusations of 'human zoos' being created and financial exploitation of hill tribe villages by outside tour operators.

Besides, the increasing link of eco-tourism to the multi-million dollar biotechnology industry through bio-piracy in key eco-tourist sites like rainforests, and the use of eco-tourism by the World Bank's Social Investment Project to support massive development projects, some involving logging operations are becoming common in many developing countries. The revolution in information and communication technologies would enable both the promoters and the tourists to exploit the hidden potentials ECT in a region, more efficiently than ever.

However, the lack of discipline of government and the escalating demand for growth will undermine efforts to create sustainable eco-tourism economies that are small but beautiful. Under extreme conditions of land grabbing and unplanned structures, it may create concrete jungles, surrounded by degraded vegetation, thus destroying the once tranquil zones. Hence, we have to be extremely careful while promoting ECT. Despite these problems, an International Year of Ecotourism (IYE) was declared by the United Nations for 2002. This will be co-ordinated by the WTO and UNEP and a range of activities held, including a World Ecotourism Summit from 19-22 May 2002 in Quebec, Canada plus various regional conferences. Oliver Hillel, the UNEP tourism programme co-ordinator sees the IYE as a chance to "assess what eco-tourism is, or can be, rather than only a promotional event for UN member governments, for the private sector and for recipients of development aid."

It is clear to many that nature-based tourism is presently seen as one of the most lucrative niche markets, and powerful transnational corporations are likely to exploit the IYE to dictate their own definitions and rules of eco-tourism on society, while people-centred initiatives will be squeezed out and marginalised.

While the commitment of the tourism industry in India to tackle these complex issues seems limited, a few smaller operators are keen to work closely with local people in order for the communities to support their business and out of an honest desire to protect environments and optimise benefits to local people. However, such small operators lack the know-how to tackle the issues involved. As a result, alternative tourism strategies for which India has a greater potential, make up a very small proportion of overall tourism facilities.

The Potential Alternatives

In any outdoor tourism activity, human experience, knowledge, expectation, and socio-cultural contexts interact with environmental elements and environments as entities to produce an outcome that affects both the humans and the environment.

Thus, sustainable tourism development depends in many important ways on the proper handling of the relationships between Tourism and the Environment. Sustainability, Peace and Environmental quality occupy the central table in the wake of global terrorism.

Greater sustainability of the tourism would mean more regional products, less noise and emissions, lesser solid wastes and appropriate sewage treatment measures, creation of jobs, lesser social conflicts/violence by learning to live in harmony and higher quality of life for the local populations well as improved quality of holidays for the guest. The conventional mass tourism, by its very nature cannot cater to these demands. Hence, alternative tourism strategies are emerging. Sustainable tourism is defined as "Tourism that meets the needs of the present tourists and host regions while protecting and enhancing opportunity for the future. It is envisaged as leading to management of all resources in such a way that economic, social and aesthetic needs can be fulfilled while maintaining cultural integrity, essential ecological processes, bio-Diversity and life supporting systems (soil, air and water)".

Thus, it has the inbuilt mechanism for promoting peace and harmony among the tourism stakeholders. A related alternative is Eco-cultural Tourism (ECT). ECT activities are offered by a large and wide variety of operators, and practiced by an even larger array of tourists. While there is no single universal definition for ECT, its general characteristics can be summarized as follows:

All nature-based forms of tourism in which the main motivation of the tourists is the observation and appreciation for admiring, enjoying and/or studying nature as well as the traditional cultures and Heritage (both past and present) prevailing in relatively undisturbed or uncontaminated natural areas

It contains participatory, interactive, educational and interpretation features. It is generally, but not exclusively organized for environmentally, socially conscious small groups by specialized and small, locally owned businesses. Foreign operators of varying sizes also organize, operate and/or market ECT tours, generally for small groups.

It minimizes negative impacts upon the natural and socio-cultural environment. Heritage Eco-cultural Tourism (HECT) is a newly emerging type of alternative tourism. When Heritage of the destination areas can be exploited along with the local Ecological and cultural attractions, we have a case for Heritage Eco-cultural Tourism. Heritage embraces magnificent natural, indigenous and historic landscapes (natural or man-made), wildlife and healthy, intact ecosystems, historical elements (that has helped to shape the regional/ national identity), cultural elements and human values, shaping regional, national, global identity; it also incorporates a strong connection to 'place'; that is, people come to the place by choice, they are somehow transformed by it, and they choose to identify themselves with it even if they don't live there. This may be because of the outstanding universal value of the areas visited from the point of view of science, conservation or natural beauty.

Historical places, objects and manifestations of cultural, scientific, symbolic, spiritual and religious values are important expressions of the culture, identity and religious beliefs of societies. Their role and importance, particularly in the light of the need for cultural identity and continuity in a rapidly changing world, need to be promoted.

Tourists are actively seeking such lost values. They come hoping for a profound psychic or spiritual experience in some quiet corners of the destination areas. Hence, we have greater responsibility to conserve the cultural Heritage areas.

The following are the key potential benefits of HECT:

- Protection and active conservation of natural and built heritage resources, justified by their own intrinsic value for posterity and the revenue which visitors contribute.
- Enhancement of the natural and built environment to meet rising quality standards necessary to sustain modern travel and tourism.
- Reconstruction for visitor usage of urban environments and environments degraded by the industrial practices of former extractive and manufacturing industries.
- Establishment of attractive environments for tourism destinations, for residents as much as visitors, which may support other compatible new economic activities, from agriculture and fishing to service and manufacturing industries.
- Creation of economic value and protection for

resources which otherwise have no perceived value to residents, or represent a cost rather than a benefit- livelihood opportunities—micro-enterprises?

- Opportunity to communicate and interpret the values of natural and built heritage and of cultural inheritance of residents of visited areas.
- Effective management of visitors within an environment so that it can support long-term economic development and repeat visits.
- Research and development of good environmental practices and management systems to influence the operation of travel and tourism businesses as well as visitor behaviour at destinations.

Opportunities, through the direct customer contacts that all travel and tourism businesses have, for operators to communicate and interpret the values of natural and built heritage and culture to visitors, thus helping to create a new generation of responsible consumers

The available knowledge indicate that the following may be considered as the major criteria for selecting HECT sites:

- *Geography*—proximity to mass-tourism sites; sufficiently closer for easy accessibility but adequately away from motorable roads and other human disturbances.
- *Climate and Ecology*—microclimates/habitats conducive enough for the tourists without any need for artificial comforts
- *Rarity and Uniqueness*—Ecosystems like mountains, rivers, mangroves, coral reefs and islands endowed with unspoiled beauty, unique culture and Heritage.
- *Infrastructure*—only reasonable—to the barest minimum but with desirable conditions—hygienic ethnic food (locally produced/prepared), protected water supply, natural ventilation and local architecture.
- *Diversity*—higher habitat/community/Ecosystem/ cultural (food, cloth, architecture, crafts, festivals etc.)—diversity and purity—potentials/opportunities

for viewing/appreciating more attractive species/ cultures as well as Heritage elements; Potentials for a variety of nature/adventure tourism activities such as camping for wildlife observation, traditional healing camps, caving, bird-watching, trekking, rock-climbing, mountain biking, skating, para-gliding, wind-surfing, funky jumping, canopy walkways, white water rafting, snorkeling, scuba diving, recreational fishing

- *Unpolluted/relatively undisturbed areas with higher Environmental quality*—in contrast to polluted/ degraded landscapes/seascapes
- *Minimum health/safety risks*—to avoid costly demands from the tourists
- *Opportunities for Environmental Education and interpretation*—for all the stake-holders
- *Opportunities for generating and sustaining new livelihoods*—to cater to the demands of the tourists—*e.g.* Apiculture (the science and art of raising honey bees), agriculture, horticulture, floriculture, community dairy/piggery/poultry, preparation of Ethnic foods, rich diversity of arts and crafts.
- *Community cooperation*—to make and enforce their own decisions on eco-tourism development.
- *Presence of dedicated NGOs*—for catalyzing cooperation.
- *Cooperation of other stake-holders*—Govt. and other institutions—their policies, programmes and goals.
- *Marketing opportunities*—potentials for targeting different types of eco-tourists (hardcore, dedicated, mainstream and casual); marketing linkages and potentials.

The HECT will enable the tourists as well as the local communities to find ways to live sustainably, and in peace with nature, Cultural Heritage and intact, functioning ecosystems. More importantly, we will be reconnecting ourselves with our forgotten treasure of the diverse culture and Heritage of the bygone era.

In this process, tourism will promote peace and sustainability by closer mutualistic interactions between tourists and the local communities. Among the several organizations that could be involved in the promotion of HECT, mention must be made of UNESCO (World Heritage sites programme) and the International Institute for Peace through Tourism at international levels and the Indian National Trust for the promotion of Arts and Cultural Heritage (INTACH) at the national level. The Indian Tourism Development Corporation and the State Tourism Development Corporations have to recognise the potentials of HECT and reorient themselves to the tasks ahead.

Broad guidelines for promoting HECT strategies may be modified and adopted from UNEP that has prescribed Environmental codes of conduct for tourism and Gonsalves' (1991) paper on guidelines for alternative tourism for the third world.

The adoption of the Global Code of Ethics for Tourism, the Green Globe programme, the ECOTEL Certification awarded by HVS Eco Services, Certification Programmes for Sustainable Tourism and Eco-tourism, Exemplary Practices by Canadian Tourism Commission, The National Eco-tourism Accreditation Programme of the Eco-tourism Association of Australia and the Australian Tourism Operators Association and equitable community participation in tourism are a few other such initiatives to name, globally.

Recently, Mastny (2002) from World Watch Institute has provided policy guidelines with examples for sustainable tourism. The recently emerging pro-poor tourism approaches, have to be ideally integrated into HECT.

MARKETING: CONCEPTS AND PRACTICES

The concept of marketing can be viewed from social and managerial perspectives. At its simplest, marketing can be defined as exchange transactions that take place between the buyer and the seller. Marketing is the management function, which organizes and directs all those business activities involved in assessing and converting customer purchasing power into effective demand. Philip Kotler defines marketing as "a social process by which individuals and groups obtain what they need and want through creating, offering and freely exchanging products and services of value with others".

ASPECTS OF MARKETING CONCEPT

The important aspects of marketing concept are:

- *Creation of demand*: Marketing tries to create demand through various means. The producers first ascertain what the customers want and then produce goods just as to the needs of the customers. There is a systematic effort to sell goods and services just as to the needs of the customers.
- *Customer Orientation*: Marketing involves undertaking a range of business activities directed at the creation of customer satisfying products and services.
- *Integrated Marketing*: The customer orientation alone is not enough on the part of management. To be effective must be backed by an appropriate set up within the country. The responsibility of marketing department is to ensure coordination of the various departments of the company *i.e.*, finance, purchase, research and development.
- *Profitable sales volume through customer satisfaction*: Marketing tries to realise long-term goals of profitability, growth and stability through satisfying customers' wants. All the basic activities of a company are planned to meet the wants of customers and still making reasonable profits. Modern marketing thus begins with the customer and ends with the customer.

MARKETING MIX

Marketing concepts had been originally developed in the context of tangible consumer goods. Marketing mix refers to the ingredients or the tools, which the marketer mixes in order to interact with a particular market. Kotler defines marketing mix as "set of marketing tools that the firm uses to pursue its marketing objectives in the target market". Each of the elements in the marketing mix is important and has an influence on the customer.

4 P'S OF MARKETING MIX

McCarthy has classified the main elements of a marketing programme in terms of 4 Ps- Product, Price, Promotion and Place.

- Product includes design, features, quality, range, size, models, appearance, packaging, and warranties. It also includes pre-sales and post-sale services like training for use, repairs, maintenance or replacements.
- Price includes concessions on basic price, discounts, rebates, credits, installation facilities and delivery terms.
- Promotion includes advertising, publicity media choices, messages, and frequency of exposure, campaigns, sales promotion, point-of-purchase, displays and merchandising.
- Place or channels of distribution includes retail outlets, wholesalers, transportation, warehousing, inventory levels, order processing procedures, etc.

Consumers generally form their perceptions of products and services based on prices. Pricing products and services is a complex process.

It is based on the uniqueness of product attributes and the perceived value, which the consumer is willing to pay. Pricing strategies are planned just as to consumers' cultural norms and the political, legal and social environment of the place where the tourist product is located.

Example of Price: Indian Airlines has offered Super Saver tickets in January 2006, a multicoupon ticket is being offered with each coupon valid for travel between any two domestic destinations connected by a direct flight.

The offer gives two options, one is about four-ticket option priced at ₹20000 in Economy class and the other is ₹28000 in Executive class. This is an example of good Bargain. There is also the option of buying additional ticket at incredibly low prices. Such convenience of booking provides the comforts of flying with wide choice of travel. Distribution systems or channels serve as the intermediary between consumers and suppliers and are an essential part of the travel and hospitality marketing strategy.

Many companies such as hotels or airlines use their central reservation systems to facilitate sales directly to customers. Example of Channels of Distribution: It is estimated that in the year 2004, out of a total 730 million Internet users, only 35.8 per cent use English language websites. Therefore, local language should be part of the distribution strategy and many hospitality companies also provide localized websites with several languages. Let us understand how a marketer uses the tools of marketing mix by taking the example of a product like 'Tanishq' watches by Titan Industries.

The watch is packed in plastic box, has a design, features, quality and company ensures warranty. It has list price but at times the dealer permits discount or rebate. The company distributes the watch through exclusive retail outlets. The company promotes it by using advertising and sales force.

All the activities of Titan are the ingredients that have gone into the making of 'Tanishq' for the purpose of creating exchanges with the potential customers.

TARGET MARKET

The term 'market' refers to the collective of existing and prospective customers for the product. People who need to stay outside their usual residence use a hotel. A person may not have such a need but if such a need arises later, he is a prospective customer.

The marketing effort is aimed at such prospective customers who would choose to buy the marketer's hotel services. However, all persons who need to stay outside are not prospective customers for the 5-star hotels. They may stay at budget hotels.

Hence, the market for the five star hotels is only part of the total market of total hotel users. Such parts are called segments of the market. The customers of the hotel are those who come to stay as well as users of other facilities. They are different groups and each group constitutes different segments since the needs and expectations of each one of these groups are different. For example, segmentation is possible on the basis of usage of swimming pool. The segments using the pools for training are different from regular guests in terms of age, behaviour, attention required, hours spent in the pool or cleanliness demanded and so on.

MARKET SEGMENTATION

Market segmentation is the process of identifying groups of buyers of the total market with different desires. Most markets are too large for an organization to provide all the products and services needed by all buyers in that market. This leads organizations selecting target markets necessitating market segmentation.

Market segmentation has certain obvious advantages in that the organization is:

- Better placed to spot and compare marketing opportunities,
- Cater to the specific needs of the buyers,
- Develop marketing programmes for specific market segments.

In tourism, market segmentation is very important. The strategy of market segmentation in tourism is to divide the present and the potential market on the basis of some characteristic and then concentrate marketing efforts like pricing, supply and promotion efforts to the target markets.

BASES FOR MARKET SEGMENTATION

Segmentation is usually done on the basis of one or more of the following characteristics:

- Buying behaviour- volumes of purchase, delivery requirements.
- Demographic- family size, religion, gender, income, occupation, language, education.
- Geographic- region, district, density of population, climate, urbanrural.

- Psychographics- value system, lifestyles, and personality types.

Usually the tourist market is segmented in terms of demographic, geographic, psychographic, social and economic criteria. For example the market for a particular area might be the businessmen in the age group of 40-60 years who have an income of over $100,000 per year and who live in southern parts of Germany.

The tourist market may be segmented on the basis of:

- Destinations.
- Economic status and spending tendencies.
- Place or origin of tourists.
- Preferences of staying, like camping, luxury hotels, caravans, etc.
- Preferences of travel, like air, sea, road, or rail.
- Purpose of tour like holidays, pilgrimage, sightseeing, shopping, etc.

Each segment of the market differs in terms of needs and expectations. No one organization can cater to the needs of all segments. Each organization has to decide on the particular segment or segments it would cater to. The segment so identified is called the target segment. Having identified the market, all activities will have to be planned keeping this target market in mind.

The services being offered, the messages in communication, the media used for communication, the pricing policies, the arrangements have to be consistent with the preferences and behaviour patterns of the target market. For example, if the hotel is targeting on the domestic tourists at religious places, then providing foreign food or advertising in business magazines would be the waste of resources. Instead, provide vegetarian thali food and advertise in religious magazines and on channels like Aastha and Sanskar.

TOURISM MARKETING

It is a well known fact that as long as the inherent sense of curiosity and adventure dwells in the hearts of human beings, the desire to travel in order to see new sights and experience new things, to live under different environments will always grows.

The marketing in tourism industry has evolved as part of the process initiated by the desire for travel in people. Without exception, all human beings will always nurture a desire to travel in order to see places.

The question arises that if the desire is ever present in people to travel and experience new things, why then would the tourism industry need marketing efforts at all? The marketing problems in tourism is quite different from marketing problems in other industries, and this justifies making marketing in tourism, a subject for separate and specialized enquiry.

The concepts and principles, the techniques and methods of marketing can be equally applied to tourism. The concept of tourism marketing can be better understood by identifying and considering the differences between markets for physical, tangible goods on the one hand and the market for tourism on the other. Tourism marketing could be defined as the systematic and coordinated efforts exerted by tourist enterprises at international, national and local levels to optimize the satisfaction of tourists, groups and individuals, in view of a sustained tourism growth.

Krippendorf, "Marketing in tourism is to be understood as the systematic and coordinated execution of business policy by tourist undertakings, whether private or state owned, at local, regional, national or international levels to achieve the optimal satisfaction of the needs of identifiable consumer groups, and in doing so to achieve an appropriate return."

Tourism is a very complex industry because of its multifaceted activities, which together produce the tourist products otherwise considered as independent industry. Besides, its complexity lies mostly in the fact that tourists are located in different places, have different socio-economic structures, different needs, tastes, attitudes, expectations, and behaviour patterns. The marketing concept helps the tourist organization to establish a consistent and effective communication system with actual and potential tourists in the selected markets. It also helps them to know their customers' wishes, needs, motivations, likes and dislikes.

SPECIAL FEATURES OF TOURISM MARKETING

From ancient times when travel was a prerogative of a select few who travelled in search of adventure to the present day jet travel, there have been many changes. Travel in ancient times was a simple affair. The type of facilities that were required by the people to travel was provided by a handful of suppliers of such services. In the present scenario of travel expansion, markets necessitated the application of marketing techniques. Marketing of tourist products has certain peculiarities.

The difference arises due to peculiar nature of tourist products:

- *A tourist product is assembled by many producers*: The tourist product cannot be provided by a single enterprise. In tourism, airline provides 'seat' to travel, hotels provide 'accommodation', a travel agent 'bookings' while a museum provides 'place of experience'. So, the tourist product is an amalgamation of many components, which together make a complete product.
- Intermediaries play a dominant role: In tourism, sales intermediaries like tour operators, travel agents, reservation services and hotel brokers play a dominant role. They determine to a large extent which services will be sold and to whom.
- *Production and consumption of tourist services are closely Interrelated*: The travel agent who sells his product cannot store it since there is a close link between production and consumption of tourist services. Production can only take place or can only be completed if the customer is actually present.
- *Tourism demand is highly unstable*: Tourism demand is influenced by seasonal, economic, political and other such factors. For example, political unrest affects inflow of tourist to a particular destination.
- *Tourism is an intangible, non-material product*: Unlike a

tangible product, no transfer of ownership of goods is involved in tourism. Instead certain facilities are made available for a specified time and for a specified use like a seat in an aeroplane or room in a hotel.

- *Travel motivations are diverse in nature*: The reasons, expectations, and desires, which influence tourists' choice for certain holiday destinations, types of accommodation and vacation activities are varied. Very often people make exactly the same choice for entirely different reasons.

To a considerable extent, tourism marketing depends on various market factors. Therefore, marketing of tourism as compared to other industries needs a somewhat different approach.

PRODUCT IN TOURISM

The needs of the tourist relate to comfort and pleasure in travel, stay, food arrangements and visiting spots of interest and attraction.

Hence, the tourist expectations are:

- Able to experience the new places–their life-styles, food, culture, heritage, etc. as per one's own choice.
- Be able to visit places of interest, spend adequate time at such places.
- Facility of transportation available.
- Facing no risk to one's person or belongings, etc.
- Getting suitable food to one's tastes and health.
- Not to be hurried or hustled against the preferred place.
- To be looked after and cared for.

The three basic components of a tourist product are:

- Attractions,
- Facilities, and
- Accessibility.

Attractions constitute an important feature of the product. Attractions are those elements in the tourist product, which determine the choice of the particular tourist product, to visit one particular destination rather than another. These are things to see and enjoy like cultural sites, historical buildings, beaches, mountains, national parks, or events like trade fairs, exhibitions, music festivals, etc. Facilities are those elements in the tourist product, which are a necessary aid to the tourist centre. The facilities complement the attractions. These include accommodation, food, communications, guides and so on.

Accessibility is a means by which a tourist can reach the areas where attractions are located. Tourists' attractions are of little importance if their locations are inaccessible by the normal means of transport. It also relates to the formalities in reaching the places like visas, customs, bookings etc.

In Tourism, the products are varied. A travel agent may arrange for itineraries and airline bookings and may also help in getting passport, visas, foreign exchange clearances, embarkation facilities at airport and so on. Similarly attractions are added to a destination. For example, 18 rooms of Buckingham Palace have been opened to visitors, which are a major tourist attraction to visitors. Apart from the Throne Room, Drawing Room and the Picture Gallery, the Souvenir shop selling white china mugs with Buckingham Palace written on it or Crystal Balls with details from the State Dining Room is also a part of the attraction. A product in tourism is the place of destination and what one may experience while proceedings to and staying at that destination.

For example:

- Sentose islands of Singapore, is packaged as a place where there are no shops, no skyscrapers, no offices- a place of quiet and tranquility, to relax and be with nature, so different from Singapore. Travelling by cable car to the island is also a part of the package.
- Places in Rajasthan like Jaisalmer are being offered as tourism products to experience the life-style of Maharajas, living in real palaces with kingly comforts, travelling on ' Palace on Wheels', the luxuriously fitted railway train, going hunting on elephant back and so on. The product is not merely the city of Jaisalmer and what it may offer as historical and cultural importance. The product is the

total experience of travel and other attractions, all related to the royalty of Jaisalmer.

The tourism product may be developed with emphasis on art, architecture, culture, religion, history, sports, leisure, temples, life-styles, etc.

- Himalayas are a product not only for sports and adventure tourism, but also for nature lovers and spirituality.
- Varanasi is a product based on religion, the Ganges capturing the essence of Oldest Hindu heritage.
- The accommodation provided, is as much a part of the safari in the African forests as the prospect of seeing wild-life. Many prefer and pay more to live in the open country 'with nature' instead of in five-star comfort.

CHARACTERISTICS OF TOURISM PRODUCTS

A product is something that a producer makes and offers to consumers to provide satisfaction of needs. Like all products, tourism also needs marketing and it is different from marketing of manufactured goods since tourism product has different characteristics.

Intangible

Manufactured goods are tangible in the sense that they have physical dimensions and attributes and can be seen, felt, or tasted. The tourism product is an intangible product. Take for example, an aviation industry.

One can see the airplane, the facilities provided within, etc. But none of these would determine the nature and quality of services imparted by the airline. One cannot see, feel, smell, touch or measure a service performed. It can only be experienced from the effects produced during the journey.

Inseparability

A physical product is produced in the factory, bought in the shop and consumed in the customer's premises at his convenience. But when the customer buys a service like travelling in an airline, the production and consumption of the services takes place at the same time. The experience of the tourist product exists when it is produced as well as consumed. The service in the airline is the promptness of delivery of baggage or courtesy of the airhostess or safety of travel.

Perishability

A manufacturer of a physical product can anticipate the demand in advance and store the goods in warehouse and deliver them to the customers at the time of need. But the supply of the tourism product cannot be stored because tourism products are highly perishable.

A seat in the plane or a room in the hotel not used today is a total waste. If an advertisement placed in the media channel is not seen or read, it is a waste. If the supply is not used, it perishes. So, the seats in an aircraft, the rooms in the hotels, the space in the ship, the services of a tourist guide, the time of the travel agency, etc. all perish if not utilized when available. What is not sold cannot be carried forward like stocks to be sold the next day or at any other time.

Ownership

No ownership passes from seller to buyer in a service. The buyer only acquires the right to certain benefits of what the seller offers. One may have the right to use a hotel room or a railway berth for a period of time, but the ownership of the room or berth remains with the hotel or the railways.

MARKETING MIX IN TOURISM MARKETING

Tourist marketing mix is largely a complex group of factors to achieve the 'end products', which helps the marketing manager to understand the demand in relation to supply and marketing investments. A balanced mix is necessary to reach this targeted result.

The tourist marketing mix can include the following elements:

The Product:

- Image, reputation, positioning

- Size and facilities offered
- Staff members and their attitudes
- The characteristics of the product

The Price:

- Corporate
- Discounted
- Normal
- Promotional
- Seasonal
- Wholesaler rates

The Promotion:

- Advertising
- Direct mail
- Public relations
- Sales promotion

The Distribution:

- Airlines
- Channels of distribution
- Clubs/Associations
- Intermediaries
- Reservation systems

'Marketing mix' has both short-term as well as long-term aspects. Long-term plans are based on study of natural, economic, social and technological aspects of the markets and customers. The short-term aspects relate to price reduction, aggressive promotion, or introduction of a new product in the market.

TOURISM MARKETING STRATEGY

One of the basic considerations for successful marketing strategy is the need for research. It provides the information base for effective marketing. It relates to providing answers to various questions pertaining to the marketing activities. Market research can be defined as the "systematic collection of information relating to supply and demand for the product in such a way that the information may be used to make decisions about its policies and objectives". In order to formulate any marketing strategy, it is essential for a tourist organization and others engaged in marketing of tourist products to know the answer of following questions:

- Who are the persons engaged in tourism and where do they live?
- Who are the potential customers and where do they come from?
- What are their likes and dislikes?
- What are their travel preferences and interests?
- What do they buy and where do they stay?
- What mode of transport do they use?
- What are their entertainment preferences?
- What are the trends in competition?
- What type of marketing programmes would be needed?

Market research provides answers to all the above questions. To make the overall marketing efforts effective and successful, as in the case of manufactured products, the tourist organization has to be totally aware of the trends in travel habits, vacation habits and complete knowledge about potential customers. It is very important to have detailed information on all aspects of a market. Results of such research will work as a guideline for designing and launching a successful marketing programme. A lot of data can be collected through publications, commercial analysis, trade information, press cuttings, previous studies etc.

Other ways to obtain data are:

- Tourism Departments,
- Discussion with tourists,
- Observation of customers at premises,
- Observations and discussions with visitors in exhibitions and trade shows,
- Attitudes, image perceptions and awareness studies,
- Advertisement and other media response studies,
- Studies of usage pattern.

Bibliography

Airey, D.: *Tourism Education*, New Delhi: Oxford University Press, 2001.

Botterill, M.: *Making Connections between Industry and Higher Education in Tourism*, London: The National Liaison Group for Higher Education in Tourism, 2003.

Grgona, J.: *Role and Importance of Tourism Staff at the Turn of the Millennium*, Hyderabad: Perspectives Publishers, 2000.

Kasper, C.: *Tourism Marketing and Management Handbook*, New York: Prentice Hall, 1997.

Ladkin, A.: *The Profile of Tourism Studies Degree Courses*, London: The National Liaison Group for Higher Education in Tourism, 2004.

Moilliet, D.: *Hospitality Research Journal*, London: Macmillan, 2001.

Payne, K.: *Tourism and Hospitality Research*, Guwahati: United Publishers, 1998.

Shea, L. J.: *Journal of Hospitality and Tourism Education*, Kolkata: ICSP Publication, 2001.

Sheldon, P. J.: *Training Needs Assessment in the Travel Industry*, Mumbai: Sabrang Publications, 2000.

Tao, H.: *The Development and Construction of Tourism Personnel*, London: Yale University Press, 2003.

Umbreit, T.: *The Role of Education in the Tourist Industry*, Salt Lake City: University of Utah, 2002.

Vroom, J. A.: *Tourism Education: A Model Program*, New Delhi: Manas Publications, 2004.

Vukoniæ, B.: *Tourism in Central and Eastern Europe: Educating for Quality*, Tilberg: Tilberg University Press, 2000.

Walle, A.H.: *Journal of Hospitality and Tourism Education*, New Delhi: Indian Institute of Public Administration, 2000.

Walsh, M. E.: *Tourism Management*, New Delhi: Government of India Press, 2007.

Watson, J.: *Developing Tourism Managers*, New Delhi: Government of India Press, 2005.

Xiao, H.: *Annals of Tourism Research*, New Delhi: Oxford University Press, 2004.

Index